379619

191 NOV

£14.20

MONEY ON THE MOVE

M. S. MENDELSOHN

MONEY ON THE MOVE

THE MODERN INTERNATIONAL CAPITAL MARKET

McGraw-Hill Book Company

New York   St.Louis   San Francisco   Auckland   Bogotá
Düsseldorf   Johannesburg   London   Madrid   Mexico
Montreal   New Delhi   Panama   Paris   Saõ Paulo
Singapore   Sydney   Tokyo   Toronto

Library of Congress Cataloging in Publication Data

Mendelsohn, Stefan.
  Money on the Move

  Bibliography: p.
  Includes index.
  1. Capital market. 2. Capital movements.
  3. Euro-bond market. 4. Euro-dollar market.
  I. Title.
  HG3891.M45   332.4'5   79-17297
  ISBN 0-07-041474-2

1234567890   DODO   89876543210

The editors for this book were Kiril Sokoloff, Virginia Fechtmann Blair, and
Joan Matthews, the designer was Elliot Epstein, and the production
supervisor was Thomas G. Kowalczyk. It was set in Gael by ComCom.

Printed and bound by R.R. Donnelly & Sons, Incorporated.

for Ingrid and Katherine

CONTENTS

PART THREE   FOREIGN BOND MARKETS AND FINANCIAL
CENTERS

APPENDIXES

FOREWORD

There are two kinds of mystery. There is subjective mystery, where things are hard to understand because, although they have rational explanations, their solutions are complicated and require special or even unavailable knowledge. Of such a kind are a Strategic Arms Limitation Treaty, n-dimensional geometry, the causes of cancer, the explanation of the Kondratieff cycle, the unraveling of Trent's Last Case, and the laws of American football. There is also objective mystery, where things are hard to understand because they are in themselves incapable of rational explanation, however subtle and knowledgeable the investigator. Of such a kind, one may suppose, are the doctrine of the Trinity, French foreign policy, and Hegel's writings.

For a long time and for most people international currency and capital markets have belonged at least to the first category, with perhaps a lingering suspicion that they really belonged to the second category. It is a fair appraisal of Stefan Mendelsohn's achievement in writing this book that he has demonstrated that they do not belong in the second catagory and that for anyone with the ability to read plain English for a few hours they need not belong in the first category.

For anyone familiar with his writings in *The Economist*, *The Banker*, the *American Banker*, and elsewhere over the years this will come as no surprise. Nonetheless, it is welcome that that prodigious talent for penetrating financial obscurity and laying out the results in clear and easily intelligible prose should have been harnessed to the single large achievement represented by this book.

It does not, of course, set out to raise, let alone resolve, all the great tangle of theoretical and policy issues that has proliferated in recent years about the significance and management of world money and its interaction with the real economy at both the domestic and international levels. It seeks rather to tell us what the thing is, how it arose, how it works, and whither it has led. A firm grasp of financial technicalities, economic analysis, and concrete historical processes is rare in one person; but it is this combination which makes this book so useful, so readable, and perhaps most remarkable, so pleasurable.

The most useful fruit of this debamboozlement is the dissipation of the nightmarish notions, which were current in the 1970's and keep recurring, of an imminent financial crash arising from the excessively rapid expansion of international banking credits and the specific weakness of the dollar. One of the most striking features of the 1960s and the 1970s has been the speed and facility with which private financial processes have accommodated the dramatically expanding and changing needs of the world economy, while governments and official international institutions struggled and frequently failed to provide even quite modest succor to the system they believed they were managing. Whether it was the expansion of international liquidity in the 1960s or the recycling of petrodollars in the 1970s, the brunt of the burden was borne—albeit very profitably—by nonofficial institutions and individuals in world currency and capital markets.

There has, of course, been a "price" or at least a consequence. The control which governments had in the 1940s and 1950s over the direction, politically and economically, of the flows of international investment has been eroded in favor of market and private criteria. This may or may not have contributed to the signs of strong and rapid economic development in some formerly underdeveloped countries; and it certainly has borne hard on other very poor non-oil-producing countries which may nonetheless deserve support for economic as well as political reasons. But it is reasonably clear that, while flexible and resilient monetary markets are certainly not capable of preventing the consequences of real economic adjustments and failures, they have proved very successful in their proper role of temporarily accommodating huge economic shocks and they are not likely through catastrophic failure of their own to cause or aggravate real economic disasters.

> Peter Jay
> *Former British Ambassador
> to the United States*

Acknowledgments

My main help in writing this book came from my friend and colleague Christopher Davis, formerly of Grindlays Bank and now at Simon and Coates, London. I cannot thank him enough.

I am indebted to all those in the markets and the official world who generously helped with my inquiries and particularly those who read parts of the book in draft. I am especially grateful to Günther Bröker, Marinus Keyzer, Rinaldo Pecchioli, and Niels Westerlund at the OECD; Norman Robson at the Bank of England; Martin Thomann, formerly at the Swiss National Bank; Helmuth Mayer at the Bank for International Settlements; and Jo Saxe at the World Bank. I am equally grateful to Guy Field, formerly of Samuel Montagu and now at Derby and Company; Giovanni Ortolani, of the European Banking Company and Continental Bank in Brussels; Hans Bär of Bank Julius Bär in Zurich; Hans-Christian Donnerstag of the Deutsche Girozentrale-Deutsche Kommunalbank; Ian Peacock of Kleinwort Benson; Michael von Clemm, David Potter, and Philip Seers at Credit Suisse First Boston; Antony Constance and his colleagues at Manufacturers Hanover Ltd.; Michael Mortara at Salomon Brothers International; Johannes de Gier at the Amsterdam-Rotterdam Bank; Armand Middernacht and Joseph Nerincx at the Kredietbank, Brussels; Stan Yassukovich at the European Banking Company; and last, though far from least, Susan Strange of Chatham House and the London School of Economics.

Brad Henderson, my editor at the *American Banker*, showed me every kindness and forbearance while I was writing this book.

The illustrations were drawn by my friend Richard Natkiel of *The Economist*.

M. S. Mendelsohn

PART ONE

THE MARKET'S ROLE AND ORIGINS

CHAPTER ONE
AN OVERVIEW

After the 1973 oil crisis, a wider public was suddenly made aware of the international capital market, although not under that slightly unwieldy and forbidding name. But words such as "petrodollars" and "recycling" quickly became sufficiently recognizable for use in headlines. The role of Western banks in channeling large surplus oil revenues to countries in deficit was far too important to be left to the financial pages. It became a matter of legitimate concern for governments and electorates, extensively reported in the general news columns of the press, and a topic for serious public discussion.

This new interest in the international capital market is fully justified, because that market has become the most important single channel for the transfer of savings from surplus to deficit countries, with considerable implications for public policy and, ultimately, the living standards of individuals throughout the world.

But it would be wrong to think that the mechanism which recycles oil surpluses was created overnight and for that purpose alone, that the only players in the game are the world's biggest commercial banks, and that the whole apparatus will be dismantled when a crisis no longer requires it. On the contrary, the transformation of short-term deposits into international medium-term credits by the Western banking system is only one part of the international capital market. The market is made up also of uncounted individuals around the world investing their savings in bonds issued by international borrowers. It was this market as a whole, consisting of banks and individual investors, which helped tide the world over the aftermath of the oil crisis. The market was able to do so because it had already become well established by the time that particular emergency arose. Indeed, by 1978 the market had once more become

3

less concerned with recycling petrodollars than with redistributing the surplus international earnings of Japan, Germany, and Switzerland and also France, which had recovered to overtake the dwindling but more publicized current surpluses of the world's oil exporting countries, taken as a group. But by 1979, oil surpluses had reemerged.

It is axiomatic that national balances of payments must balance. The current account of a country's balance of payments with the rest of the world consists of net earnings on merchandise trade, plus investment income, plus net "invisible" earnings from services such as shipping, insurance, and tourism. Countries in current surplus are net exporters of capital by definition, just as those in current deficit are net importers of capital. A current surplus is always exactly matched by a rise in national reserves, exports of capital, or some combination of the two. A current deficit has to be financed by imports of capital (meaning international borrowing and the attraction of investment from abroad) to the extent that it cannot be financed by a drawing down of reserves.

The international capital market (see Figure 1) contributes to this balancing process by providing medium- and long-term finance in three main ways: (1) by the issue of *Eurobonds* sold internationally

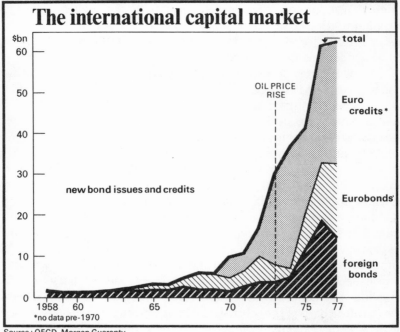

Source: OECD, Morgan Guaranty

FIGURE 1

outside the jurisdiction of any single national authority; (2) by the sale of *foreign bonds* on behalf of nonresident borrowers in national capital markets; and (3) by the granting of medium-term foreign currency credits (or *Eurocredits)* by international syndicates of banks.

The borrowers are governments, government agencies, international organizations like the World Bank (which then re-lend the proceeds to their member countries) and private business companies. A large part of the short-term deposits transformed by banks into international medium-term credits consist of funds deposited by oil exporting and other surplus countries. But nearly half the funds mobilized by the international capital market during most of the 1970s were raised by the sale of bonds, largely to individual investors. The greater part of the market's liabilities therefore consist of funds deposited in Western banks by the governments and official agencies of surplus countries and an even larger part of the market's assets consist of money lent to the governments and agencies of deficit countries. But a significant minority of the market's funds are drawn from and lent to the private sector, and the financial intermediaries around which the market revolves are nearly all private enterprise institutions like commercial banks, investment banks, and securities firms.

The market's importance for the world economy is considerable. In the four critical years following the quadrupling of world oil prices at the end of 1973, it provided about one-half of the capital needed to finance the current external payments deficits of all the world's oil-importing countries combined, meaning the industrial countries, the non-oil developing countries and the Communist countries as well (see Table 1).

In bridging greatly enlarged current payments gaps not filled by other international capital, such as official flows, the private market made it possible for industrial countries to meet the higher world oil price without an even deeper and longer recession than they actually suffered. And it did even better for the non-oil developing countries. As a group, they avoided recession. Their economic growth in the years immediately following the oil crisis remained very close to the average 5 percent of the preceding 20 years and in some of them growth actually quickened after 1973. In the case of the poorest developing countries, which do not have access to private international finance, this was due mainly to the mercy of good weather and harvests. But in the case of the more advanced, higher-income developing countries, "most were able to borrow heavily from private sources to maintain their investment," in the words of the World Bank's report for 1977.

At another level, the greatly enlarged role of the international capital

TABLE 1

THE MARKET'S PART IN FINANCING THE WORLD'S DEFICIT COUNTRIES

($ billion)

	1971	1972	1973	1974	1975	1976	1977
Current deficits:							
OECD*	0	5	4	40	13	39	51
non-oil LDCs	10	6	8	25	40	26	27
other†	2	3	5	10	19	14	11
Total	12	14	17	75	72	79	89
Rise in reserves	38	28	7	33	17	31	47
Financing requirement	50	42	24	108	89	110	136
Eurocredits	4	7	21	29	21	39	40
International bonds	6	10	8	7	20	32	33
Total market financing	10	17	29	36	41	71	73
Other financing	40	25	5	72	48	39	52
Total financing	50	42	34	108	89	110	125
Market financing as percent of total financing	20	40	120	33	46	65	58

*Except Germany, Japan, Switzerland, and the Netherlands.

†Mostly U.S.S.R., Eastern Europe, and China, but also includes South Africa.

SOURCE: IMF, OECD, Morgan Guaranty.

NOTE: In 1973 the world's deficit countries as a group attracted more capital than they needed to finance their combined current deficits plus a rise in their reserves, and were thus able to reexport capital. "Other financing" includes official capital and private financial flows like short-term trade credits which are not raised in the international markets. Figures rounded.

market has made an impact on the Western banking structure. There is no way of calculating the income which the market generates for banks, but gross earnings of between $4 billion and $5 billion by 1977 seem to be a fair guess. What is evident is that such earnings are highly concentrated among about 20 of the world's biggest commercial banks, which dominate Eurocredit lending because they alone have the resources, plus another 20 to 30 international investment banks and securities firms which dominate the issuing and trading of international bonds. An expansion of international business on the part of leading American, European, and Japanese financial institutions has been a natural accompaniment of the market's growth. Eurocredit income was certainly one reason for the 70 percent increase in the earnings of America's 13 biggest commercial banks between 1970 and 1976, when their domestic earnings virtually stagnated for lack of business loan demand at home. During those years, their combined domestic earnings rose by only 4 percent. But their foreign earnings rose no less than $7\frac{1}{2}$ times from 17 percent to 49 percent of total earnings,[1] although the banks felt compelled to reassure the authorities and their shareholders about this achievement rather than trumpet it.

Last but not least is the importance of the market for investors, because nearly one-half of all international bonds (Eurobonds and foreign bonds) are sold to individuals. By the end of 1978, the value of outstanding Eurobonds had grown to about $70 billion and annual turnover in the secondary market to about $90 billion. The volume of traditional foreign bonds outstanding and traded was slightly higher. Taken as a whole, the market for international bonds had therefore grown to a respectable size in absolute terms. Nevertheless, it does not do to exaggerate. From the time it began functioning on a regular basis in 1963 until the end of 1978, even gross issues of Eurobonds amounted to less than 5 percent of new issues on the domestic bond markets of the 24 member countries of the Organization for Economic Cooperation and Development, and the proportion of new foreign bond issues was about the same. The value of the international bond market is in the marginal contribution it makes toward the movement of capital around the world.

All books must have a beginning and an end. This one concentrates on the years from 1945 to 1978. Part One tries to describe the events which brought the modern market into being, its evolution, and its implications for the world economy. Part Two deals with the offshore markets, the Eurocredits, and Eurobonds arranged outside the jurisdiction of any single national authority. Part Three deals with foreign bonds issued by nonresident borrowers in the world's main domestic capital markets under the laws of the countries in which they are sold. One aim is to describe as plainly as possible how the market works for investors, borrowers, and financial intermediaries such as the commercial banks which provide Eurocredits, and the investment banks and securities firms which arrange the sale of international bonds. Another aim is to set the market into a perspective of the past and present in the hope of contributing, also, to an understanding of the further developments which will inevitably take place.

---

[1] Thomas H. Hanley, *United States Multinational Banking: Current and Prospective Strategies,* Salomon Brothers, 1976 and 1977.

CHAPTER TWO
ECONOMIC ORIGINS

General Economy since 1944

Markets are created by their environment and then contribute to it. The era which brought the modern international capital market into being was characterized by an astonishingly quick economic recovery from the Second World War followed by more than 20 years of very rapid growth, though accompanied by increasing financial strains from the early 1960s onward, culminating in the inflationary boom of 1972 and 1973, the deep recession of the two following years, and a fragile recovery thereafter.

One starting point is the contrast between the unwieldy international negotiations of the 1960s and 1970s and those which led to the Bretton Woods Agreement on a new international monetary system in 1944. That negotiation, of a generation ago, was confined for all practical purposes to only two countries and indeed two individuals, which is undoubtedly one reason why something was achieved, even though that agreement was not quite what either of the two principal negotiators had wanted.

The two principals were Maynard Keynes, representing the United Kingdom, and Harry Dexter White, of the U.S. Treasury, and they came to the negotiations with very different memories of the interwar years. Keynes was obsessed with the unemployment which had been created by the overvalued exchange rate into which Montagu Norman, the Governor of the Bank of England, had locked sterling when Britain "returned to gold" in 1925. Keynes therefore wanted the new system to leave national authorities the freedom of altering their exchange rates when necessary to preserve exports and employment, and he was particularly anxious to secure this freedom for a trading nation such as Britain.

The American authorities, on the other hand, were anxious to avoid any repetition of what they regarded as the destabilizing exchange rate movements which had followed Britain's abandonment of the gold-bullion standard in 1931. This was partly because they believed that the ensuing competitive European devaluations had damaged American farm exports, and also because they wanted a system of stable and indeed fairly rigidly pegged rates for the protection of their assets if they were going to act as bankers to the world.

In the end, the American Congress, which had the deciding voice, gave the new system a far greater rigidity than either Keynes or even White had sought. Both men were aware that a growth of world trade would require a growth of world reserves and therefore hoped for some form of deliberate reserve creation through an artificial asset which Keynes wanted to call "bancor" and White "unitas." Keynes envisaged such a reserve asset as being valued ("but not unalterably") in gold. He foresaw that there could be no acceptable expansion of world reserves over the long run without periodic increases in the value of gold against currencies, so long as gold had to be at the center of the system, since there could be no relying on the production of new gold to keep in step with the world's need for new reserves. He himself did not think that gold would always need to be at the center of the system, but he was diplomatically content to leave that to an undefined future.

However, the U.S. Administration was obliged to give the Congress a near-veto over the dollar–gold price to secure Congressional approval for the International Monetary Fund (IMF), and the rules finally agreed for the IMF were therefore biased towards a very rigid system, although with some concessions. Automatic exchange rate alterations were allowed, but only within strict limits, and greater adjustments only in the largely undefined extremity of a "fundamental disequilibrium" of payments.

In practice, although this was not so laid down in the IMF Articles of Agreement, the system was based on gold through the dollar alone, and there has since been wide agreement that this particular reserve structure ultimately broke the system, rather than the more direct constraints which were put on exchange rate adjustments. Reserve creation came to depend on American payments deficits supplemented by British deficits and the diminishing proportion of new gold which national authorities were able to claw from the markets.

This imposed an impossible rigidity on exchange relationships. The United States, as the principal reserve center, was left with a passive exchange rate. Britain, as the second reserve center, could not alter its exchange rate without the greatest difficulty and without undermining confidence in the system. Surplus countries were inhibited from revaluing (up-valuing) their exchange rates against the dollar, which would have had the same result as a dollar devaluation, but which was the only way in which a realignment could be achieved under the rules of the game as they then existed, since the rules effectively stopped the dollar from being devalued directly against gold. But the surplus countries were inhibited from "taking the action" by revaluing because of the supposed risk to their exports and employment and the supposed need for prior consultation about accompanying action by their trading partners. Paralyzed, the surplus countries therefore imported dollars and inflation during the 1960s and grumbled about what was happening.

The whole monetary debate of the 1960s therefore centered on the weakness of the reserve structure—and the drive for deliberately created reserve assets, like the emergency apparatus of central bankers' currency swaps and gold pools, all took for granted the desirability of preserving a system of pegged if somewhat more flexible exchange rates. But the creation of Special Drawing Rights (SDR) on the IMF from the beginning of 1970 was too late, too small, and too timid in its conception to save the system.[1]

It is worth recalling, in the very different climate of the late 1970s, that all the financial powers were very strongly committed to a system of pegged exchange rates throughout the troubled 1960s, prominently including successive American administrations. The decisive American support for the creation of Special Drawing Rights (SDR) provided evidence of that commitment, as did America's leading role in the defense of sterling's $2.80 exchange rate from 1964 to 1967. Indeed, the U.S. authorities remained, if no longer wholeheartedly committed, then at least willing to cooperate in one last attempt at pegged exchange rates when they took part in the unsuccessful realignment agreed at the Smithsonian at the end of 1971.

---

[1] The alternative of increasing the value of official reserves and hence the level of international liquidity by raising the official gold price was not seriously considered for several reasons. They included the near-veto over the official dollar–gold price which had been given to the U.S. Congress in return for its ratification of the Bretton Woods Agreement; the belief that an increase in the gold price would have inflationary potential, that it would encourage speculation on future increases, and that it would leave international reserve creation even more openly and therefore provocatively in the hands of the United States than the back-door method of increasing world reserves through American payments deficits. There was also the objection that an increase in the official gold price would unfairly benefit the half-dozen industrial countries holding most of the world's gold reserves, and a subsidiary objection was the benefit which would be conferred on South Africa and the U.S.S.R. as the world's biggest gold producers. But, in purely practical terms, it proved no easier to achieve deliberate reserve creation through SDR issues dependent on the agreement of more than 100 finance ministers than it had been to secure reserve creation through increases in the official gold price.

Whether the Bretton Woods system contributed to world prosperity during the 25 years preceding 1970 is one of those arguments that can never be settled. In this, it is exactly like the unresolved argument about the contribution which the world gold standard may or may not have made during the 40 years of its operation to 1914. The advocates of each of these systems argue that they provided a stable framework; the detractors claim that the two systems "worked" only so long as conditions happened to be favorable and that each broke down in its turn when conditions were no longer propitious. There is no need to pursue such arguments here, because we are concerned only with what actually happened and specifically with the combination of financial and economic circumstances which brought a set of modern financial markets into being.

There are certainly sufficient explanations for the prosperity which followed the Second World War, by contrast with the instability and depression which followed the First. After 1918, there was general and rapid disarmament, but soon after 1945 governments again started spending heavily on defense. After World War I, the victors weakened Europe by demanding reparations,[2] but after World War II, America, as the most powerful victor, sensibly and generously financed the recovery of former allies and enemies alike. Moreover, all governments spent heavily on infrastructure and social services (as well as on defense), having become converted to policies of full employment.

Governments were able to pursue full employment policies for a considerable time after the World War II without generating inflationary pressures, partly because of the large slack which existed after 1945 and partly because of rapid advances in technology. Those advances received a large initial boost from the accumulation of military research and development which became available to civilian economies after the war and which continued thereafter, though on a lesser scale, as the spin-off of further defense and space research. Another reason for rapid increases in productivity during the 20 years prior to 1970 consisted of massive shifts of farm workers to more productive employment, partic-

---

[2]An additional factor between the wars was Germany's hyperinflation of 1923. Contrary to folklore, this was not caused by reparations but by the fact that the Kaiser's government financed its *entire* war expenditure through borrowing. The idea was to win the war and collect the cost from the losers. When this plan miscarried, the only alternative was to wipe out the government's debt to German investors by debasing the currency. That done, the Reichsmark stabilized of its own accord rather than because of the "wizardry" attributed to Dr. Hjalmar Schacht, the president of the Reichsbank. There was, of course, also the American stock exchange boom and bust of the 1920s. So far as anyone can make out, this seems to have occurred because the authorities were at first prepared to finance mass lunacy and then, taking fright, stopped financing it.

ularly in countries like France, Italy, and Spain, while other countries such as Germany and Switzerland were able to draw easily trained and highly productive additional labor from the less developed Mediterranean areas.

There was yet another stroke of luck (for the industrial economies) in the general weakness of commodity prices during the 20 years up to 1972. The years immediately after 1945 saw a boom in raw material prices created by the revival of civilian demand and later reinforced by the Korean war, at a time when supply was still lagging because of low investment by commodity producers during the depressed 1930s, which was not fully made up even during the Second World War and its aftermath. But by the early 1950s supply had again caught up while new industrial techniques were economizing ever more in the use of many raw materials. Last but far from least was the decline of 30 percent in real oil prices during the 20 years to 1969, which occurred because under the arrangements then existing with the major oil companies, producing countries could increase their revenues only by increasing output. The weakness of oil-based products helped, in turn, to drag down the prices of competitive raw materials like natural fertilizers, rubber, and fibers (just as the steep rise in oil prices after 1973 helped drag up the prices of other commodities).

Early warning of impending strains between a dynamic world economy and a rigid international monetary system came in 1957 when the International Monetary Fund extended large credits for the first time, to Britain and France, following a flight out of their currencies after the Suez invasion at the end of 1956. More significant, in 1958, was a first flight out of the dollar into European currencies when a recession and falling interest rates in the United States coincided with a boom and high interest rates in Europe. Here was dramatic evidence that the postwar "dollar gap" had been decisively closed and within two years the opposite fear of a dollar glut had gathered sufficient force to produce a brief, unnerving flight into gold in October 1960. The London bullion price suddenly rose above the then sacrosanct official $35 an ounce to more than $40, until a combination of alarmed central bankers rushed in to stabilize this lynch pin of the pegged exchange rate system, to which the financial powers then attached so much importance.

This was the event which swung President Kennedy's new administration to the quest for international monetary reform and artificial reserve creation immediately after he took office in January 1961. But by the time the international negotiations had entered their dilatory and ultimately inconclusive course, the strains which finally broke the system were building up ever more force.

The most visible strain was the tiresome soap-opera of sterling's three-year crisis, which ended with the pound's devaluation from $2.80 to $2.40 in November 1967. Mr. Henry Fowler, the Secretary of the U.S. Treasury, correctly interpreted this event when he said, "It puts the dollar in the front line." The markets felt exactly the same and pressure switched abruptly from the world's second to the world's first reserve currency in the form of a stampede out of dollars into gold. Within four months the central bankers' gold pool had lost one-tenth of its stocks, at which point the authorities gave up the attempt to hold down the market price at the official level. The emergence of a free gold price on the market turned the system of pegged exchange rates anchored to an official gold price into a fiction, but it was a fiction which was to endure for another three years.

The ultimate pressures were meanwhile building up less immediately obviously from the incompatability of policy into which President Johnson became trapped from 1965, when he decided that it was necessary to make an extended commitment to Vietnam. However, it was also necessary for Johnson to maintain the Great Society program for social advancement in the United States, which he had inherited from President Kennedy. As a very broad generalization, Americans who supported one of these policies tended to oppose the other. This made it extremely difficult to abandon either policy or to tax the electorate with the full cost of both. The dilemma produced a series of rising American budget deficits from 1965, when the American economy was already stretched to the limits of capacity after the Kennedy expansion of the earlier 1960s. As a result, the domestic purchasing power of the dollar and the American balance of payments began to weaken and the dollar came under growing pressure on the exchanges, especially after sterling's 1967 devaluation, as noted earlier. The surplus countries, notably Germany and Japan, could have responded by letting the value of their currencies rise but, as already described, they did not do this, or did not do it sufficiently. This was the combination of circumstances which broke the Bretton Woods system of pegged exchange rates in August 1971, when President Nixon suspended the gold convertibility of the dollar, thus leaving the dollar and all currencies to float against each other.

The most important immediate consequence was that all major countries activated their economies at the end of 1971 to counter the presumed shock which the Bretton Woods collapse had given to business confidence. The combined effect was far greater than intended by any single government and the result, in 1972 and 1973, was the most concentrated boom in output and trade that the world had ever experienced. That in itself was enough to drive raw material prices to their highest levels since the Korean war, although the pressure was compounded by large-scale hedging out of currencies into commodities. Moreover, all this happened to coincide, by the rarest ill fortune, with exceptionally bad weather and harvest failures throughout the world's food growing areas, plus the depletion of the Peruvian anchovy shoals, an important source of animal feed. The whole sorry process then culminated with the Middle Eastern war of October 1973, which provided the occasion rather than the reason for a long overdue though very large increase in world oil prices. The sequel of the deep recession (see Figure 2) of 1974 and 1975 (the worst in a generation), of uncertain recovery after 1976 and the possibility of profound structural changes in the world economy are all too recent for an historical judgment. But a tentative evaluation will nevertheless be attempted at the end of Part One of this book.

The world recession

Industrial production in relation to pre-recession trends.*

* Monthly indices (fourth quarter 1973 = 100) and log-linear trends based on quarterly data for the period 1955–74. The inset figures represent the average annual growth rates implicit in these trends.

Reproduced with permission of BIS

FIGURE 2

CHAPTER THREE

THE BIRTH OF EUROCURRENCIES

Every step in the evolution of the modern international financial markets resulted from the private financial community's spontaneous responses to the world's growing political and economic strains; the markets which did so much to bridge the cracks of the 1970s were born of the premonitory stresses of the 1950s and 1960s. This was true in turn of the birth of the Eurocurrencies, Eurobond, and Eurocredits markets. It is just as well that commercial instinct drove the markets to innovation, because the striking feature of what happened was the large gap at each stage between private achievement and official failure. Two examples are particularly relevant.

Almost the whole of the 1960s was taken up by an "urgent" international negotiation on the need for official liquidity creation. The net result was an addition of less than $10 billion to world reserves in the form of Special Drawing Rights on the International Monetary Fund, issued during the three years to 1972. As already remarked elsewhere, this came far too late and was far too small to underpin a system of pegged exchange rates, which had been its object. To the extent that additional liquidity was needed to finance the growth of world trade, it was provided without fanfare by the Eurocurrencies market, whose net size expanded by more than $350 billion during the dozen years to the end of 1977. Market lending to official borrowers made a major contribution to the $250 billion increase in world reserves which took place during those twelve years, helping to keep the ratio of world reserves close to six months of world imports in 1977, as in 1970 and 1960. Looking back, the 1977 annual report of the IMF was disarmingly frank about what had happened, saying of SDR creation that "things did not turn out as expected in the short or longer run" and adding that the international capital markets "have, in effect, become major suppliers of reserves."

A second example of the chasm between official and private achievement is provided by the likewise "urgent" international negotiations which took place on the need for official recycling of oil exporters' surplus earnings. During the four years leading to the end of 1977, these negotiations had produced two IMF special oil financing facilities totaling $7 billion. In the same period, the international capital market mobilized more than $200 billion, or almost 30 times as much as the official negotiators. This, too, was frankly acknowledged by the IMF's 1977 report, which said:

Very substantial payments imbalances have developed in recent years, and there was a time when official agencies would have been expected to be the principal intermediaries between surplus and deficit countries. When the need arose, however, private international markets had already developed to the point at which they were able to perform this function effectively for a number of countries, and have continued to do so.

So, at this stage it becomes useful to move back and try to trace, step by step, just how the international market developed to the point of being able to perform functions which the international agencies could not.

Neither the Eurocurrencies nor the Eurobond and Eurocredits markets is wholly new in concept, but then hardly anything ever is. The late Paul Einzig cited evidence of transactions in sterling deposits in foreign countries in the nineteenth century, the issue of United States loans in dollars in Europe during the same period, and a fairly active business in sterling and dollar deposits in Berlin and Vienna in the 1920s.[1] But, as he rightly remarked, the difference in degree between those occasional earlier precedents and the modern markets was so great, even by the early 1960s, as to have constituted a difference in kind.

The first of the modern international markets to emerge during the past generation was the Eurocurrencies market. It is a market in which foreign currencies are lent and borrowed as distinct from the foreign exchange market, where they are bought and sold. It consists of a pool of predominantly short-term deposits which provides the biggest single source of funds that commercial banks transform into medium- and occasionally long-term international loans, or Eurocredits. In addition, international investment banks and securities firms borrow Eurocurrencies to finance their portfolios and trading of international bonds.

---

[1]Paul Einzig, *The Eurodollar System,* Macmillan, London, 1964.

And borrowers in the international capital market often deposit in the Eurocurrencies market the temporarily idle part of funds they have obtained for the medium or longer term. In brief, the Eurocurrencies market is the international money market on which the international capital market is largely based.

A Eurocurrency is simply a foreign currency deposited in a bank outside the country where the currency is issued as legal tender. A dollar deposited in New York is a plain dollar, but it becomes a Eurodollar when deposited in a bank outside the United States. Similarly, Deutschemark becomes Euro-Deutschemark in London or Zurich, while sterling becomes Euro-sterling outside the United Kingdom. It is the location of the bank where funds are placed and not the ownership of the bank or the ownership of the funds which determines whether they are domestic or foreign currency. Deutschemark on the books of an American branch bank in Frankfurt are ordinary Deutschemark, but dollars on the books of that American bank in Germany are Eurodollars, even if they have been placed in Frankfurt by the American bank's own head office in the United States or by a corporation in the U.S. Obviously some international transactions involve domestic currency for one partner but foreign or Eurocurrency for the other. If a bank in Paris advances French francs to a bank in London, the French bank has created a domestic currency asset, but the London bank has run up a foreign or Eurocurrency liability in Euro-French francs.

Ultimately, however, there is nowhere a dollar can be held excepting in the United States, even when title to it resides elsewhere. So, when a bank in Frankfurt advances dollars to a bank in Zurich, instructions have to be sent to New York, where the account of the German bank is debited and that of the Swiss bank credited. The ultimate settlement of Euro-Deutschemark, Euro-Swiss franc, Euro-French franc, and Euro-sterling transactions are similarly made in Frankfurt, Zurich, Paris, and London.

The origins of the modern Eurocurrencies market go back to 1949 when the new Chinese Communist government began disguising its dollar earnings by placing them with the Russian-owned Banque Commerciale pour l'Europe du Nord in Paris. This happened even before Peking's identifiable dollar balances in the United States were blocked under American legislation forbidding trade with the enemy, following the outbreak of the Korean war in 1950. Soon after, the Russian bank in Paris and the Moscow Narodny Bank in London began disguising their dollar balances too, for fear that they might be similarly blocked.

The disguise and safeguarding of Communist countries' dollar balances took the form of placing them with banks in Western Europe rather than directly in New York. This incorporated them into the claims of Western banks on the United States (the Communist depositors having, on their part, claims on Western European banks). Hence the origin of what was at first known as the European market for dollar deposits. In the jargon, such deposits soon became known as Eurodollars and, later, Eurocurrencies, even after the business in foreign currency deposits had spread beyond Europe, notably to the Caribbean and to Asian centers. In the latter, such balances were dubbed Asian dollars by the Bank of America in 1969, with the aim of adding to their local appeal. But, whatever their tag, all are identical in being foreign currency assets or liabilities for the banks dealing in them.

In placing dollars with Western European banks, Communist banks were not motivated by fear alone. They were also building up relationships for the purpose of eventually securing access to dollar loans, which were not at that time available to them from American banks. And, within a few years, Communist banks had become takers as well as givers of funds in the Eurodollar market.

The next milestone in the market's development was the freezing of Egypt's official sterling balances in London during the invasion of the Suez zone by British, French, and Israeli forces in October 1956. This coincided exactly with the suppression of the Budapest uprising by Russian tanks and a renewal of East-West tensions, thus reinforcing in two different ways but simultaneously the kind of fears which had led to disguised reserve currency placements in the first instance.

These events also gave the fledgling Eurodollar market fresh impetus of another kind, because the sterling crisis which resulted from Britain's intervention in Egypt (and helped stop that intervention) led to restrictions on the use of sterling for the financing of third-country trade to which neither the United Kingdom nor any of the Overseas Sterling Area countries were partners. By this time, the practice of dollar depositing had become known in the market, though not beyond, and it inspired some enterprising British bankers to turn to other currencies when stopped from using their own. They therefore started bidding for dollar deposits, which they then re-lent to finance foreign trade.

The London banks which first began making a regular practice of dealing in dollar deposits were mostly merchant banks (approximately equivalent to American investment banks and French banques d'affaires) and British overseas banks (meaning banks headquartered in London but having most of their operations abroad, mainly in countries which had formerly belonged to the British empire or those in which British finance and influence had been especially strong, like Argentina).

Indirectly, Winston Churchill played a part, as he seems to have done in almost everything that happened in the world during his long life.

It happened as follows. In 1952, three senior British officials proposed making sterling freely convertible once more so that it could again become a world currency. The plan was named ROBOT for its authors, Sir Leslie Rowan and Sir Richard (Otto) Clarke of the Treasury, and Sir George Bolton, of the Bank of England. Their idea was for restoration of convertibility at a floating exchange rate, accompanied by initial blocking of most nonresident sterling balances, but their gradual and progressive unblocking thereafter.

In British tradition, the penultimate verdict on this financial proposal was left to the government's scientific adviser, Lord Cherwell, who did not understand its technicalities. Churchill, who turned it down, did not understand the technicalities either. But he understood that Cherwell did not like the plan, and that was enough for him. More important, Churchill remembered having been bamboozled by Montagu Norman into the disastrous "return to gold" of 1925 and never thereafter lost his healthy distrust of financial experts, reinforced by the disaster of sterling's brief and premature return to external convertibility under American pressure in 1947. And indeed, Cherwell and Churchill had common sense on their side; no technical plan, however subtle, could have restored the currency of a declining power to a world role.

However, the upshot was useful. Sir George Bolton left the Bank of England where he had been overseeing foreign exchange controls, "because I didn't want to spend the rest of my life as a prison warder." He thereupon became chairman of a British overseas bank, the Bank of London and South America (since merged into Lloyds Bank International) where, having been forced to accept that there was no international future for sterling, he became the best known and influential of all British bankers in deliberately building up a Eurodollar market with its center in London.[2]

---

[2]These events were recounted to the author by Sir George Bolton. They are described also in *A Banker's World, The Revival of the City, 1957–1970,* edited by Richard Fry, Hutchinson, London, 1970.

CHAPTER FOUR
THE GROWTH OF EUROCURRENCIES

The nature of the Eurodollar's origins at the end of the 1940s obviously precluded publicity. But the British innovators, like their Communist predecessors, also kept rather quiet about what they were doing. The Bank of England was, of course, informed and was sufficiently far-sighted not to stifle the market when it might have done so by a fussy application of its authority. But there was some fear that the authorities might dampen this new market if it threatened to grow too quickly as a result of the participants trumpeting their actions. In reality there was little danger of excessive, premature publicity because transactions in foreign currency deposits were always grafted onto the foreign exchange operations of the participating banks, as they still are. And during the 1950s foreign exchange dealing was still shrouded in sufficient mystery to deter inquiry. A note in the *Economist* in 1958 was probably the first public reference to the market. Eurodollars were not once mentioned by name in the 350 pages of a major official report on the British financial system which appeared in 1959, or in the four volumes of evidence on which the report was based, although it is fair to add that the report showed awareness and prescience by remarking at one point that it mattered less whether international trade was financed in sterling so long as much of it continued to be financed through London.[1]

As it happened, the trading of currencies on the foreign exchanges and the lending of foreign currencies in the Eurocurrencies markets expanded very rapidly after the late 1950s. This was because a number of European countries relaxed their exchange controls for the first time

---

[1]*Report of the Committee on the Working of the Monetary System,* Command 827, 1959 (known as the *Radcliffe Report* for its chairman, Lord Radcliffe).

since the Second World War and because the American domestic money market was reopened for the first time since the Depression of the 1930s. The result was to give investors and borrowers a new range of choices in their use of the dollar while at the same time allowing them to move money more freely between currencies and national markets.

In Europe, 10 countries restored external convertibility for the first time since the Second World War in December 1958, followed by another 20 European and associated countries in 1959.[2] All these 30 countries undertook to make their own currencies freely convertible into other currencies for nonresidents. This made the currencies of the 30 countries indirectly convertible into gold (through the dollar) and the dollar thus lost the unique status it had enjoyed since 1939. In other words, the return of convertibility increased the range of comparably backed currencies available to international investors and borrowers.

The European action represented a formal acknowledgement that the postwar dollar famine had come to an end. The current account of the American balance of payments recorded its first postwar deficits in 1958 and 1959 (leaving aside the freak deficit of 1953 which resulted from the Korean war). The leading European countries therefore felt it safe to restore current convertibility and had a strong motive for doing so following the creation of the European Economic Community in 1958. The object was to facilitate the further growth of international trade and this was achieved by the cooperation of the EEC and the relaxation of exchange controls; the value of world exports rose by 43 percent in the five years from the end of 1958 compared with 28 percent in the five preceding years.

On the other hand, the relaxing of exchange controls had not been intended to unleash flows of hot money from one currency to another, although such flows soon built up, initially in response to differentials between high interest rates in Europe, which was trying to cool a boom in the late 1950s, and low interest rates in the U.S., which was then in recession. Such flows were then followed by the first panic flight out of the dollar into the London gold market in 1960 and by hedging into the Deutschemark and Dutch florin, which were revalued in 1961.[3]

Interest arbitrage from lower-yielding dollar into higher-yielding and newly convertible European investments had the same result no matter whether such switching was being done by American or other

---

[2]Britain was the only European country which had tried to restore current convertibility at an earlier stage—prematurely, briefly, and disastrously in 1947, as already mentioned.

[3]In retrospect, it is difficult to recapture the excitement caused. The value of the two currencies against the dollar was raised by all of 5 percent. But exchange rates were then believed to be as immutable as the laws of nature and the world was therefore as thunderstruck as though the boiling point of water had been altered by official decree.

investors. The logical counterpart of every dollar sold is a dollar bought. To the extent that dollars were acquired by foreign central banks in support of exchange rates, they increased the "overhang" of official foreign dollar holdings which were at that time eligible for conversion into gold at the U.S. Treasury, although most foreign official dollar reserves were and still are invested in U.S. Treasury bills. But, dollars acquired by foreign private holders can be placed either in the U.S. domestic money market or in the offshore Eurodollar market, where the returns to investors are nearly always higher than those obtainable in the U.S. itself (for reasons to be explained later).

As a result of the new opportunities opened up at the end of the 1950s, the net size of the Eurocurrencies market increased almost threefold in 1959 and then doubled again in 1960, as far as can be determined from the very rough estimates which are the only ones available for that early period of the market's history. Moreover, although 17 currencies were being dealt in the Euromarket from 1967, the market was and remains predominantly an external dollar market and any increase in its size is usually caused mainly by an increase in dollars being lent and borrowed outside the United States.

A development which approximately coincided with European relaxation of exchange controls in the late 1950s was the reopening of a range of choice for investors and borrowers in the American domestic money market after almost a quarter of a century of cheap money. Interest rates were first allowed to rise in 1956 to help dampen the economy after the Korean war boom. But partial monetary restraint also accompanied President Kennedy's fiscal stimulation in 1961. By a highly technical manipulation known as "Operation Twist," American long-term interest rates were kept down to encourage investment, while short-term rates were allowed to rise. Thus, from 1961 to 1963, the rate on overnight federal funds rose by 125 basis points but long-term U.S. government bond yields rose only by 10 basis points.[4] This combination of fiscal stimulation and partial monetary restraint was outstandingly successful in producing a prolonged and stable expansion of the American economy during the five years prior to the end of 1966, when real growth averaged almost 6 percent a year while consumer price increases averaged less than 2 percent. But the incidental effects on the American and international money markets were profound.

During the 24 years following the 1932 Depression, the American authorities almost never allowed short-term interest rates to rise above

---

[4] A basis point is $\frac{1}{100}$ of a percentage point and is usually used to describe changes in or differentials between interest rates, rather than the level of interest rates themselves. For instance, an increase in an interest rate from 7 percent to $7\frac{1}{2}$ percent is an increase of 50 basis points; the differential between 5 percent and $5\frac{3}{4}$ percent is 75 basis points.

2 percent and often kept them below 1 percent. For corporate treasurers and other investors, this made active money management more trouble than it was worth. But the abandonment of cheap money policies after 1956 changed that by producing a variety of competing money market assets. This made treasurers increasingly reluctant to leave balances idling at their banks, particularly for very short periods, because the Federal Reserve Board's Regulation Q does not allow commercial banks to pay interest on deposits of less than 30 days (while also limiting the interest they may pay on time deposits beyond that maturity). To get around such restrictions and recapture their market share, American banks began issuing negotiable Certificates of Deposit (CDs), the invention in 1961 of First National City Bank of New York (as it was then called before its name was shortened to Citibank).

Being issued at more than 30 days, CDs were allowed to carry interest but, being negotiable in a secondary market, they can provide a return also to investors selling before maturity. For five years, the authorities allowed the CD market to take root and flourish unimpeded, but this changed in the credit crunch of 1966. Regulation Q ceilings, limiting the return commercial banks may pay on time deposits, including CDs, were held below the rising market rates of competing assets like Treasury bills, commercial paper issued by business companies, and the returns paid by savings and loan associations which provide home mortgages. This resulted in massive shifts out of CDs and other commercial bank time deposits, partly into nonbank financial assets in the U.S., but partly also into the Eurodollar market, where there are no regulations to stop banks from paying whatever the traffic dictates.

This gave an enormous boost to the Eurocurrencies market in 1966 and again in 1969 and the first half of 1970, when the process was repeated (the market's net size growing by an average of about 50 percent in each of those three years). Those events contributed also to the growth of the Eurocurrencies market in a more fundamental, longer-term way. American banks virtually stampeded to open branches abroad to circumvent the discretionary American credit squeeze of 1966 and any future such squeezes. Thus the invasion of the world by American banks, which had begun early in the 1960s, accelerated rapidly after 1966. In that year, 13 American banks had 244 foreign branches; by 1977 130 American banks had 738 foreign branches. As a result, American banks replaced British and continental European banks as the dominant force in the Eurocurrencies market after the mid-1960s. Restricted from competing for funds at home, U.S. banks simply borrowed unimpeded from their growing chain of foreign branches. The liabilities of banks in the U.S. to their foreign branches shot up from about $2 billion to almost $15 billion between 1966 and the end of 1969, and then plummeted to less than $1 billion by the end of 1970. (This followed the suspension of Regulation Q interest ceilings in June 1970, to provide the liquidity which the American authorities thought their domestic banks would need to absorb the backwash of the Penn Central Railroad Company's collapse).

The net effect of Regulation Q was distinctly odd. By limiting the ability of American commercial banks to compete for funds in their domestic market, it forced them to bid for dollars abroad. At the same time, large American corporations were attracted to place their surplus funds at freely competitive rates with the foreign rather than the domestic branches of their banks. So, what was acclaimed at the time as a massive expansion of international lending amounted in reality to a rather artificial shift of a large part of the American domestic money market from New York to London and other foreign centers.

Because the vagaries of Regulation Q had played such a large part in the growth of the Eurodollar market during the latter 1960s, it was widely believed that market growth would slow down after the easing of Regulation Q restrictions in June 1970. But in fact, growth slowed down only slightly from an annual average of 40 percent during the four Regulation Q years from 1966 to 1970, to an average of 35 percent during the three years from the easing of the Q restrictions to the oil crisis at the end of 1973.

A factor which became increasingly important for the expansion of the Euromarkets in the late 1960s was the growing participation of central banks and other official agencies. The attitude of central bankers to the Euromarket has always been ambivalent. They have welcomed the market's contribution to the financing of world trade and investment, while worrying about the channel it provides for large hot-money flows which can transmit inflation across borders and upset exchange relationships. Few central bankers have ever wanted to regulate the Euromarket and fewer still have believed they could do it effectively without killing the market altogether. From the earliest days, therefore, central bankers have compromised by trying to use and influence the market.

At first, central banks intervened only indirectly by inducing their commerical banks to place funds in the Euromarket or borrow from it. From 1959 onward, Italian commercial banks were encouraged sometimes to lend and sometimes to borrow; at various times from 1960, the Deutsche Bundesbank gave German commercial banks special inducements to recycle into the Eurodollar market hot money which had flooded into Germany from abroad; and the Tokyo authorities encouraged their banks to borrow Eurodollars to help finance Japan's current balance of payments deficits from 1961 to 1964.

Beginning in 1965, central banks started entering the Euromarkets themselves, initially on a small scale and mainly through the Bank for International Settlements, in Basel. Even when official participation became still more direct, it remained limited as long as it was confined to the central banks of the main industrial countries. Indeed, in 1971 they agreed to reduce their Euro-deposits because they found that dollars which they put into the market were promptly converted by private borrowers back into Deutschemark and other promising currencies.

However, the developing and smaller industrialized countries were not inhibited in this particular way. One of the few problems developing countries do not have is an excessive demand for their currencies. They could therefore deploy their reserves in the Euromarket with far greater freedom than the main industrial powers. From the latter 1960s, they took advantage of this freedom to switch a growing proportion of their reserves out of traditional investments in U.S. and British Treasury bills, partly into higher-yielding Eurodollar and Euro-sterling balances. But they also switched some of their balances out of the two reserved currencies altogether, diversifying into stronger currencies like the Deutschemark and Swiss franc. However, given the restrictions on foreign investment in the domestic financial markets of surplus countries, the move was largely into Euro-Deutschemark, Euro-Swiss franc, and other Eurocurrencies (see Figure 3).

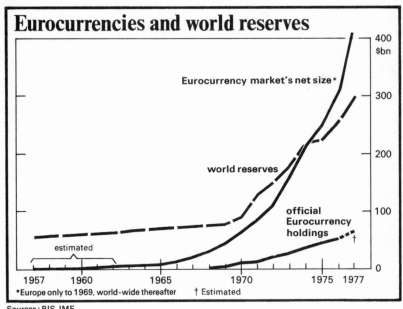

Sources: BIS, IMF

FIGURE 3

Such switching by developing countries gathered momentum as they gained reserves during the world commodities boom which began in 1972. Thus during the five years prior to the end of 1972, the Eurocurrency balances of developing and partly industrialized countries rose almost sixfold to more than $40 billion and from 20 percent to 30 percent of all funds in the Euromarkets. During those years their liabilities to (that is, their borrowings from) the market grew even faster, increasing sevenfold to about $35 billion. But, as a group, this still left them net creditors at the end of 1972 and in a position to start drawing heavily on the market when the need arose after the oil crisis a year later. Finally, the special factor which contributed to market growth after the beginning of 1974 consisted of the surpluses of the oil exporting countries which were invested in Eurocurrencies either directly, but also indirectly, through Western banks.

CHAPTER FIVE
EUROCURRENCY INFLUENCES

One of the enduring influences on the Eurocurrencies market is the trend of international balances of payments, but the connection is not as straightforward as sometimes suggested. Thus the growth and size of the Eurodollar market is in no way a direct counterpart of American balance of payments deficits. This is obvious from the fact that the net amount of Eurodollars outstanding has always been far larger than America's cumulative payments deficits, however measured. Moreover, the Eurodollar market has sometimes expanded very rapidly when America's external account happened to be in equilibrium or surplus (such as 1966, 1968, and 1969); at other times the net amount of Eurodollars outstanding has grown very slowly despite an exceptionally large American payments deficit (as in 1971). Other external markets, such as those in Euro-Deutschemark and Euro-Swiss franc, have tended to expand as a result of German and Swiss surpluses, not deficits.

The real connection between balances of payments and the Eurocurrency markets is more subtle than an appealingly simple mirror image. External payments deficits are usually associated, at least partly, with a faster rate of money creation in the deficit than the surplus countries. When surplus countries buy deficit currencies for the support of their own exchange rates (whether under a system of pegged rates or dirty floating), excess liquidity is spread to the surplus countries and some of this spills over into the Eurocurrency markets. For instance, when the Deutsche Bundesbank creates Deutschemark in order to buy dollars and thus arrest the appreciation of the mark's exchange rate, there is almost no way in which this process can be stopped from adding some liquidity to the German banking system. The resulting fall in German interest rates will then induce some investors to switch to higher yields on Eurodollar deposits, although they will usually protect themselves against the exchange risk by repurchasing Deutschemark forward at the same time as they buy dollars spot. Thus the Eurocurrencies market is influenced mainly by the exchange rate expectations and interest rate differentials which are symptoms of differences between national rates of inflation and balance of payments trends, and funds can be attracted (on a covered basis) into weak currencies by relatively high interest rates, just as they can be attracted into strong currencies despite low interest rates.

However, interest arbitrage takes place not only between currencies, but also between the domestic and external markets for the same currency. The dollar provides a good illustration. The return on Eurodollar deposits has nearly always been higher than on comparable New York money market investments (as shown by Figure 4). At first glance this seems puzzling, because banks are not required to hold noninterest earning reserves against Eurocurrency liabilities as they are against domestic liabilities. Since this makes it effectively cheaper for a bank to borrow dollars outside rather than inside the United States, it is not immediately obvious why Eurodollar deposit rates should in fact be higher than the rates offered in New York.

Part of the explanation offered by bankers is that some unquantified premium must be offered to depositors outside the country where a currency is issued. In other words, a depositor is deemed to be taking a marginally greater risk in placing dollars with the foreign rather than the domestic office of a U.S. bank. In the case of some external assets, this is clearly spelled out. For instance, dollar Certificates of Deposit issued in London carry a written stipulation making them the liability of the issuing branch alone. Branch banks everywhere are subject to the laws of the countries in which they are located. So, if banks in Britain were ever nationalized or their funds frozen, the holder of a dollar CD issued by the branch of an American bank in London might have difficulty getting his or her money out of that bank's head office in the U.S. The same applies in other centers outside the U.S.

But there are other factors as well. Banks outside a currency's country of issue often have to bid more actively for deposits than do banks in a domestic system, to which funds flow almost automatically. There will obviously always be more dollars available for placement in the domestic than in the Eurodollar market (about four times as many at the end of 1977, when the net total of Eurodollars outstanding was about $280 billion compared with commercial bank assets and liabilities of more than $1,145 billion in the United States). Moreover, banks in the Euromarket are under pressure to acquire the constant supply of short-term deposits on which

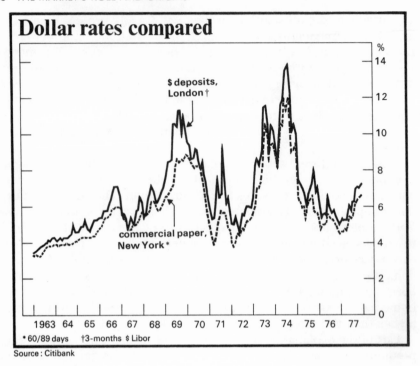

Dollar rates compared

$deposits, London †

commercial paper, New York *

1963 64   65   66   67   68   69   70   71   72   73   74   75   76   77

* 60/89 days   †3-months $ Libor

Source : Citibank

FIGURE 4

they largely depend for financing relatively longer term loans to their nonbank customers.

But, possibly the most important factor is that banks in the Euromarket can afford to offer higher deposit rates without in fact paying more for their money than banks in the domestic market. The following example explains why. Banks in the U.S. are required by law to hold noninterest bearing reserves (in vault cash or at Federal Reserve Banks) averaging at least 3 percent against time and savings deposits. So, when a bank in the U.S. offers 8 percent for a three-month deposit of $100 it has the use of only $97 and the true cost of that money to the bank is therefore $8\frac{1}{4}$ percent. Banks outside the U.S. are not required to hold any noninterest earning reserves against foreign currency deposits, and therefore have the full use of the money they receive. In this example, the true cost of money will thus be exactly the same to a bank in London offering $8\frac{1}{4}$ percent for three-months Eurodollars and a bank in the American domestic market offering 8 percent. The Euro-depositor is better off; the Eurobank is no worse off.

The same asymmetry works on the lending side. Banks in the United States usually require their customers to maintain compensating balances of 10 to 20 percent of any funds they have borrowed. This obviously drives up the true cost of money to the borrower above the stated interest rate being paid to the bank. If the borrower of $100 is required to keep $10 as a noninterest earning sight deposit with the lending bank, he or she has the use of only $90 and the true cost of that money to the borrower, at a stated interest rate of 8 percent, is close to 9 percent. In the Euromarket it is far less common for banks to demand that their customers keep compensating balances, so that the true cost of Eurodollars is often lower than of dollars borrowed in the United States, even when the stated rate of interest on Eurodollar loans is above comparable stated loan rates in the U.S. domestic market.[1]

What all this boils down to is that the Eurocurrency markets are freer and therefore in some ways more efficient than domestic money markets. And that helps to explain the huge size and continual expansion of the Euromarkets, quite apart from the special factors which helped growth along at various stages in the market's development.

Indeed, it seemed a sign of market maturity when Eurocurrency growth in the 1970s came to depend on special factors far less than in the past, reflecting instead changes in the world economy more closely than it used to. Market growth speeded up during the world boom of 1973, slowed down during the recession of 1974 and 1975, and then picked up again with the world economy in 1976 and 1977. Among the first to point to this new and closer link between Eurocurrency growth and the world economy was the Bank for International Settlements, which observed in 1975 that the market had been "visibly affected by the recession."

---

[1]Figure 4, showing that Eurodollar interest rates are usually marginally above money market rates in the U.S. domestic market deliberately compares two "clean" instruments, namely Eurodollars and U.S. commercial paper, neither of which are subject to reserve requirements. The Bank of England has shown that Eurodollar rates have usually been higher, also, than U.S. secondary market CD rates even after correction for U.S. domestic reserve requirements and the cost of Federal Deposit Insurance (*Quarterly Bulletin,* March 1979).

CHAPTER SIX

THE BIRTH OF EUROBONDS AND EUROCREDITS

The seminal event in the evolution of the Eurobond and Eurocredits markets was found in the controls imposed in the early and mid-1960s on the outflow of capital from the United States for the preservation of the gold-linked dollar at the center of an international system of pegged exchange rates. The U.S. Interest Equalization Tax (IET) was the main factor in the development of the Eurobond market and subsequent controls were mainly responsible for bringing the Eurocredits market into being.

President Kennedy's Interest Equalization Tax was announced on July 18, 1963, and came into effect immediately, even before its approval by the Congress. The tax was levied on the income of American investors from the new and outstanding securities of designated foreign borrowers. This drove down the price of outstanding securities and drove up the return which had to be offered on new securities to the extent needed to cover the American investor's new tax liability.

The tax was calculated so as to increase the cost of foreign portfolio borrowing in the U.S. market by 1 percent (increased to $1\frac{1}{2}$ percent from January 1967). World Bank issues were exempt, on the understanding that the Bank would not sell in the U.S. market portions of loans for on-lending to countries whose borrowing was subject to the IET. Canadian issues were exempted provided they did not exceed what was needed to keep Canada's gold and foreign exchange reserves at certain agreed levels. Japanese government and government-guaranteed issues were exempted from 1965 up to a total of $100 million a year—an empty gesture since Japan's balance of payments moved into strong surplus from 1966, making such borrowing "unnecessary," as the Organization for Economic Cooperation and Development (OECD) pointed out at the time. Issues by developing countries were also exempted, another empty gesture given their limited appeal to U.S. investors, then as now.

In practice, the IET applied to loans issued in New York for selected industrial countries and mainly for European and Australasian borrowers. The total of these had approximately tripled to $645 million during the four years prior to 1963, mainly because American monetary policy was kept very easy during those years to underpin recovery from the American recession of 1957–1958 and the lesser recession of 1960–1961. As a result, interest rates in the U.S. fell well below those in Frankfurt and Amsterdam and almost to the level of those in Zurich, attracting a growing number of foreign borrowers from the main European foreign bond markets to New York. This threat of a growing capital drain deeply troubled the American authorities, given the large and steady fall in America's reserves from 1957 onward despite the recovery of the current account of the balance of payments to consistent surpluses after the deficits of 1958 and 1959.

Following another fall in American reserves in 1963, the IET was extended in February 1964 to apply also to lending by U.S. financial institutions at one to three years to designated foreign borrowers. And from 1965 the IET was reinforced by the Voluntary Foreign Credit Restraint Program (VFCR) and the rules of the Office for Foreign Direct Investment (OFDI). These latter programs, which were progressively tightened over the years, required U.S. companies to improve their individual balances of payments with industrial countries by any combination of several ways, including a better trade balance, a reduction of foreign direct investment, larger repatriation of earnings, or greater borrowing abroad to finance foreign direct investment. Since American corporate plans for large increases in foreign direct investment were well advanced at that time, the main result was a large increase in borrowing abroad by the foreign subsidiaries of U.S. companies. In February 1967, the IET on dollar loans made at more than one year by the overseas branches of U.S. banks was therefore waived to allow those branches to compete on equal terms in the new and as yet statistically uncharted Eurocredits market, in which syndicated banks loans were initially made mainly to the foreign subsidiaries of American corporations. This was, indeed, the most important single development in the birth and initial growth of international medium-term Eurocredit bank lending.

The introduction of the VFCR and OFDI controls coincided almost exactly with the growing limitations imposed by the Federal Reserve Board's Regulation Q on the ability of banks in the United States to compete for large interest-bearing time deposits at home, thus forcing them to bid abroad, although mainly from the same American business corporations who simply switched funds from the U.S. to the foreign branches of their American banks. At the same time, these corporations switched their medium-term borrowing for overseas expansion from the domestic to the foreign branches of their banks. The combined effect of all this nonsense was therefore little else than to remove a large part of the American money and capital markets offshore where, having discovered many advantages (like lower taxes and freedom from officially imposed reserve requirements), much of the markets have remained.

"To what extent U.S. corporate borrowing abroad has improved the U.S. external payments position is difficult to say." This was the verdict of an OECD study in 1968 and a judgment has not become any easier since that time. The IET certainly succeeded in pushing European and other designated borrowers out of the New York market; the volume of new issues for such borrowers fell from $645 million to a nominal $20 million between 1963 and 1966. But this in itself did not amount to much in terms of an American external payments deficit of $4½ billion on an official settlements basis during those years (see Figure 5). Much play has therefore been made of what would have happened if the IET had not been imposed, along with the other controls which followed. Here, it is possible to point to more than $10 billion of identified borrowing by American companies in the Eurobond and other foreign bond markets during the decade of American controls. It seems a reasonable deduction that much of this finance would have been raised in the American domestic market in the absence of controls, and the proportion of U.S. borrowing in external markets dropped sharply after the controls were lifted in 1974. Those who defend the controls point also to about $30 billion raised by non-American borrowers in the Eurobond market and in foreign bond markets outside the U.S. during the ten years prior to the end of 1973. But it would be unsafe to guess how much of this might have been raised in the U.S. market had there been no controls; certainly not all of it, as demonstrated by the limited return of previously debarred foreign borrowers to New York after the controls were lifted in 1974.

Finally, a retrospective case for the effectiveness of controls might be argued from the partial data available for the Eurocredits market. Although this came into being in the middle 1960s, borrowing estimates are available only from 1970. But they show that the proportion of identified American borrowing in this market dropped sharply after the lifting of American capital controls, from 13 percent in 1972 to a mere 2 percent by 1977.

Yet all the available evidence does no more than show that the

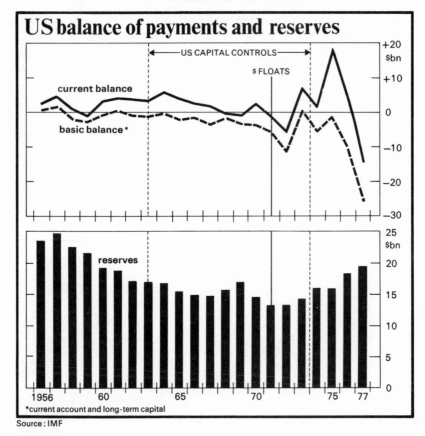

US balance of payments and reserves

*current account and long-term capital

Source: IMF

FIGURE 5

location of a great deal of international dollar capital financing was shifted from the U.S. to other centers. The net effect which this may have had on the American balance of payments remains highly obscure. However, it is fair to add that no illusions were held by Mr. Robert V. Roosa who, as Undersecretary of the Treasury for Monetary Affairs during the Kennedy and Johnson Administrations, was mainly responsible for the many financial reenactments of Custer's last stand during the 1960s. He made clear that he did not think his emergency measures would of themselves save the situation; he was merely trying to hold out for an orderly reform of the international monetary system.[1] But the cavalry did not clatter to the rescue in time; indeed, it did not arrive at all.

---

[1]Robert V. Roosa and Fred Hirsch, "Reserves, Reserve Currencies and Vehicle Currencies: An Argument," *Essays in International Finance,* No. 54, Princeton, May 1966.

Only two points can be made with certainty: that the controls did not ultimately save the fixed dollar and the Bretton Woods system, as intended; and that they brought into being new markets which have become so well established in their own right that they probably could be killed off only by some dramatic change in the international financial situation, or new and very different controls, or a combination of the two.

CHAPTER SEVEN

LINKS BETWEEN THE EUROCURRENCIES AND THE INTERNATIONAL CAPITAL MARKET

Extensive links exist between the predominantly short-term Eurocurrencies and the medium- and longer-term international capital markets, as shown in Figure 6. It is easiest simply to list some of the more obvious.

The main connections with the *Eurocredits* market include the following:

1. Banks secure in the Eurocurrencies money market a large part of the funds which they lend to their customers at medium-term, usually five to seven years. This puts them under constant pressure to bid for Eurocurrency deposits and helps explain why Eurocurrency deposit rates are usually marginally higher than the returns offered by banks in domestic money markets for the same currencies (although, as explained earlier, the true cost to the banks is no higher). The agreed margins

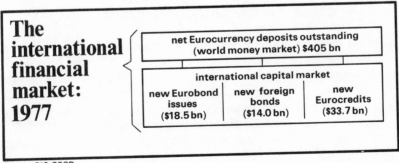

The
international
financial
market:
1977

net Eurocurrency deposits outstanding
(world money market) $405 bn

international capital market

| new Eurobond issues ($18.5 bn) | new foreign bonds ($14.0 bn) | new Eurocredits ($33.7 bn) |

Source: BIS, OECD

FIGURE 6

paid by borrowers over the cost of short-term funds to the banks gives the banks an assured return on their medium-term Eurocredits. The borrower is assured only of an agreed amount of credit for an agreed maturity, but has no assurance about the cost of his or her money. This cost is determined by the largely unpredictable fluctuation of short-term Eurocurrency deposit rates, for which the borrower pays a margin agreed for the term of credit but adjusted, usually at intervals of six months, in order to maintain that agreed margin above the level of short-term interbank Eurocurrency deposit rates.

2. The interplay between the Eurocurrencies and Eurocredit markets is reinforced because borrowers usually make temporary deposits in the short-term market of the proportion of medium-term Eurocredits they have secured but not yet used. Such redepositing helps to increase the gross volume of Eurocurrency deposits outstanding and may also have some influence in driving down Eurocurrency deposit rates and hence the cost of Eurocredits, although it is difficult to estimate the former of these influences and almost impossible to estimate the latter, which is probably marginal. It should be emphasized, however, that the temporary redepositing of unused portions of Eurocredits by borrowers in the Eurocurrencies market provides a return to the borrowers and therefore differs from the noninterest bearing compensating balances which borrowers in the U.S. domestic market are required to hold with the banks from which they borrow. However, the redepositing of temporarily unused portions of Eurocredits in the Eurocurrencies market reduces the net indebtedness of the borrowers and in this way increases to some extent their eligibility for additional Eurocredit facilities.

3. The Eurocurrencies market facilitates interest and currency arbitrage on the part of banks and borrowers, usually in connection with exchange rate cover in the forward market. Banks can therefore draw on a variety of Eurocurrencies to convert into the short-term Eurodollars which they mainly use to transform into medium-term Eurodollar credits. The borrowers likewise have a range of choice for the temporary redepositing in the Eurocurrencies market of temporarily unused Eurocredits. Possibly more important is that many Eurocredit agreements give borrowers a qualified option to choose alternative currencies at each six-monthly roll-over date. This in turn influences relative demand and interest rates of the various currencies dealt in the short-term Eurocurrencies market. The redepositing of temporarily unused Euro-

credits has a similar influence, although in both cases such influence is probably marginal.

The main connections with the *Eurobond* market include the following:

1. The most common measure of the yield curve on Eurobonds is the differential between the return on Eurobonds and the cost of short-term Eurocurrency deposits—usually three-month LIBOR, the London inter-bank offered rate for dollar deposits. This has a crucial influence on the volume of new Eurobond issues, which rises whenever the yield curve does (as in 1975 to 1977) but falls when the yield curve narrows or in fact turns into a negative yield curve (as in 1974, when Eurocurrency deposit rates rose above Eurobond yields), causing investors to switch from medium- and long-term to short-term assets. Fluctuations in short-term rates seem to have the greater influence, since they are often more volatile than long-term interest rates.

2. The yield curve on Eurobonds, determined so largely by Eurocurrency deposit rates, has an important influence also on the volume of new Eurocredits in relation to new Eurobond issues and the volume of new foreign bond issues. High short-term Eurocurrency rates, which make it difficult for borrowers to secure international bond financing, force them to borrow more heavily in the Eurocredit markets. When short-term Eurocurrency interest rates fall and reopen the yield curve on international bonds, borrowers fund the floating rate Eurocredits they were forced to take up during the preceding period of high short-term rates and switch to international bond financing. However, although the proportion of international bonds and Eurocredits changes in response to such influences, the total of international capital provided by the combination of the two increased steadily during the 1970s.

3. Another link between the Eurocurrencies and Eurobond markets is that investment banks and securities firms which manage and sell new Eurobond issues and which make a secondary market for Eurobonds finance themselves to a large extent in the Eurocurrencies market. This tends to increase their voluntary holdings of Eurobonds for profit when depressed Eurocurrency deposit rates help to create attractively large yield curves on Eurobond investment. Conversely, it increases their involuntary Eurobond holdings when rising Eurocurrency deposit rates narrow or reverse the Eurobond yield curve. The latter happens because banks do pro-

vide some support to the secondary market during bad times, partly by being trapped into doing so and partly out of longer-range self-interest in trying to provide the relatively stable markets necessary to encourage continuing investor interest.

4. The relationship between Eurocurrency deposit rates and Eurobond yields naturally influences Eurobond prices creating real or paper capital gains or losses for investors and banks in the market. This naturally affects the profits of investment banks and securities firms in the primary and secondary Eurobond markets, although that effect is often disguised in consolidated balance sheets and can only be guessed at by shareholders.

5. Investors switch between Eurocurrency and Eurobond assets to some extent, but they do so to a far lesser extent than the investment banks and securities firms in the market. This is true particularly of individual investors, who commonly switch to a greater extent between external bonds in various currencies, or between fixed-interest securities and equities, or between short-term domestic and longer-term international assets (as between commercial paper in the United States and Eurobonds or foreign bonds).

CHAPTER EIGHT

THE INTERNATIONAL CAPITAL MARKET'S SIZE IN THE WORLD ECONOMY

Most aspects of the international capital market are extensively documented. Estimates of the volume of new financing are published regularly and so are breakdowns of currencies used, maturities, terms, yields, and classifications of borrowers by country and their public or private standing. But the attempt to put the market's size into some perspective in its relationship to the world economy is seldom made and is, admittedly, almost impossible because some global magnitudes cannot be more than what may be termed "guesstimates." So what follows here is intended only as an extremely broad-brush picture and does not pretend to a precision which would be spurious.

During 1977, the year chosen for illustration because it was the latest for which even preliminary guesstimates were available at the time of writing, the gross amount of new financing on the international capital market was very roughly $70 billion, averaging the guesstimates of the OECD and Morgan Guaranty. There are no published estimates of the market's net new lending but, given that the really big surge in new lending started only in 1973, it seems a reasonable assumption that the proportion of new net to gross lending was still very high in 1977, probably over 80 percent or close to $60 billion.

At first glance this seems trivial in the context of a world economy whose 1977 output was about $7,000 billion (or $7 trillion). But the importance of any market lies in its contribution at the margin, which is usually out of all proportion to the market's size. Equilibrium is all; a weight need not be big to balance the scales. And this is precisely what a seemingly tiny international capital market contributes in helping to balance the world economy at any given level of output, which is always considerably higher than it would have been in the absence of such financing or some equivalent balancing counter.

Of the guesstimates set out in Table 2, that for 1977 world output is derived by taking the weighting of the Organization for Economic Cooperation and Development of United States gross national product at just under 40 percent of OECD GNP, and then taking the World Bank's estimates that the industrial countries have, for several years, accounted for about 63 percent of world output, the centrally planned (or Communist) economies for about 21 percent, the non-oil developing countries for about 13 percent, and oil exporting countries for about 3 percent. This is not wholly out of line with guesstimates of world output of $5,385 billion for 1974, by the *Economist,* and about $6,700 billion for 1976, by the Development Assistance Committee of the OECD.

Now although countries are deeply dependent on each other, they nevertheless remain largely self-contained. Most of the world's goods and services are consumed in the countries which produce them. Thus the International Monetary Fund estimated the value of world trade at about $1,000 billion for 1977, meaning that the countries of the world supplied, on average, about 85 percent of their own goods and services. Nevertheless, it is the very substantial minority of about 15 percent of

TABLE 2   5548t

THE INTERNATIONAL CAPITAL MARKET IN THE WORLD ECONOMY, 1977

($ billion)

World output	7,000
Domestically consumed	6,000
Goods and services internationally traded	1,000
World savings	1,500
Investment financed by domestic savings	1,400
International capital flows	100
International capital requirements:	
To finance current external deficits	90
For additions to world reserves	60
	150
Financing:	
Official aid and nonmarket capital*	80
International market capital	70
	150

*Official aid included about $14 billion net from OECD countries, about $8 billion net from OPEC, and about $1 billion net from Communist countries. Nonmarket capital includes trade credits, foreign direct investment (the creation or purchase of a business in one country by residents of another), and foreign portfolio investment (the purchase of domestic securities in one country by residents of another). All guesstimates very approximate and very rounded.

SOURCE: IMF, OECD, IBRD (World Bank).

goods and services entering world trade which makes a disproportionately large contribution to the world's living standards. Even a supremely rich and well-endowed country like the United States could not enjoy the life style it has without importing the raw materials it lacks, or lacks in sufficient quantity, as well as goods and services which other countries produce more efficiently, while exporting some of its own output to foot the import bill.

In terms of savings, countries are likewise far more self-sufficient than often supposed. On the World Bank's estimates, the world's gross domestic savings and investment have averaged just over 20 percent of output for many years, suggesting a total of world savings and investment running at roughly $1,500 billion in 1977. But even the very poorest African countries generally provide at least 70 percent of the savings needed to finance their investment and developing countries as a whole self-finance well over 90 percent of their development. Here again it is the all important margin that counts, filled in this case by exports of capital from the richer industrial countries and from oil exporters, who channel the largest part of their financial surpluses through the Western banking system.

Estimating the gap which needs to be filled by capital exports is a very rough and ready business, mainly because of the notorious asymmetries in world current payments totals which have so far defeated official statisticians and computers everywhere. This is partly because countries record exports more promptly than imports and partly because the national returns on which international agencies have to rely are often sketchy, to put it politely. Thus the asymmetries in world current payments totals averaged no less than about $30 billion a year on the IMF-OECD estimates during most of the mid-1970s, this being the amount by which the total of recorded current deficits regularly exceeded the total of recorded current surpluses.

One way of trying to get around the difficulties and arriving at some approximate global picture is to total the current deficits as estimated by the IMF and the OECD for the world's non-oil developing countries, plus the centrally planned Communist economies, plus those of the whole of the OECD area minus those OECD industrial countries running large current payments surpluses, notably Japan, Germany, Switzerland, and the Netherlands. On that basis, the world's current deficits totaled about $90 billion in 1977 while world reserves rose by about $60 billion. Adding the two sums therefore suggests a world financing gap of about $150 billion in that year.

In practice, the official data attempting to reconcile global current balances of payments are grotesque because of the enormous "asymmetries, errors, and omissions" conceded by the International Monetary

Fund and attributed largely to "official placements of foreign exchange in the Euromarkets[1]". The important conceptual point is that countries whose domestic investments exceed domestic savings are, by definition, in current external deficit and the other way around. The figures in Table 2 are therefore unashamedly fudged. They are intended to give an impressionistic view of the international capital market's place in the world structure and nothing more.

[1]*IMF Survey,* International Monetary Fund, May 8, 1978, p. 133.

CHAPTER NINE
WORRYING ABOUT EUROCURRENCIES

Worrying about the international financial markets is a thriving industry of its own, quite literally for financial journalists as well as for bankers who write for the financial press while also advertising in it. But it is significant that the focus of anxiety keeps shifting in a neurotic way, never fixing permanently on any single aspect. Many people have an instinctive feeling that they *should* be troubled by markets which have grown so quickly, which are so big and in many ways so little understood. But they are unsure precisely what it is they ought to be nervous about and so a limited number of topics succeed each other endlessly as the fashionable concern of the moment. Each is discussed learnedly, exhaustively, and inconclusively until attention switches to the next. Whenever the round has been completed it starts again, the roster as unvarying as the questions about eternal verities posted on wayside pulpits outside churches. Contradictory beliefs flourish easily in a field where knowledge is elusive and emotions strong, as in the answers to a poll of international bankers in February 1978.[1] Nearly 60 percent thought there was a danger of "overtrading" in the Euromarkets (presumably by other banks), but 75 percent believed control of the markets would be undesirable even if possible.

Those who worry about the Euromarket are usually concerned about the soundness of the banks in it and about the market's supposed potential for monetary disruption. Under the first heading they fear that lack of conventional regulation creates a danger of

---

[1]Poll by *The Financial Times* and *The Banker*, London, February 1978.

imprudent banking and chain collapse. Under the second heading they worry that the market does or may generate excess liquidity, add to inflationary pressures, complicate domestic monetary management, and aggravate exchange rate disturbances. Fears about the international capital market concern the financial, economic, and political risks of extensive lending to governments, especially by commercial banks which depend on short-term Eurocurrency deposits to finance a large part of their medium- and long-term loan commitments. Because of the close link between the Eurocurrencies market as a pool of supply to the international capital market, worries about the two markets overlap, but it is convenient to try to examine some of the main worries separately.

Nearly all fears about the Eurocurrencies market are rooted in the fact that banks are not required by supervisory authorities to keep reserves against their foreign currency (i.e., Eurocurrency) deposits, as they must against their domestic currency liabilities. One purpose of the classic banking reserve base is to contribute to sound banking by helping to ensure that banks will be able to meet sudden withdrawals by depositors. But reserve requirements are also an instrument of monetary management. A reserve base at any level holds down the creation of credit by a banking system below what it would be in the absence of such a base. The base is also used more flexibly by the authorities in many countries, who require the maintenance of reserve ratios at different levels against different maturities of deposit liabilities and periodically vary the levels to reduce or increase the rate of credit expansion.

The absence of a reserve base in the Eurocurrencies market could indeed permit imprudent banking if reserve requirements were the only safeguard of sound banking, but they are not. The Eurocurrencies market is by no means simply left to its own devices. National authorities in the major countries improved their supervision of Eurobanks during the 1970s, especially in London. The Bank of England treats foreign currency operations as an integral part of the total business of banks in its jurisdiction for purposes of supervision. It requires an adequate matching of assets and liabilities by currencies and maturities. It also requires banks in its jurisdiction to maintain specified ratios of capital and liquid assets (such as Treasury bills) against their deposit liabilities as a whole, including foreign currency liabilities. In an emergency, such liquid assets can be mobilized just about as quickly as mandatory reserve assets (which banks are usually required to keep as vault cash or sight deposits with their central banks). Indeed, exemption from reserve requirements (as distinct from capital and liquidity requirements) is the only significant element of permissiveness in Eurobanking.[2] Although the Eurocurrencies market is not regulated as such, the banks in it are supervised—and extensively so in the major countries, where the biggest Eurobanks operate.

The past can give no assurance for the future, but in almost 30 years of market evolution from the first beginnings in 1949, no bank has failed solely or even mainly because of unsound Eurocurrencies lending. There were certainly losses on Eurocurrency loans, including several to oil-tanker owners in the early 1970s, but they were no different from and, on the whole, smaller than losses incurred by banks on domestic loans, especially against real estate.

The worst shock suffered by the Eurocurrencies market up to the time of writing was the collapse of Bankhaus Herstatt, a relatively small German bank, in June 1974. What happened was significant in several ways. The collapse of Herstatt resulted from gambling in the sale and purchase of currencies on the foreign exchanges and not from unsound lending of foreign currencies in the Euromarket. Nevertheless, the event did show the Euromarket's vulnerability to a panic chain reaction. For a few months, smaller banks had great difficulty in obtaining Eurocurrency deposits even at premiums above quoted market rates, for no other reason than being smaller banks. But, equally instructive, although less remarked, was how quickly market forces reasserted themselves. Bigger banks, inundated with deposits, had no use for the excess funds except to plough them back into the Euromarket, where deposit rates for all banks soon settled back into their normal pattern.

Yet recovery from the Herstatt scare did not permanently reassure everyone, perhaps in part because it was relatively quick. The next panic, it is argued, might last longer and some banks might then find themselves unable to obtain at any price the continuing flow of short-term Eurocurrency deposits which they need for their longer lending commitments. And that fear is rooted, in its turn, in concern about the degree of maturity transformation and the market's supposed vulnerability to some big outside depositors, especially oil exporting countries. But there seems to be more emotion than logic in this.

---

[2]An important qualification is that reserve requirements are not wholly absent from the Euromarket. When a bank in Amsterdam makes a dollar deposit with a bank in London, the balances of the two European banks are adjusted accordingly on the books of their correspondent banks in the United States (the only place where dollars can ultimately be banked). And the banks in the U.S. are required to maintain reserves against those dollars, which are domestic currency liabilities on *their* books, even though they are foreign currency (i.e., Eurocurrency) assets and liabilities on the books of the European banks.

The persistent worry about maturity transformation by Eurobanks is another way of alleging that they do not maintain adequate liquidity ratios and that, in turn, is the basis of widespread fears of chain collapse. But there is not enough information to know whether the degree of maturity transformation in the Euromarkets is indeed greater than in the main national banking systems and the phenomenon in itself is not disturbing; indeed, maturity transformation is the essence of banking because, without it, bankers would be acting simply as cloakroom attendants for money.

The market's supposed vulnerability to powerful outside depositors is more dubious still. Among those who have raised this particular specter was the U.S. Senate Subcommittee on Foreign Economic Policy. In September 1977, it warned gravely of the "weapon" which Arab oil exporters had built up in the form of short-term bank deposits in the West, allegedly liable to withdrawal at any time. Withdrawal to where? The only way in which oil exporters or any one else can withdraw deposits from the international banking system is by cashing them into bank notes for burial in the ground.[3] As Mr. Walter Wriston of Citibank remarked about similar doom-mongering at an earlier stage, anyone who talks in this way does not understand how money markets work. Investors who withdraw deposits from one bank or several have no alternative but to switch them to other banks. This leaves the deposits exactly where they were before, in the international banking system. The deprived banks then simply go into the market to bid the deposits back. That could prove a nuisance and add marginally to costs, but it could not threaten the world banking system.

All this might seem to imply that the stability of banks in the Eurocurrencies market can be taken for granted, but that would be going too far. After the Herstatt scare, arrangements were made through the Bank for International Settlements (the BIS) under which commercial banks in the major countries gave formal undertakings of ultimate responsibility for their foreign branches. At the same time central banks formally undertook to provide help of last resort to any of their commercial banks facing difficulties as a result of the operations of foreign branches. Those agreements usefully spelled out what had merely been implicit before, although some questions were left about supervision and responsibility for the operations of branch banks in brass-plate centers.

---

[3]Even money spent, or invested in nonfinancial assets like gold, would still find its way back into the banking system through the deposits of the recipients. The Senate Subcommitee seemed to be confusing money market deposits, which a bank can replace by bidding for them in the market, and noninterest bearing current accounts, which cannot be similarly replaced by a bank from which they are withdrawn.

But, that said, there seems ultimately no obvious or logical reason why the Eurocurrencies market should be inherently more vulnerable than the international banks which make it. The possible weakness may be a subtle one. Because the Euromarket mushroomed so quickly in ways not fully understood, it arouses greater uneasiness than traditional markets with longer histories. To adapt President Franklin D. Roosevelt's phrase, it may be that the one thing the Euromarket has to fear is fear itself. It is inevitable that reckless Eurocurrency lending will lead to one or more bank failures sooner or later. When that happens, there is a danger of a reaction far more traumatic than to similar domestic banking failures. This may prove the Achilles heel of the Euromarket, if it has one.

Whether the Eurocurrencies market contributes to world financial instability is a different question. The assertion that it does rests on the argument that the absence of a reserve base allows Eurobanks to create credit faster than banks in a domestic system, who are obliged to keep part of their funds frozen as reserves. The remedy usually prescribed is the imposition of reserve requirements at internationally agreed levels to be held in some internationally agreed form against Eurocurrency deposit liabilities. However, many bankers have argued against both the need and feasibility of such control, among them Mr. C.W. McMahon, an executive director of the Bank of England. He found the evidence of a larger Eurocredit multiplier inconclusive. But, he added, even if the possibiliity of a larger multiplier were conceded, that itself would not imply any net addition to world credit because of the scope for "leakages" from the Euromarket into domestic banking systems. Much of the credit extended by the Euromarket was a substitute for domestic credit, said Mr. McMahon. "It cannot be emphasised too strongly that the Euromarkets are very largely an alternative channel for, rather than a net addition to, credit flows that would take place in some form or other in any event."[4]

Besides, Mr. McMahon argued that control would be impractical. On the technical level, it would be difficult to decide whether reserve ratios should seek to equalize conditions between Eurobanks and banks in a currency's country of issue, or between Eurobanks and banks in countries supplying the foreign currency deposits. More important, imposition of reserve ratios, in Mr. McMahon's view, "would probably induce banks to divert a large part of their business through alternative channels, particularly brass-plate companies outside the scope of control."

This speech has been singled out as a lucid expression of widely held

---

[4]C.W. McMahon, speech reprinted in the *Bank of England Quarterly Bulletin,* March 1976.

and strongly established views. The portrayal of the Eurocurrencies market as a channel rather than a source of international financial instability is persuasive. Inflation, excessive imbalances of world payments, and disruptive exchange rate fluctuations result almost wholly from the policies of the major financial powers. At worst, the Euromarket may make a very marginal contribution to the spread of instability through its sheer efficiency as a transmission channel.

However, a critic could point out that the intellectual argument against the need for control is compromised, even if it is not invalidated, by special pleading about the difficulty of applying it. Logically, reserve requirements either are a useful tool of monetary management or they are not, in which case they should either be abandoned everywhere or extended to all banking operations. To this, the answer would be that the difficulties of trying to apply reserve requirements to Eurocurrency operations would far outweigh any advantage, and there the argument must be left. It is, in any case, the sort of matter ultimately decided by events rather than debate. If an upheaval should ever persuade the international authorities that control of the Euromarket should be tried after all, then it will be, effectively or otherwise, and the intellectual arguments for it will be found. The last word on this subject remains to be written.

As stated above, worry about the Eurocurrencies market centers mainly on its alleged credit-creating and inflationary potential and on the contribution which many believe that this market makes to the instability of exchange rates by providing a ready channel for international hot-money flows. There are also those who fear a special degree of commercial risk because banks are not required by law to maintain reserves against their Eurocurrency deposits as they are against their domestic deposits. By contrast, worry about the international capital market is concerned mainly with commercial risk. In the international bond markets this proved minimal during the 15 years prior to the end of 1977. About $72 billion were raised through more than 2,700 Eurobond issues and losses amounted to less than 0.24 percent from the default of 10 small American companies for a combined $170 million. The record of the foreign bond markets was better still.

Worry about the international capital market has therefore been concentrated almost exclusively on medium-term international Eurocredit bank lending. The narrowly defined commercial or banking risks of such lending are examined in some detail in Chapter 17. Its main conclusion is that there is hardly any worry about Eurocredit lending to industrialized and oil-exporting countries; there is caution but no deep concern about lending to the U.S.S.R. and Eastern Europe; and that concern about Eurocredit lending to non-oil developing countries is concentrated upon some rather than all. Moreover, a clear distinction is made between the Eurocredit debt of a handful of highly advanced, rapidly growing developing countries and the very different question of the generalized debt burden of all developing countries as a group.

However, one observation can be inserted here to put into perspective the commercial stakes in Eurocurrency and Eurocredit lending. At the end of 1977, the total assets of commercial banks in the world's 11 biggest industrial countries and their branches in Luxembourg and the Caribbean amounted to about $4,150 billion. The gross foreign currency (i.e. Eurocurrency) assets of those banks and branches then amounted to about $660 billion, or just over 15 percent of their total assets—a ratio corresponding almost exactly, as it happens, to that between world output and world trade. The total of Eurocredit lending then outstanding was between $130 and $140 billion, or between 3 percent and $3\frac{1}{2}$ percent of total Western banking assets. It is therefore one thing to observe that Eurocredit lending expanded very rapidly during the 1970s, providing a useful service to the world economy and making an important contribution to the earnings of banks in the market, especially the biggest international banks which dominate it. But it is simply untrue to state that the Western banking system has been putting all of its eggs into the Eurocredit basket.

CHAPTER TEN
ECONOMIC AND POLITICAL IMPLICATIONS

The emergence of the modern international capital market has been associated with two changes of great importance to the world economy which began to take place in the early 1960s. One of these changes was that the main burden of transmitting capital across the world was once again shifted onto the private sector by a combination of events and fiat. The other is that more developing countries finally started to emerge and, as a result, have increasingly competed with the mature industrialized countries for capital, raw materials, and world markets. The contemporary international capital market was born out of the first of these developments and contributes to the second.

For about 20 years after 1945, the movement of capital across the world was largely an act of official foreign and economic policy in which governments and international agencies played the major part. Resources were transferred initially for the reconstruction of Europe and Japan after the Second World War and then for the development of the poorer countries. The United States, which started this process, wanted political control over capital transfers, directly in the case of the implementation of the Marshall Plan and its subsequent bilateral aid, and indirectly, at least to a large extent, over the World Bank's disbursals. When other Western countries became aid donors, they were motivated by similar considerations.

Development aid by the Western industrialized countries was regarded as desirable partly on humanitarian grounds. But at a more prosaic level it was sold to Western legislatures as a form of foreign policy and to Western industry as a disguised form of export subsidy. It was also believed on both idealistic and realistic grounds that stimulating the growth of the world economy as a whole would benefit all in the longer run.

During the 20 years leading to 1965 there were private international capital transfers too, but they were not financed in an international capital market. After 1945, American industry once again began to make substantial direct investments abroad, building or buying plants in other countries. In the immediate postwar years there was no alternative because the rest of the world did not have the dollars to import goods made in the United States, the only major country to have emerged from World War II with its industry not only intact, but much enlarged. Besides, foreign direct investment offered American industry tax advantages and the benefits of what was then cheaper labor abroad. But until controls were imposed on the export of capital from the United States in the mid-1960s, American companies financed their foreign direct investment from the American domestic capital market.[1] See Figure 7.

Meanwhile, the industries of other Western countries were in no position to export capital for many years after the World War II. When German industry was eventually able to do so once again, memories of expropriations after 1918 and 1945 proved a psychological deterrent for a long time, prompting the import of labor rather than the export

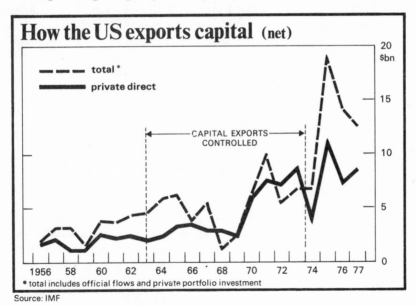

FIGURE 7

---

[1]Another form of international investment is foreign portfolio investment, consisting of the purchase of domestic securities in one country by the resident of another. But nearly all such investment has been financed in the financial markets of the investor's country or that in which the securities are bought, thus bypassing the international capital market.

of capital ("capital" exports being made only indirectly through the wages sent home by Turkish and other foreign workers in Germany). Japan, for its part, concentrated heavily on direct investment abroad, mainly to secure access to raw materials and later to foreign markets. But, as in the case of American industry, such investment was financed for many years mainly in the Japanese domestic capital market.

The result was to leave the international capital market no more than a residual role over the two decades following 1945. And, during that time, the international market consisted exclusively of the "classical" market in foreign bonds issued for nonresident investors in the domestic capital markets of other countries, this being the only part of the contemporary international capital market with a long history, the regular issue of foreign bonds in Europe dating from the beginning of the nineteenth century and periodic issues going further back.

However, in the two decades after 1945 the amounts raised on "classical" foreign bond markets did not amount to much. Access of foreign borrowers to New York, even when officially unimpeded, was and remains limited by American investor resistance, the deterrence of the Securities and Exchange Commission's disclosure requirements, and the cold scrutiny of the American credit rating agencies. To that extent New York remains largely a neighborhood rather than an international capital market (for Canadian borrowers) and an international capital market only at one remove (for World Bank issues). Meanwhile, foreign borrowers' access to the London bond market, the world's biggest international market until 1914, was restricted by the British authorities as long ago as 1938, still more tightly restricted after 1945, and stopped completely after 1972. And access of foreign borrowers to Frankfurt, Zurich, Tokyo, and Amsterdam was and remains limited by the capacity of those markets to provide international capital and by the concern of their national authorities to control the impact of foreign borrowing and especially investment on their balances of payments and exchange rates.

The innovation of offshore markets in Eurobonds and Eurocredits, which now supply the bulk of international market capital, dates back only to the mid-1960s. The birth of those markets resulted from a revival of international demand and the restrictions imposed on the export of capital from the United States, whose authorities were unwilling to allow the American market to meet this upsurge of international demand because of the adverse effect they feared on the American balance of payments and the stability of the dollar.

The supply of funds to the new international capital market and the demands on it increased suddenly and dramatically during the world's economic boom of 1972 and 1973, with its accompaniment of steeply rising food and raw material prices, and then grew very considerably once again after the quadrupling of world oil prices in the final quarter of 1973. That event expanded supply and demand in the international capital market for several reasons. Non-oil developing countries were forced into the market to help finance greatly increased current payments deficits resulting from the higher price of oil, oil-based products like fertilizers, the higher cost of freight, and the stagnation or decline of their export earnings because of the recession in the Western industrial countries. Since most of the Western industrialized countries were themselves plunged into large payments deficits which they, too, financed extensively in the international capital market, they were in no position to maintain let alone augment official aid flows to the developing countries. Since those aid flows actually declined in real terms, the LDCs (less developed countries) were made still more dependent on the international capital market.

On the supply side, the revenues of oil exporters, or at least the biggest exporters with the smallest populations, rose much faster than their ability to spend them on new imports. This had the deflationary effect of an indirect or purchasing tax imposed by oil exporters on the rest of the world. It also had the effect of geographically shifting the ownership of a significant part of the world's savings from the Western industrial countries (the traditional suppliers of capital to the rest of the world) to oil exporting countries, particularly in the Middle East. But those countries did not have a sufficiency of trained personnel, financial institutions, or international financial connections and experience to undertake the task of reexporting their new capital surpluses themselves. Nor did the richest and least populous of them have the political power necessary for the job, the bailiffs which every lender ultimately needs at his back. They therefore shifted the task to the Western financial system, placing most of their surpluses in the Eurocurrencies market and in the United States (as shown in the Table 3), and the role of the Western industrial countries was suddenly changed. Instead of remaining the principal suppliers of capital to the rest of the world, they became intermediaries for the provision of international capital, except for Germany, Japan, Switzerland, and the Netherlands, whose current payments surpluses allowed them to continue supplying capital to other countries.

The pattern of growth in the issue of foreign and Eurobonds, mainly to individual investors, is strongly influenced by national controls on private capital flows. But within that framework, the trend of issuing volume is determined mainly by differentials of yield between international short- and long-term fixed-interest securities and by investors' currency preferences. Eurobond issuing volume has fluctuated extremely widely on those influences, falling from about $6 billion in 1972

TABLE 3
INTERNATIONAL CAPITAL FLOWS 1974/1977
($ billion)

Current surpluses:	
OPEC	170
Germany	22
Japan	10
Switzerland	10
Netherlands	7
Total	220*
International market capital, 1974/1977:	
Eurocredits, Eurobonds,	
foreign bonds	200
OPEC assets, end 1977:	
Eurocurrencies	60
Investments in U.S.	42
Investments/loans	
other industrial countries	28
Investments/loans	
to LDCs	20
Loans to international	
organizations	10
Total	160

*Rounded figures do not add.

Note: All the OPEC surpluses listed above except the $20 billion of investments and loans to developing countries were channeled internationally through the Western system. Eurocurrency placements and loans to international organizations were thus channeled directly. Investments in the U.S. and other Western countries released equivalent amounts of domestic savings for transmission abroad.

SOURCE: OECD, BIS, Arab Monetary Fund, Abu Dhabi.

to about $2 billion in 1974 and then rising to about $18 billion in 1977. However, an important factor is that the market seems to have been given structural strength by the participation of more institutional investors and more strongly capitalized securities firms and investment banks in the secondary market, so that succeeding peaks and troughs in Eurobond issuing volume during the 1970s were at progressively higher levels.

To some extent periodic declines in international bond issues have been offset by increases in publicized Eurocredits and the other way about, but the total financing provided by the international capital market as a whole increased rapidly during the 1970s, at least to the time of writing in 1978–1979. The main influence here is that the sparsely populated oil exporters have no alternative to the international market as a direct or indirect channel for moving their capital surpluses to the rest of the world. It follows that the market can be expected to go on playing a very important part in plugging the world's financing gaps for at least as long as a structural imbalance persists in world payments as a result of petroleum prices remaining historically high in terms of the prices of other goods and services.

The term "recycling" for the redistribution of funds from surplus to deficit countries acquired such vogue after the oil crisis that it came to be used in almost every context, including a new biography of Lord Byron referring to the poet's habit of "recycling" lines from his earlier to his later poems. But in financial terms recycling is merely a new and more graphic expression for the classical banking function of transforming savings into investment within or between economies.

The part played in recycling by the international capital market will depend not only on the persistence of the structural or long-term imbalance in world payments created by the 1973 increase in world oil prices, but also on the duration of payments imbalances caused by a structural change in the world economy which seems to have coincided with, rather than to have been caused by, the rise in oil prices. This structural change consists of the fact that a break seems to have occurred after a generation of unprecedented economic growth in the Western economies at the very time when several advanced developing countries began to emerge as producers and even exporters of machinery and consumer goods, whose output was formerly a near-monopoly of the West. The extent of the connection between these trends is uncertain, but they do not appear to have been an exact counterpart of each other.

In the Western industrialized world, warning signs began to appear in the early 1970s, but they became acute and widely noticed only from the recession and stagnation of 1974 onward. The flattening or decline in the share of profits in national income and of fixed capital expenditure in most Western countries predated the 1973 oil crisis. The considerable excess capacity which became apparent in certain industries, notably steel, shipbuilding, textiles, synthetic fibers, and some petrochemical industries in most Western countries after 1974 were partly cyclical. But they were almost certainly partly structural too, resulting from earlier synchronized investment booms.

The coincidence of economic stagnation and a probable structural change in the Western economies with the emergence of new competition from advanced developing countries has had the inevitable result of intensifying conflict among social and economic groups within countries as well as conflicts between countries, the latter mainly in the form of growing pressure for trade protection. In January 1978, Mr. Oliver

Long, the director general of the General Agreement on Tariffs and Trade (GATT), estimated that import restrictions since 1974 had depressed world trade by between 3 percent and 5 percent below the levels it might otherwise have reached, meaning aborted trade flows of $30 billion to $50 billion by 1977, with a multiplied effect on total economic activity. In the same month, the Japanese prime minister, Mr. Takeo Fukuda, went as far as to warn of the possibility of an "economic and political equivalent of the third world war" unless the slide to protectionism were halted. It should be noted that a less obvious but increasingly widespread form of trade protectionism is achieved indirectly through government subsidies to declining industries and areas. "Job creation," which consists by definition of the creation of jobs for which there is no market demand, insidiously undermines efficient allocation of resources not just within the countries where such policies are pursued, but also between countries through distortions of international trade.

The ending or at least interruption of a generation of exceptional economic growth has had other side effects. One of them has been an increasing shrillness and downright ill-temper among the theologians of rival economic dogmas. At the same time, governments and their advisers have tended to blame factors beyond human control for adversity, although they were happy to take credit for competent economic management when matters were going well. Theories suggesting the hand of providence have been resurrected. In its annual report of June 1978, the Bank for International Settlements (BIS) joined the growing number of observers who had come to worry that Kondratieff's theory of long-term economic cycles may have contained some truth.

That such cycles actually occurred at approximately regular intervals since the late eighteenth century has been demonstrated. But exactly why they occurred is uncertain, although that is crucial to the implication of inevitability and the belief therefore expressed by the BIS in "the possibility of a slowdown of the Kondratieff type after several decades of virtually uninterrupted fast growth."

In fact, the more one looks at the record, the greater the number of random explanations which undermine the concept of an immutable law of nature foreshadowing the future on the basis of the past.[2] The

---

[2]Nikolai Kondratieff, the Russian economist born in 1892, detected economic cycles of about 50 years, consisting mostly of about 20 years of rising output followed by a few years of floundering and then by about 20 years of recession. For different reasons, this worried Stalin even more than it did the BIS a generation later, the Marxist objection being that the theory challenged the inevitability of capitalism's permanent decline. Kondratieff was arrested in 1930, "tried" the following year, and never seen again. But the worry he caused was probably needless, given the endless explanations which can be found for the

world may indeed be facing a generation of misery, but it is by no means a foregone conclusion. The very opposite may come to pass, with an investment boom bringing the mature industrialized countries into a new era of advanced technology (possibly based, at least in part, on the microcircuit revolution) while traditional manufacturing is taken over to an increasing extent by developing countries moving to the next stages of industrialization.

But there is no disguising the great difficulties of a transition in which new competition is created for some countries and industries while new opportunities are created for others. The development of Japan, to cite only the most obvious example, has created not only new markets for raw material producers but also new competition for American and European industries, while countries such as South Korea, Singapore, Taiwan, the Philippines, and the Colony of Hong Kong are competing increasingly with Japan.

However, what is happening is not an unfortunate accident. It is the outcome of a consistent Western policy since 1945, and there is no need to abandon the belief that growing prosperity in more countries will ultimately contribute to the greater prosperity of all, despite the pain of the present transition.

But because the main role in bridging current payments imbalances has been left to the international capital market, the market has filled a policy vacuum and not merely a financing need. One effect has been to thrust Eurobanks into a political role. Nor is it true that bankers assume that role only when imposing conditions in cases of default; they do so by the very act of lending on a large scale. Such lending involves them, at least passively, in helping to determine priorities both for exporting and importing countries: guns or harvesters, turbine generators or jet fighters. The answers help to decide which Western export industries are helped or threatened by the creation of new competition

---

peaks and troughs he traced. A 20-year upturn from 1790 coincided exactly with the Neopleonic Wars and the 20-year downturn which followed accompanied (by chance or otherwise) the stultification imposed on Europe by Metternich at the Congress of Vienna. The next upturn, from about 1840 to 1865, spanned the Crimean War and the American Civil War. More important was that it coincided with the first railway and steamship booms. The very speed with which these helped dump more goods onto markets may or may not have contributed to about 25 years of recession to the 1890s. The next upturn came soon after the injection of fresh liquidity into the world from South Africa's new gold mines and, with booster shots from the Anglo-South African War of 1899 to 1902 and the First World War, lasted to the end of the 1920s. The cycle then contracted to a downturn of less than a decade to 1938 before lengthening again to an upturn of about 35 years to 1973. That upturn began with Hermann Goering's preference for guns over butter and was given a different, constructive, and more lasting impulse in 1947 by the Marshall Plan for the reconstruction of Europe.

from foreign industry, as well as patterns of consumption, display, and development in borrowing countries.

The delegation of a greatly increased share of international financing by Western governments to international banks has other implications. One of them is that each party gives itself as a hostage to the other; governments by abandoning what they formerly regarded as part of their responsibility and banks by risking their independence if any widespread collapse of their international loans should ever make official rescue necessary.

Another aspect is that as long as the international transmission of capital mainly took the form of official flows and foreign direct investment, the process was, in a sense, more controlled. When international capital is provided by governments there is at least a presumption that the donor governments know and are willing to face the eventual consequences for their electorates of helping to bring new foreign trade competitors into being.

When the international transfer of capital takes the form of foreign direct investment it is controlled in another way. Multinational companies with specialized knowledge of international trends in their fields can at least be presumed to concentrate new investment where it will dovetail with existing investment elsewhere.

On the other hand, market capital flows are "controlled" to a far lesser extent by the considerations described above. International market capital tends to go in a highly concentrated form to a relative minority of advanced developing countries, unlike official aid which is spread far more evenly around the developing world and which is often provided for political, and not merely economic, reasons. At the same time, it is almost certain that market capital makes a greater contribution, directly or indirectly, to industrial development in the recipient countries than most official aid or than a great deal of private foreign direct investment, which has tended to be heavily concentrated on mining and other extraction of raw materials. And, to the extent that market capital is thus more efficient than aid or foreign direct investment, it speeds up the process by which industrial countries are faced with new competition from developing countries in the quest for raw materials and export markets for manufactured goods.

However, in the present transition, an apparent conflict of interest has arisen between Western bankers on the one hand and the more old-fashioned, beleaguered Western industries on the other. Debt is deferred trade, and bankers depend on an expansion of Western markets so that borrowing countries can earn the export income needed to service their external debt. Many older Western industries, on the other hand, have come to see their survival in terms of greater restrictions on imports.[3] This would provide an enjoyable gladiatorial contest if Western bankers and industrialists were wholly unconnected caricatures, but while their interests may seem to conflict in some ways they are closely entwined in others. A large American commercial bank having an interest in the industrial development and debt servicing capacity of a country like Brazil also has a considerable interest in the welfare of important domestic corporations such as U.S. Steel and General Motors. Moreover, the pension and trade union funds of Western workers are often invested partly in Western commercial banks. The conflict of interest is therefore one which has to be settled with kid gloves.

It is time to sum up. During the 1970s, the international capital market played a growing part in financing greatly enlarged imbalances in net current payments between countries, caused by a coincidence of a steep rise in energy costs and a quickening change in the structure of the world economy. The market filled a gap left by governments and international agencies. It saved the industrialized world from an even deeper recession than it actually suffered and allowed many developing countries to maintain an almost unchecked economic expansion.

The market itself cannot "solve" the problems of adjusting to higher energy costs and profound changes in the world economy. That adjustment requires conservation of energy, the development of new sources and forms of energy, and a shift to new industries in the advanced economies. It is an adjustment which cannot be made by economic management alone, because of the great political difficulties in reconciling strong differences of interest.

The international capital market plays a double role in this process. In acting efficiently to allocate resources to growing economies, it speeds the changes in the structure of the world economy to which older economies must adjust. But the market also allows deficit countries to make a less abrupt and painful adjustment than might otherwise be forced on them. However, the market does not let countries postpone adjustment indefinitely, as shown by the curtailment of lending to Italy in 1974 and Britain in 1975. In the words which the International Monetary Fund first applied to its own lending many years ago, the international capital market provides "time, but not time to waste."

---

[3]In April 1978, Mr. Frederick Jaicks, the chairman of Inland Steel, one of the larger American manufacturers, blamed international finance for contributing to the world's excess steel capacity and the "dumping" of foreign steel onto the U.S. market, although he did focus his blame on the World Bank rather than on international lending by commerical banks.

PART TWO

THE OFFSHORE MARKETS: EUROCREDITS AND EUROBONDS

CHAPTER ELEVEN

EUROCREDITS — THE WHOLESALE MARKET

Eurocredits and Eurobonds constitute the offshore sector of the international capital market because they are arranged outside the jurisdiction of any single national authority. The contrast is with foreign bonds, which are sold in a domestic capital market on behalf of a nonresident borrower under the laws of the country in which they are issued. Foreign bonds are discussed in Part Three. Part Two deals with Eurocredits and, thereafter, with Eurobonds.

Eurocredit lending is the wholesale sector of the international capital market. Eurocredits are medium-and sometimes long-term loans provided by international groups of banks in currencies which need not be those of the lenders or borrowers; for instance, a five-year dollar credit extended to a Norwegian company or government agency by a group of American, Japanese, and European banks.

The fact that banks alone provide finance in this sector of the international market is one feature distinguishing it from the retail bond markets, where most capital is supplied by individual investors and institutions such as pension funds and insurance companies.

Another distinctive feature is that nearly all Eurocredits are provided at floating rates of interest, unlike international bond financing which consists mostly of fixed-interest capital. Banks provide Eurocredits at margins or "spreads" above the cost of their own deposits. The margins are fixed for the duration of the loan, but the total interest paid by the borrower is adjusted at regular intervals, usually every six months, to reflect changes in the underlying cost of short-term deposits to the banks. The banks are thus assured of a fixed return. The borrower is assured only of a fixed sum for an agreed period, but at a floating and unpredictable cost. This arrangement is the single most important feature of the Eurocredits market and has become the foundation of its existence.

The fluctuating and unpredictable cost is a serious disadvantage for borrowers, but represents the price for international capital which would otherwise be unobtainable. Protection from interest risk helps make it possible for banks to provide Eurocredits to borrowers lacking the public appeal to compete for fixed-interest capital in the international bond markets. It also allows banks to provide Eurocredits in far larger amounts than could be raised on the international bond markets by even the most highly rated borrowers. Most large official borrowing for balance of payments support and nearly all international market borrowing by developing and Communist countries is therefore by means of Eurocredits.

The banks' insulation from interest risk is the most important but not the only factor making possible the provision of Eurocredits in large amounts and to a wider range of borrowers. The banks protect themselves also from currency risk by lending only those currencies they are first able to obtain as deposits in the amounts and for the maturities needed. The one risk common to the Eurocredit and international bond markets is that of a borrower's default. But the resources of Eurobanks are very much greater than those of international bond investors, many of whom are individuals, and the syndication of most Eurocredits among groups of banks spreads the risk of default and further helps to make possible the assembling of very large loans.

In a market of heavyweights, borrowing and lending are extremely concentrated. The Organization for Economic Cooperation and Development has estimated that the market had served about 400 borrowers from 77 countries by the end of 1977. But during the five years from 1973 through 1977, four countries received nearly one-third of all publicized Eurocredits and ten countries received more than half. Ranked in order, they were the United Kingdom, Brazil, Mexico, Italy, France, Spain, Iran, Algeria, Venezuela, and Indonesia, and nearly all of their borrowing was official or officially guaranteed.

On the lending side, the number of banks in the market has been estimated at up to 500, but the number of large and regular participants is not much more than 100 and a decisive role is played by only a handful of the world's biggest commercial banks. Circumstantial evidence suggests that 10 banks arranged about one-half of all publicized Eurocredits in 1976 and 1977 while providing approximately one-quarter of the money themselves, and that 20 banks arranged about two-thirds of the total while providing about one-third of the money. In a market of whales and minnows, the minimum participation normally offered to any bank in a Eurocredit syndicate is $1 million, but partici-

pations of $10 million are common and there have been participations
of more than $100 million by individual banks in some very large
credits (like Citibank's $115 million participation in a $3 billion credit
to the Canadian government in May, 1978).

It is in the nature of wholesale markets that transactions will be
larger but fewer than in retail markets and the rule has held for the
Eurocredits and international bond markets. The number of Eurocredits has been fewer and their average size larger, but the total financing
provided by the Eurocredits and international bond markets was not
significantly different (at least until 1978, when the volume of new
Eurocredits shot up).

During the eight years leading to the end of 1978, the fullest period
for which comparisons were available at the time of writing, the total
of publicized Eurocredits, at about $210 billion, compared with about
$160 billion of international bond financing, and during the three years
prior to the end of 1977 the volume of Eurocredits and international
bond financing was roughly equal.

But the average size or Eurocredits during the middle and latter
1970s was about $75 million, or nearly double that of Eurobond issues
at about $40 million. And the difference between the biggest Eurocred-
its and Eurobond issues has been even more pronounced. At the time
of writing, the biggest international bank credit ($3 billion for the Cana-
dian government in May 1978) was 6 times the size of the biggest
recorded Eurobond placements (of $500 million each for the European
Community in 1976 and Shell Oil in 1977) and $8\frac{1}{2}$ times the size of the
biggest publicly offered Eurobond issue ($350 million for the Australian
government in March 1978).

TABLE 4(a)
THREE MEASURES OF PUBLICIZED EUROCREDITS*

($ billion)

	Morgan Guaranty	World Bank	OECD
1970	4.7		
1971	4.0	4.1	
1972	6.8	8.0	
1973	21.9	20.8	20.8
1974	29.3	28.5	28.5
1975	21.0	20.6	20.6
1976	28.8	28.8	27.8
1977	41.8	32.3	33.7

*Publicized commitments only. World Bank estimates unavailable before 1971 and OECD unavailable
before estimates before 1973.

TABLE 4*(b)*

INTERNATIONAL CREDITS AND BONDS

($ billion)

	Eurocredits	International bonds*
1970	5	5
1971	4	6
1972	7	10
1973	22	8
1974	29	7
1975	21	20
1976	29	33
1977	34	32
Total	150	120

*Eurobonds plus foreign bonds. Figures rounded.

SOURCE: Morgan Guaranty (excepting for 1977 Eurocredits total, which is OECD's).

TABLE 5

EUROCURRENCY BANK CREDITS

(by country of borrower, in millions of dollars)

	1970	1971	1972	1973	1974	1975	1976	1977
Industrial countries	4,246	2,601	4,097	13,783	20,683	7,231	11,254	17,201
Australia	53	239	155	3	127	124	12	360
Canada	45	25	29	51	30	113	885	3,292
Denmark	27	171	41	254	393	341	607	868
Finland	36	47	20	433	308	399	300	314
France	19	40	176	50	3,224	719	586	2,325
Greece	10	65	270	510	419	239	323	204
Ireland	30	0	0	0	321	338	433	440
Italy	1,387	317	928	4,761	2,321	120	355	1,024
Japan	5	35	80	195	372	448	370	112
New Zealand	80	30	32	0	490	313	0	538
Norway	0	15	128	265	402	159	472	182
South Africa	60	226	149	333	587	510	650	0
Spain	230	317	136	479	1,151	1,147	2,037	1,973
Sweden	48	38	115	99	203	302	440	1,446
United Kingdom	48	462	689	3,150	5,655	160	1,671	1,992
United States	1,827	428	864	1,649	2,221	764	677	826
Yugoslavia	10	0	226	303	551	73	125	433
Other*	330	145	60	1,248	1,905	961	1,310	872
Developing countries	446	1,286	2,414	7,288	7,318	11,098	15,017	20,852
Non-OPEC countries	300	936	1,481	4,537	6,252	8,199	11,019	13,427
Argentina	41	185	20	87	499	72	957	849
Brazil	87	257	579	740	1,672	2,152	3,232	2,814
Chile	0	0	0	0	0	0	208	591
Hong Kong	0	0	10	72	67	533	85	408
Ivory Coast	0	22	0	95	63	50	154	265

Korea	25	49	100	205	133	347	738	1,265
Malaysia	0	24	50	0	140	425	207	212
Mexico	56	295	196	1,588	948	2,311	1,993	2,700
Morocco	0	0	0	0	0	200	641	772
Peru	0	0	139	434	442	334	395	189
Philippines	5	0	50	187	843	363	970	698
Taiwan	0	0	0	0	297	135	219	524
Other	86	104	337	1,129	1,146	1,276	1,218	2,140
OPEC countries	146	350	933	2,751	1,067	2,899	3,999	7,424
Algeria	0	50	172	1,302	0	500	643	691
Indonesia	0	0	93	192	668	1,347	469	817
Iran	123	211	335	722	114	265	1,411	1,209
United Arab Emirates	0	0	18	310	151	156	55	1,086
Venezuela	23	79	200	137	57	38	1,185	1,666
Other	0	10	115	88	75	593	235	1,955
Communist countries	38	66	285	779	1,238	2,597	2,503	3,394
Germany (East)	0	0	35	0	12	280	215	832
Hungary	30	50	50	90	150	250	300	300
Poland	0	0	0	430	509	475	525	19
Soviet Union	0	0	0	0	100	650	282	234
COMECON institutions	0	11	140	50	120	480	600	1,100
Other	8	5	60	209	347	462	581	909
International institutions	0	10	0	0	24	65	74	190
TOTAL	4,730	3,963	6,796	21,851	29,263	20,992	28,849	41,637

*Includes multinational organizations.

SOURCE: Morgan Guaranty, *World Financial Markets*, March 1978

TABLE 6
INTERNATIONAL BOND ISSUES AND EURO CURRENCY BANK CREDITS

(by country of borrower, in millions of dollars)

	1970	1971	1972	1973	1974	1975	1976	1977
Industrial countries	8,046	7,531	11,512	19,612	26,073	22,446	35,454	39,755
Australia	159	360	402	31	244	814	1,068	1,434
Austria	14	37	92	142	673	1,231	682	1,449
Belgium	2	0	25	135	20	31	134	277
Canada	1,091	874	1,530	1,246	2,110	4,612	10,221	8,521
Denmark	119	312	358	424	517	547	1,602	1,589
Finland	83	143	282	565	352	752	642	643
France	261	326	431	142	3,609	2,544	3,307	3,988
Germany	140	77	97	58	116	194	745	647
Greece	10	65	330	525	419	239	323	204
Ireland	72	100	30	95	456	408	454	526
Israel	0	0	30	0	300	2	119	111
Italy	1,727	466	1,038	4,838	2,371	226	440	1,336

Japan	125	156	186	272	609	2,187	2,453	2,047
Netherlands	521	279	235	456	1,025	738	625	533
New Zealand	91	122	96	0	523	780	413	1,105
Norway	94	115	239	362	478	1,104	1,878	1,831
South Africa	159	441	430	549	637	957	727	33
Spain	260	414	222	566	1,151	1,264	2,281	2,271
Sweden	113	125	340	270	278	1,302	1,551	2,946
Switzerland	50	52	35	108	59	152	301	135
United Kingdom	306	1,115	1,550	4,384	5,876	435	2,707	3,897
United States	2,623	1,726	3,071	3,069	2,408	1,093	1,139	2,115
Yugoslavia	10	0	226	333	551	73	196	553
Multinational companies	15	214	192	985	996	638	1,309	1,144
Other	0	10	47	56	293	122	137	420
Developing countries	**520**	**1,385**	**2,978**	**7,953**	**7,581**	**11,683**	**16,612**	**24,417**
Non-OPEC countries	374	1,035	1,960	5,102	6,453	8,716	12,474	16,179
Argentina	110	185	20	87	499	88	957	942
Brazil	87	263	695	802	1,697	2,187	3,500	3,546
Chile	0	0	0	0	0	53	208	591
Hong Kong	0	15	10	155	117	558	85	537
Ivory Coast	0	22	0	104	63	50	165	265
Korea	28	61	100	205	133	347	797	1,334
Malaysia	0	24	75	17	140	425	217	255
Mexico	56	342	404	1,764	998	2,604	2,441	3,859
Morocco	0	0	0	0	0	228	685	800
Peru	0	0	139	434	442	334	395	189
Philippines	5	0	50	212	861	393	1,337	816
Singapore	0	10	51	60	24	12	204	314
Taiwan	0	0	0	0	317	135	219	524
Other	88	112	417	1,262	1,161	1,301	1,263	2,207
OPEC countries	147	350	1,018	2,851	1,128	2,967	4,138	8,237
Algeria	0	50	197	1,373	60	535	753	930
Indonesia	0	0	93	192	668	1,365	469	817
Iran	123	211	355	743	114	265	1,441	1,290
United Arab Emirates	0	0	18	310	151	156	55	1,128
Venezuela	23	79	240	144	59	38	1,185	2,099
Other	0	10	115	88	75	608	235	1,973
Communist countries	**38**	**91**	**335**	**779**	**1,278**	**2,836**	**2,599**	**3,642**
Germany (East)	0	0	35	0	12	280	215	832
Hungary	30	75	100	90	190	352	325	474
Poland	0	0	0	430	509	496	596	93
Soviet Union	0	0	0	0	100	650	282	234
COMECON institutions	0	11	140	50	120	480	600	1,100
Other	8	5	60	209	347	578	581	909
International institutions	**686**	**1,241**	**1,719**	**1,345**	**1,189**	**3,938**	**6,700**	**6,029**
Total	**9,290**	**10,247**	**16,545**	**29,689**	**36,120**	**40,903**	**61,366**	**73,842**

SOURCE: Morgan Guaranty, *World Financial Markets*, March 1978.

CHAPTER TWELVE
EUROCREDIT MECHANICS

To move to a more detailed explanation, beginning with some unapologetic repetition: Eurocredits are medium-term foreign currency bank credits from the point of the borrower, the lending banks, or both. Most are provided on the borrower's name, without collateral in the form of a lien on the borrower's property or revenues. The World Bank and OECD define medium-term credits as those provided for more than a year, but during the middle and latter 1970s more than 85 percent of publicized Eurocredits were provided for five to eight years. Only about 5 percent had maturities ranging from one to five years, while the remaining 10 percent had maturities stretching in rare instances to as long as 15 years.

The bank syndicates making the credits are not permanent groupings, but are formed in each case by banks willing to take participations of varying size in a particular credit.

The total amount and maturity of a credit and the schedule of drawings and repayments are agreed with the borrower in advance. So is the lending margin or scale of margins which will apply throughout. As already mentioned, the total rate of interest which the borrower pays to the banks is adjusted at regular intervals, usually every six months, to reflect changes in the underlying cost of funds to the banks. The credit is "rolled over" or technically renewed on its original terms every six months, when the banks theoretically go back into the Eurocurrencies money market to finance themselves for the following six-months' "rollover" or interest period. Hence the unwieldy name of "medium-term syndicated Eurocurrency roll-over bank credit"—mercifully capable of abbreviation to Eurocredit. In essence, the banks make a commitment to provide a succession of short-term loans over a medium-term period.

Although there are many variations in practice, the basic mechanics are illustrated by the example of a dollar credit provided for seven years at a fixed margin of 1 percent above the cost of six-months' deposits in the London inter-bank market, where banks in deficit secure funds from those in surplus in a roughly similar way as in the federal funds market in the United States. If LIBOR (the London inter-bank offered rate) for six-months' Eurodollar deposits is 5 percent when the credit is first granted, the borrower pays the banks in the Eurocredit lending syndicate 6 percent per annum during the first six months. If LIBOR then rises to $5\frac{1}{2}$ percent, the borrower pays $6\frac{1}{2}$ percent for the ensuing six months. If LIBOR then falls to $4\frac{1}{2}$ percent, the borrower pays $5\frac{1}{2}$ percent during the following six months, and so on.

There are many refinements of this basic arrangement. Some credit agreements provide for an increase in lending margins during the latter years of the loan to compensate banks for a longer commitment and to protect their return on fixed lending margins from the erosion of inflation. There are also loan agreements giving the borrower the option of choosing the length of each succeeding interest period on condition that the lending banks are able to obtain market funds for the selected maturity. This allows a borrower to take a view of interest rates, but without risk to the banks. Borrowers will choose a short roll-over period when interest rates are high, but expected to fall, and a longer period when rates are low, but expected to rise. A ten-year, $2\frac{1}{2}$billion credit arranged for the British government in March 1974, incorporated both features. The lending spread was fixed at $\frac{3}{8}$ percent above LIBOR for the initial two years; $\frac{1}{2}$ point above for the next three; $\frac{5}{8}$ percent above for the following two; and $\frac{3}{4}$ points above LIBOR for the final three years. But there was an option for the British government to take a view of interest rates by selecting each succeeding interest period for three, six, or twelve months ahead.

Most Eurocredits are provided, at least initially, in dollars; the World Bank has consistently estimated the proportion at about 97 percent.[1] But many loan agreements give borrowers a choice of currencies for each roll-over period provided that the lending banks declare themselves able to obtain the currencies in the market in the amounts and for the periods required. This allows borrowers to take a view of exchange rates at each roll-over but, once again, without risk to the lending banks.

Whatever currency is chosen, the base rate is the inter-bank rate for Eurocurrency deposits. In the case of dollar credits, this is customarily

---

[1] In 1978, there was evidence of a growing proportion of Eurocredits being provided in Deutschemark.

LIBOR, the London inter-bank offered rate for Eurodollar deposits. In the case of Deutschemark credits, the base rate is often LUXIBOR, the Luxembourg inter-bank offered rate for Deutschemark deposits, Luxembourg being the main center for the inter-bank Euro-Deutschemark market. And, for similar reasons, the Paris inter-bank rate is used as the base for Eurocredits provided in external sterling.[2]

However, no matter which currency is chosen, an identical problem arises in determining an applicable base rate. Inter-bank offered rates for all Eurocurrencies and maturities fluctuate ceaselessly throughout every business day. More important, no single quotation applies equally to all banks. The biggest and strongest banks are usually able to obtain deposits from the inter-bank market at marginally lower rates than smaller banks. This makes the choice of a common base rate for all members of a Eurocredit syndicate a delicate matter at all times. And it became a highly contentious issue during the panic following the collapse of Bankhaus Herstatt in Germany in June 1974. Differences between inter-bank Eurocurrency deposit rates offered to larger and smaller banks widened very considerably for a time, a development reflected by a pronounced increase in lending margins on new Eurocredits to allow the participation of smaller banks. Even at that, smaller banks were so squeezed that the volume of new Eurocredit lending fell from an annual $40 billion in the first six months of 1974 to exactly half that level during the remainder of the year and through 1975, before a recovery began in 1976.

In an effort at fairness to all participating banks, Eurocredit agreements nominate reference banks to determine the base rate which will be deemed to apply equally to all syndicate banks for each roll-over period of a Eurocredit. The reference banks are usually chosen as a representative cross section of banks in the lending syndicate and a few agreements aim at still greater neutrality by nominating reference banks which are not members of the lending group. In the case, say, of a Eurodollar credit, the LIBOR determined as applying to all syndicate members for each roll-over period is the one quoted in the market to the reference banks for the maturity required. Moreover, it is the rate quoted at a stipulated time. This is often 11 A.M. London time two business days before the start of the next roll-over and for delivery of the required currency deposits to the syndicate banks on the first day

---

[2]The terms on Canada's $3 billion credit in May 1978 were an innovation, consisting of New York prime rate during the initial four years and New York prime plus $\frac{1}{4}$ point during the latter years. Since U.S. prime had averaged 40 basis points above 6-months' LIBOR during the preceding 18 months, the terms to Canada were the equivalent of a shade above LIBOR plus $\frac{3}{8}$ percent ($37\frac{1}{2}$ basis points) during the first four years and a shade above LIBOR plus $\frac{5}{8}$ percent ($62\frac{1}{2}$ basis points) during the final four years.

of the roll-over period. Any differences in LIBOR quotations to the reference banks are averaged upward to the nearest $\frac{1}{8}$ percentage point.

The base rate thus chosen plus the prearranged lending spread is the rate of interest at which all banks in the lending group are obliged to supply their share of funds to the borrower for the following roll-over period. For instance, if base LIBOR is determined by the reference banks as being 5 percent and the agreed lending margin is $\frac{1}{2}$ percent, then all banks in the syndicate are required to provide their share of funds to the borrower at $5\frac{1}{2}$ percent for the ensuing roll-over, or interest period. In practice, some banks in the syndicate will be able to obtain deposits in the inter-bank market at slightly below the LIBOR deemed to apply to the group as a whole, while other banks may have to bid slightly more. The return to banks in the group will not therefore be exactly equal.

FEES

The lending margin is only one part of the return to banks, the other part consisting of management, participation, and commitment fees. Since lending margins are usually publicized while fees are seldom disclosed, borrowers are often prepared to concede higher front-end fees in return for the credit standing implied by relatively lower lending margins. Front-end fees are a flat sum paid once only at the start of the loan. It follows that the longer the maturity, the readier borrowers are to bargain a higher level of fees against lower lending margins. Banks who play a leading role in arranging a credit without themselves providing any significant share of the money have a greater interest in a high managing fee than in wide lending margins. The reverse is obviously true of banks providing a large share of funds (and also of lesser participants in a lending group who receive only a small share of fees or none).

The management fee, representing a flat percentage of the loan, is paid by the borrower at the time the credit agreement is signed to the bank or banks who have arranged (or "managed") it. Part of that fee is then passed on by the managing banks in the form of participation fees related to the share of funds provided by other banks in the lending syndicate. An example was a $600 million 10-year credit arranged in July 1977, for Nacional Financiera S.A. the Mexican state development bank. The managers were Lloyds Bank International and Libra Bank. In addition to a lending margin rising from $1\frac{1}{4}$ to $1\frac{3}{4}$ percent over the life of the credit, the borrower paid a management fee of $\frac{3}{4}$ percent, amounting to $4\frac{1}{2}$ million.

Out of the $\frac{3}{4}$ point management fee, which they were entitled to take in full on their own subscriptions, the managing banks passed on participation fees to other banks of $\frac{1}{8}$ percent on subscriptions of $2 million to $4 million; $\frac{1}{4}$ percent on $4 million to $7 million; $\frac{3}{8}$ percent on $7 million to $10 million; and $\frac{1}{2}$ percent on subscriptions exceeding $10 million.

An example of a slightly different arrangement was provided by a $1 billion Eurocredit to the Nigerian government in October 1977, at a margin of 1 percent plus a management fee of $\frac{1}{2}$ percent. Three lead managing banks, Chase Manhattan, Morgan Guaranty, and the Deutsche Bank, underwrote $50 million each at a fee of $\frac{7}{16}$ percent; an additional seven banks acting as subordinate comanagers underwrote $25 million each at a fee of $\frac{5}{16}$ percent. Each of the 22 banks in the extended management group committed itself to provide the amount it had underwirtten, either on its own or with the recruitment of other participants. The three lead managers passed on part of their management fee to the two categories of comanagers and all banks in the management group passed on part of their fees to yet other banks in the form of participation fees.

Management fees are passed on as participation fees only down to a certain level. Banks taking no more than a small part of a credit often get no participation fee at all, as in the case of banks subscribing less than $2 million each to the Mexican credit cited above. The part of the total fee left to the lead manager or lead managing banks after payment of participation fees to other banks is known as the *praecipium* (from the Latin verb *praecipere:* to take a prerogative share).

In addition to the front-end management fee, borrowers are usually required to pay a commitment or "facility" fee at an annual rate on undrawn portions of a credit to compensate banks for keeping funds ready. This often ranges between $\frac{1}{4}$ and $\frac{3}{4}$ percent; in the case of the Mexican credit already referred to it was $\frac{1}{2}$ percent. On top of that, a few loan agreements require borrowers to maintain compensating balances with the lending banks, but this is far from usual.

The level of margins and fees fluctuates for the market as a whole according to the liquidity of major banks and their readiness to provide international medium-term credits at times of slack domestic loan demand in their own markets. The margin to prime borrowers fell to $\frac{3}{8}$ percent during the first half of 1974, but shot up to $1\frac{1}{4}$ percent during the post-Herstatt panic in the second half of that year. It remained at $1\frac{1}{4}$ percent in 1975, but fell to 1 percent in 1976 and back to $\frac{5}{8}$ percent by late 1977, when the faltering of the industrial world's inherently weak economic recovery left Western banks scrambling to deploy in the Eurocredits market the cash surpluses for which there was insufficient demand in their domestic markets. Margin cutting is always led by those banks which happen to be most liquid; the pace was set by American banks until about 1977 and by German and Japanese banks in 1978 and 1979, by which time prime margins had come down to $\frac{3}{8}$ percent.

There are also wide differences at any time between margins and fees quoted to individual borrowers according to their credit standing. At one extreme, the rare and possibly unique example has been cited of a Eurocredit granted to an international oil company without any lending margin at all, presumably because the banks hoped to obtain other business from a powerful borrower.[3] At the other extreme, margins of no less than 9 percent were charged to some Turkish borrowers in 1977, a level on the borderline of usury and refusal. Between those extremes, margins reported for sovereign borrowers at mid-1977 ranged from $\frac{7}{8}$ percent for Britain, France, Iran, and Sweden, through $1\frac{1}{4}$ percent for Spain, $1\frac{3}{8}$ percent for Italy, $1\frac{5}{8}$ percent for Mexico, $1\frac{3}{4}$ percent for the Philippines and South Korea, $1\frac{7}{8}$ percent for Brazil, $2\frac{1}{4}$ percent for Peru, and $2\frac{1}{2}$ percent for Burma. The terms are never uniform for all of any country's borrowers; governments can usually borrow more favorably than their agencies, even when the agencies' debt is government-guaranteed, and business companies can often raise money at better terms than official borrowers, particularly when credits are linked to an investment promising to generate foreign exchange.

DRAWINGS AND REPAYMENTS

While a loan may be defined as a sum of money lent and repaid in a lump, a credit suggests a facility on which a borrower may draw only under given conditions and within stipulated limits. It is for this reason that the market is usually referred to as one for Eurocredits rather than as a market for international medium-term bank loans.

Conditions for drawings and repayments vary considerably and depend mainly on the kind of Eurocredit granted. There are two principal varieties. One is called a revolving credit and resembles an overdraft facility or credit line made available for a given period, either as a standby for use in case of need or else to meet temporary but recurring financial requirements. The borrower may draw the credit up and down as circumstances dictate. Interest is paid on the amounts actually drawn, while a commitment or facility fee is usually charged on the undrawn portion. The loan is cleared not by a schedule of repayments, but by a progressive reduction of the credit line. An example was

---

[3]A.A. Weismuller, "Trends in Medium-Term Lending," *The Banker*, London, March 1976.

provided by the $3 billion credit arranged for the Canadian govern-
ment in May 1978. The full amount was available to the borrower
during the first four years, 83.3 percent during the fifth year, 66.6
percent during the sixth year, 50 percent during the seventh year, and
33.3 percent during the final year.

The second basic variety of Eurocredit, and the more common kind,
is the term credit. This usually provides for a schedule of drawings at
the beginning, a schedule of repayments towards the end, and an intervening period of grace during which the full amount is available to
the borrower, no repayments being required during that time. An
illustration is again provided by the $2½ billion British credit of 1974,
which allowed drawings as and when needed during the initial year and
required repayment in four equal annual installments from the end of
the seventh year. The Nigerian credit mentioned earlier required the
full amount to be drawn during the first year, with nine equal semian-
nual repayments from the end of the third year.

A variant of the conventional term credit, usually provided to help
finance the development of mineral resources, links the amount and
timing of repayments to the flow of revenues from the investment and,
in that respect, includes what the World Bank has called "an element
of equity." Besides this, there are some Eurocredits for project finance
which provide for one or more large "balloon" repayments at the end,
for instance a credit for the building of an oil refinery which will take
time to produce a return, but which is likely to generate large revenues
once it starts working.

The main difference between a revolving and a term credit is the
borrower's ability to run drawings up and down according to need
on a revolving credit. By contrast, a term credit obliges the borrower to stick to the agreed schedule of drawings and repayments.
Once the borrower has given written notice, usually required seven
days in advance, that he intends to make a drawing to which he is
entitled under a term credit, he is irrevocably committed to making
it. It is true that the borrower may forego a drawing to which he is
entitled, likewise on seven days written notice, but having done so
the borrower forfeits his right to that drawing and cannot later
change his mind. Similarly, if the borrower should decide to recon-
stitute part of a term credit ahead of time, he cannot subsequently
redraw it.

However, many loan agreements and probably a majority, allow
prepayment of the full amount without penalty at 30 days or sometimes 60 days notice. This is a feature of cardinal importance for
borrowers. Those with sufficient market strength, who have nevertheless had to concede wide margins in a lenders' market, can re-

place such credits with new ones when conditions change in favor of borrowers.

This is precisely what happened when a borrowers market for Eurocredits in 1977 allowed "consolidation of existing loans at more favorable terms," according to OECD.[4] New Zealand renegotiated a $400 million five-year credit (arranged three years earlier at a margin of 1 percent) to get more money for a longer period at a lower spread, namely $500 million for seven years at a margin rising from $\frac{5}{8}$ percent to $\frac{3}{4}$ percent. Ireland did likewise, obtaining $300 million for eight years at a flat $\frac{7}{8}$ percent to replace a credit for an identical amount arranged a year earlier for a shorter maturity of seven years and at a margin rising from $1\frac{3}{8}$ percent to $1\frac{1}{2}$ percent.

The provision for cancellation of Eurocredits is particularly valuable for borrowers with the credit standing to switch flexibly between the international credit and fixed-interest bond markets. This is especially true of business companies, many of which prepaid Eurocredits arranged in 1973 and 1974 to take advantage of a return of favorable borrowing conditions on the Eurobond market after 1975. The volume of corporate Eurocredit borrowing fell from about $9 billion to $6 billion between 1974 and 1977, while the proportion dropped from more than 30 percent to less than 20 percent of total Eurocredit financing. As OECD remarked of the Eurocredits market in 1977, "It did not provide particular advantages for corporations compared with the international bond market".[5]

---

[4]*Financial Market Trends,* OECD, No. 3, February 1978.
[5]OECD, op. cit.

CHAPTER THIRTEEN
PRACTICES AND PARTICIPANTS

The nature of the Eurocredits market has changed over time and, with it, that of the participants. Most borrowing in the early years was by business companies; the preponderance of official borrowing came only later. The syndication of credits among groups of banks was a feature from the start, an import from the United States where legal limitations on the loans of any single bank to any single customer had long made loan syndication a necessary practice. But commercial banks, which have always provided most of the money for Eurocredits, were originally content to leave the arrangement of credits to British merchant banks, institutions which specialize in matching borrowers and lenders, although having limited lending resources of their own.[1] Floating interest rates became common only after a time. In the early years, most Eurocredits were made at fixed rates of interest (and a minority, estimated at up to 10 percent of the total, still are, although such credits are usually provided by single banks to single customers and are rarely publicized).

The beginnings of the modern market in medium-term international bank credits date back to 1965, when controls on the export of capital from the United States forced American companies to finance overseas

---

[1]A precedent here was the syndication of acceptance credits in the London market. These credits are promissory notes "accepted" by a bank, whose endorsement or guarantee makes it possible to trade the notes at a discount in the money market. Most acceptance credits have maturities of 90 days and are used for trade financing, but in some cases acceptance credits provided by groups or syndicates of banks were renewed for extended periods to finance capital expenditures. In Great Britain, merchant (or investment) banks have traditionally specialized in acceptance finance and are often referred to as "accepting houses." It was natural for such banks to be among the pioneers in arranging syndicated Eurocredits when that market began to develop in the 1960s, largely centered in London.

investment by borrowing abroad. They immediately became major borrowers on the fledgling Eurobond market, but also financed foreign investment by means of medium-term Eurodollar bank loans. These were willingly supplied at fixed rates of interest by American commercial banks rushing to follow customers abroad and by other international banks anxious to establish themselves in a new market. But the banks were painfully reminded of the classic dangers of borrowing short (at fluctuating rates) to lend long (at fixed rates of interest) by the American credit crunch of 1969, when short-term interest rates in the United States and the Eurodollar market shot up by almost 300 basis points in the space of six months. Chastened by that experience, banks generally became unwilling to lend even to the strongest borrowers excepting at the floating rates of interest which have remained the market's most distinguishing feature ever since.

As a result, the composition of borrowers began to change. Those with sufficient credit standing and needs of a size encompassable by the international bond markets switched to more fixed-interest financing in the international bond markets. At the same time, the protection which banks obtained from the innovation of floating interest rates made it possible for them to start providing balance of payments financing on a large scale, initially to Italy in 1970, to many developing countries from the following year, and to all of the world's deficit countries excepting the poorest after the oil price explosion at the end of 1973. It is impossible to be precise about longer-run trends in a market for which comprehensive official data go back only to 1973 and data of any kind only to 1970. But impressionistic evidence suggests that business companies were the main borrowers during the 1960s and it is known that they still accounted for about one-half of all Eurocredit borrowing in 1970. But, thereafter, official borrowers took an ever greater share of Eurocredit finance.

The change among borrowers was accompanied by a similar transformation in the composition of lenders. In the early years, the "management" or arrangement of Eurocredits was dominated by British merchant banks and other specialized investment banks, who were quick to seize an opportunity of earning high fee incomes on a small capital base, because they could usually count on placing with other banks about 80 percent of any Eurocredit they arranged.[2] They were ideally suited to the role by their traditional willingness to pioneer new business and by their wide international connections with banks and borrowers, particularly strongly established in some cases with certain

---

[2]Andrew Liddell, *The Banker,* London, November 1976, p. 1221.

areas of the world, such as the connections of Hambros Bank with Scandinavia and those of Kleinwort Benson with Latin America.

Commercial banks were originally willing to play the relatively passive role of merely providing funds. They did not yet have the specialized personnel or the established international connections to arrange the credits themselves and the market provided an easy way of building up international loan portfolios and clientele.

Even when the stakes grew larger, commercial banks still hesitated to undertake the arrangement of Eurocredits directly. Their initial foray into this part of the business was largely through consortium or joint-venture banks, created by groups of large commercial banks to undertake specialized international operations for all the shareholders. The first consortium bank was created in 1964; by 1971 there were 46. But the number represented in London then declined to 34 by 1977, following a realization in many cases that a pooling of international business had drawbacks as well as advantages for the partners.

Although consortium banks and British merchant banks continue to play a part in arranging Eurocredits, the management of most credits had passed to the world's biggest commercial banks by the early 1970s. It was inevitable that this should have happened. They alone had the resources to meet the huge increase in demand for credits and, having once acquired experience of the business, there was no reason for them to continue foregoing management fees to others. Far more important was the need of the biggest lenders to protect their growing exposure by playing a more active part in the evaluation of borrowers, the negotiation of terms and the supervision of loans by acting as Eurocredit managers themselves. This development represented an important change in market structure. In the earlier days, when merchant banks dominated the arrangement of credits, participations were parceled out in roughly comparable amounts among groups of banks having an approximately equal voice in deciding terms to the borrowers. But since then, it has become customary in the market to talk of a "wholesale" sector consisting of large commercial banks who arrange credits, take the major share, and call the tune, along with a "retail" sector consisting of smaller banks taking what participations they can get.

Table 7 shows the extreme degree of lending concentration in a market of big battalions. It suggests that five banks arranged about 40 percent of all publicized Eurocredit financing in 1976 and 1977 combined; that ten banks arranged more than one-half; and that 20 banks arranged nearly two-thirds. The list is almost synonymous with that of the world's biggest commercial banks. It still includes one British merchant bank (Morgan Grenfell) and four consortium banks (UBAF, Libra, Orion, and BAII). But it is dominated by 15 major American, British, and European banks, three of which (Chase Manhattan, the National Westminster, and the Westdeutsche Landesbank) are also among the shareholders of two of the consortium banks listed (Libra and Orion).

Some sources have estimated that by the mid-1970s managing banks were taking onto their own books 60 percent or more of the Eurocredits they arranged. Even on more cautious market estimates that managing banks usually provide about one-half of the credits they manage, the list suggests that ten banks may have provided about one-quarter of all publicized Eurocredit lending in 1976 and 1977 and that 20 banks may have provided about one-third.

TABLE 7
TOP EUROCREDIT BANKS
(Credits Managed, 1976–1977)

	Millions of dollars	Percent of total publicized Eurocredits
Citicorp	7,645	
Chase Manhattan	6,395	
Morgan Guaranty	4,425	
Bank of America	3,300	
Dresdner Bank	1,850	38
Manufacturers Hanover	1,665	
First Chicago	1,640	
UBAF	1,390	
Bankers Trust	1,355	
Libra Bank	1,255	12
Deutsche Bank	1,255	
Crédit Lyonnais	1,250	
Morgan Grenfell	1,150	
Wells Fargo	1,075	
National Westminster	615	8
Chemical Bank	575	
Orion Bank	525	
Westdeutsche Landesbank	480	
BAII	400	
Lloyds Bank International	390	5

Adapted from *Euromoney*, April 1978. Figures rounded. In credits having several lead managers, the total amount has been divided equally among them. The total of publicized Eurocredits during the two years was about $63 billion (OECD).

UBAF: Union de Banques Arabes et Françaises

BAII: Banque Arabe et Internationale d'Investissement

CHAPTER FOURTEEN
ARRANGING EUROCREDITS

Whatever other advantages Eurocredits may have, such as their availability in larger amounts and to a wider range of borrowers, it is simply untrue, as claimed by many bankers, that they can be arranged more quickly than international bond issues. The time between a borrower's first approach to the Eurocredits market and the receipt of funds is usually between six and eight weeks. It is true that an established borrower with well-prepared documents may be able to obtain a credit in as little as two or three weeks but, at the other extreme, the arrangement of some credits has taken six months or longer. This is not very different from conditions on the Eurobond market, where the average time for the arrangement of a new issue is six weeks and where a few issues can be rushed through in half that time.

The main roles in putting together a Eurocredit are played by the *managing bank* or banks appointed by the borrower to arrange the credit, the *lead banks* providing most of the money, and the *agent bank* appointed by the lenders to look after their interests once the loan agreement has been signed. Sometimes, all three roles are combined by a single bank. An example of a "tombstone," which is an advertisement published by the banks to record their part in its management and sale, is shown in Figure 8.

The first and most important step is the award of a mandate by the borrower to the managing bank or banks. Their main duties are to negotiate terms and to assemble a lending syndicate. This includes helping to draw up a statement of the borrower's financial condition and the purpose for which the credit is required, as well as helping to prepare a loan agreement spelling out the obligations of the borrower and the lenders.

THIS ANNOUNCEMENT APPEARS AS A MATTER OF RECORD ONLY

Ekofisk Transportation System

Norpipe a·s

owned 50/50 by

Den norske stats oljeselskap a.s (Statoil)

and

The Phillips Group

consisting of

Phillips Petroleum Company Norway
American Petrofina Exploration Company of Norway
Norsk AGIP A/S   Norsk Hydro a·s   Elf Aquitaine Norge A/S
Total Marine Norsk A/S   Eurafrep Norge A/S
Coparex Norge A/S   Cofranord A/S

U.S. $300,000,000

EUROCURRENCY CREDIT

MANAGED BY

CITICORP INTERNATIONAL GROUP
SOCIETE GENERALE DE BANQUE S.A.
BANK OF AMERICA NT & SA
MORGAN GUARANTY TRUST COMPANY OF NEW YORK
COMMERZBANK AKTIENGESELLSCHAFT
CHEMICAL BANK
COMPAGNIE FINANCIERE DE LA DEUTSCHE BANK AG
MANUFACTURERS HANOVER LIMITED
CHASE MANHATTAN LIMITED
THE NORWEGIAN BANKING GROUP FOR PETROLEUM FINANCING
BANQUE DE PARIS ET DES PAYS-BAS

AND PROVIDED BY

ANDRESENS BANK INTERNATIONAL S.A.
BANKERS TRUST COMPANY
BANK OF AMERICA NT & SA
BANQUE DE PARIS ET DES PAYS-BAS
BANQUE EUROPEENNE DE CREDIT (BEC)
BANQUE NATIONALE DE PARIS
BARCLAYS BANK INTERNATIONAL LIMITED
BERGEN BANK INTERNATIONAL S.A.
CANADIAN IMPERIAL BANK OF COMMERCE
THE CHASE MANHATTAN BANK, N.A.
CHEMICAL BANK
CHRISTIANIA BANK OG KREDITKASSE
INTERNATIONAL S.A.
CITIBANK, N.A.
COMMERZBANK INTERNATIONAL S.A.
COMPAGNIE FINANCIERE DE LA DEUTSCHE
BANK AG

CONTINENTAL BANK
CONTINENTAL ILLINOIS NATIONAL BANK AND
TRUST COMPANY OF CHICAGO
CREDIT DU NORD
CREDIT SUISSE
DEN NORSKE CREDITBANK (LUXEMBOURG) S.A.
FIRST CITY NATIONAL BANK OF HOUSTON
FIRST NATIONAL BANK IN DALLAS
IRVING TRUST COMPANY
MANUFACTURERS HANOVER TRUST COMPANY
MORGAN GUARANTY TRUST COMPANY
OF NEW YORK
SECURITY PACIFIC BANK
SOCIETE GENERALE DE BANQUE S.A.
TEXAS COMMERCE BANK
UNION BANK OF NORWAY LTD.
UNITED CALIFORNIA BANK
WELLS FARGO BANK, N.A.

FIGURE 8   A Eurocredit "tombstone" advertisement placed by banks to record their part in arranging and providing the credit. (*Courtesy of Citicorp International Group.*)

Although the first obligation of the managing bank or banks is to the borrower who has appointed them, the terms they propose must obviously be acceptable to other lenders as well. Moreover, while the managers' functions legally end with the signing of the loan agreement, the stake and reputation of the managers requires them to keep in touch with borrowers and to help protect the interests of the lending syndicate as a whole. Legally, however, that function passes to the agent bank after the signing of the loan agreement, the agent's role being similar to that of the trustee who looks after the interests of investors in a bond issue.

Loan agreements go to great lengths to absolve managing and agent banks from any liability arising from any act or omission short of "gross negligence or willful misconduct" as construed by courts of law. Lead managers and agents are entitled to accept a borrower's statements at face value and are not bound to inquire into a borrower's affairs beyond their actual knowledge. Neither the managing nor agent banks are responsible to members of the lending syndicate for a borrower's default; nor is any bank in a syndicate responsible to the borrower for the failure of any other bank to fulfill its obligations. All banks in a syndicate sign a common loan agreement with the borrower, but the contractual relationship is between the borrower and each bank individually. Each lending bank is therefore responsible for its own credit assessment of the borrower, its own decision to participate in a credit, its own surveillance of the borrower, and its own risk.

Most prospective borrowers are required to provide a syndication memorandum setting out their financial position, although some large and well-known borrowers have obtained Eurocredits without such a document, among them the British and Swedish governments and Eléctricité de France. However, all Eurocredits are governed by loan agreements running anywhere from 30 to 200 pages, prominently including "covenants" about the borrower's future conduct. Falsification of "representations" and "warranties" about a borrower's condition in a syndication memorandum or failure to perform "covenants" in a loan agreement are regarded as defaults. But these are often overlooked, at least for a time, provided debt service is being maintained and does not seem endangered.

Because most Eurocredits are unsecured, special importance is attached to "covenants" about the borrower's conduct and to "negative pledge" clauses providing that no future loans will be raised on terms giving new creditors preference. In the case of corporate borrowers, covenants usually stipulate maintenance of given ratios between assets and liabilities, while also limiting dividends and total debt service in relation to earnings. In the case of official borrowers, there are often stipulations that no liens on property or revenues will be given to new creditors without similarly being offered to existing creditors. All agreements include "cross-default" clauses, stipulating that a default on any loan will be regarded as a default on all. This has the disadvantage of allowing any creditor to bring down the entire pack, but it does avoid a scramble to get out first and is designed to provide equal treatment for all creditors in the event of default.

Guarantees by the parent of a borrowing company or the government of an official agency are normally unconditional, irrevocable, continuing, and open-ended. In plain English, the guarantor cannot evade responsibility by claiming ignorance or loss of control over a subsidiary borrower; in the case of the subsidiary's default, the guarantor remains responsible under all circumstances. In the event of the guarantor's default the claims of the subsidiary's creditors rank equally with all claims on the guarantor.

CHAPTER FIFTEEN
THE POLITICS OF EUROCREDITS

The arrangement of Eurocredits has become more complicated in practice than theory because of shifts in the balance of power between banks and borrowers and because of the politics of relationships between banks.

If an account of Eurocredit lending politics seems confusing and sometimes contradictory, it is because practices have become exactly that in a largely unregulated market which has grown almost overnight into a major factor of the international economy. The evidence of loose conduct is overwhelming; bankers consistently testify to it not only in private conversation but also in print. This need not mean that such conduct is universal or even widespread; its prevalence is impossible to know. The offenders are, of course, always "other" banks. The truth may be that some banks act with consistent prudence, that some have a tendency to cut corners for the sake of more business, and that still others occasionally veer from greater to lesser caution according to pressure or temptation. As in all businesses, there is the traditional conflict between the salesperson's priority to drive up volume (in this case the international loan officer) and the backroom officials urging greater care (usually treasurers, accountants, and sometimes bank economists). The closeness of control exercised by boards of directors varies because there are many claims on their attention, especially in the case of outside directors with limited time and limited knowledge of banking. The description of scramble and conflict which follows is therefore a partial one; it deals with tendencies which are real enough, but whose extent is unknown.

In the early days, approaches to the market usually came from the borrower through the agency of a specialized bank or one with which the borrower had a long relationship. Moreover, the bank thus chosen to manage a credit would usually have some specialized geographical or industrial expertise; it would recruit a lending group of similar banks; and the banks in the group would have comparable stakes in the credit and comparable interests in continuing relationships with the borrower and the managing bank. The pattern was seldom quite so neat, but it was very widespread.

However, matters began to change about 1970. Bankers, alerted to the possibilities of a new market, began making regular approaches to clients and that practice had already become well established by 1974, when Mr. Yoon Park, of the World Bank, reported, "Loan demand has been maintained in large part by active solicitation from lenders . . . virtually every significant corporation and government agency throughout the world receives regular calls from the loan officers of many Eurobanks."[1]

Nearly all accounts agree that loan solicitation has become even more intensive since that time because of competition among banks to replace maturing Eurocredits and because banks try to maintain their income by increasing the volume of their Eurocredit business whenever lending margins are squeezed. Borrowers have naturally taken advantage of this situation, sometimes in a particularly open way. In October 1976, Sr. Benito Raul Losada, the governor of the Venezuelan central bank, telexed 20 international banks inviting tenders for a $1 billion credit to his government, and a group led by Morgan Guaranty undercut another led by the Bank of America. A year later, the Venezuelan finance minister, Sr. Hector Hurtado, went a step further by simply announcing in public that another $350 million was wanted by two state agencies. Offers duly poured in and a group led by Manufacturers Hanover won the bidding.

However, the net effect has been to change the form of competition between banks more than the degree of competition, and the benefit to borrowers has not been as great as might appear at first sight. When merchant banks and other specialized banks acted on behalf of established clients in putting together Eurocredits, they had an interest as well as an expertise in scouring the market for the best terms. While competition to participate in Eurocredit lending used to be filtered through a borrower's established bankers, more of the approaches are now made directly to the borrower.

What this change has done is to create a less tidy market with a growing divergence of interest between larger and lesser Eurobanks.

---

[1]Yoon Park, *Euromoney,* April 1974.

The interest of the largest banks is in obtaining mandates for the arrangement of Eurocredits and keeping or capturing ancillary business from the borrower. The main concern of lesser banks is not so much with the borrower, but to keep and cultivate relations with the bigger banks.

In this more fluid market, it is inevitable that the favors flaunted will usually outnumber those available for dispersal. Credits have been managed by banks having no previous relationship or knowledge of borrowers; some arrangements have floundered because the complexities of relationships between banks made it impossible to agree which bank should be in charge; in other instances responsibilities have been parceled out to an extreme and even ludicrous degree.

A glaring example was provided by an $800 million credit for Pemex, the Mexican state oil company, in February 1978. Three American banks were made responsible for syndication in the United States, a Japanese bank for syndication in Asia, a German bank for syndication in Europe, a Swiss bank for drawing up the documents, and a Canadian bank for arranging visits to inspect Pemex operations. A British bank was given the task of arranging champagne and other trappings for the signing ceremony. All were thus included as managers (with attendant prestige and fees) in an army of generals outnumbering privates.

In such a market, continuity of relations between borrowers and banks has often been eroded and with it standards of credit assessment and subsequent surveillance of borrowers. The efforts concentrated on obtaining a mandate and putting a credit together often exceed those devoted to keeping an eye on the borrower's affairs thereafter.

The interest of lesser participating banks has been diluted in two special ways. Credits were traditionally arranged by an initial discussion of terms between manager and borrower, with subsequent adjustments to obtain widely spread and roughly comparable participations from other banks. Many credits are still arranged in this way. But in the rush to beat competition by putting credits together quickly, it has become more common for a single major bank to agree terms with the borrower and then farm out the credit, relying on its market power and the reputation of its judgement to recruit participants. Alternatively, a small group of large banks will underwrite a credit and each will syndicate parts of it, but obvious disaffection arises when it is subsequently discovered that different levels of participation fees have been conceded by the various lead managers.

The difference of interest between banks emerges also in the appointment and role played by the agent bank. Unlike the trustee of a bond issue whose sole duty is to investors and who is never actually an investor, the agent bank of a Eurocredit, who has the same duties towards lenders, is often a major lender itself and is, moreover, usually left free to conduct other business with the borrower as well.

If in the course of its other dealings with a borrower the agent bank discovers prejudicial but confidential information it risks suit by the borrower for disclosing it or by the Eurocredit syndicate if it does not. Theoretically, an agent can escape by resigning, but this obviously creates suspicion. Mr. G.E. Putnam, a senior vice president of Citicorp International, which he himself described as a *SLOB*, or "substantial lender on own book," has naturally argued the advantages of an agent who is also a major lender. "I admit that conflicts exist, but with proper safeguards they can be neutralized."[2] Yet he did not specify how they were to be neutralized, nor can it be done. If the agent bank is a large lender engaged also in other business with the borrower, its position becomes equivocal; if not, it may prove uninterested and inactive, the agent's fee being minimal. All that borrowers and syndicate banks can do is to choose what they consider the lesser disadvantage in any particular credit.

The routine function of the agent is to arrange prompt transfers of funds between lenders and borrowers. The more difficult role is to act for lenders if anything goes amiss. Some loan agreements instruct the agent bank to act on its own initiative or to do so within limits; many others stipulate that the agent shall act only on instructions from banks who have provided or committed more than a given proportion of the total credit, usually between 50 and 66 percent. The higher the percentage, the more cumbersome the administration of the agreement, but it does have the advantage of being more democratic in giving a greater voice to smaller participating banks whose interests may not be the same as those of the biggest lenders.

The smaller interest of minor participants ties them less closely to a Eurocredit than the biggest banks with the most at stake. Banks usually retain their participation in a Eurocredit to maturity, but their right to assign or otherwise transfer all or part of their participation to another bank during the life of a credit is written into many loan agreements. In practice, the ability to withdraw is circumscribed by considerations of future relations with the borrower and with the managing banks, but banks do withdraw in certain circumstances. Examples of such circumstances include a syndicate bank itself coming under pressure, suspicions arising about the borrower, if a bank's self-imposed limits on lending to any borrower or country tempt it to switch from an existing to a new and more profitable credit to the same borrower, political

---

[2]G.E. Putnam, "Big Banks as Managers of Credit Syndicates," *Financial Times* Euromarkets Conference, London, February 1977.

pressure of any sort or (fairly frequently) for "window-dressing" of a bank's accounts at its year-end. This ability of smaller banks to withdraw was given new recognition in the $600 million credit to Nafinsa, the Mexican state development bank, arranged in July 1977 and referred to previously in another context. It provided that participants could withdraw at two-year intervals, the two managers, Libra Bank and Lloyds Bank International, offering a "gentlemen's agreement" not to reveal the identity of deserters to the borrower while using their "best efforts" to replace defectors. As an incentive to stay, a renewal fee of a flat $\frac{1}{4}$ point was offered to banks remaining after the first two years of the ten-year credit. But there were doubts about this arrangement, since any circumstances causing banks to withdraw might logically be those making their replacement difficult.

The worst awkwardness arises from the greater and understandable reluctance of smaller banks to modify conditions of repayment or to extend additional facilities to borrowers in difficulty. Having less at stake, they are sometimes more determined to enforce their rights or readier to cut their losses. This greatly complicated the efforts of Citibank to rearrange Zaire's credits after 1976. In the same year Hambros Bank found it simplest to take over voluntarily the participations of other banks in a Eurocredit it had arranged for a Norwegian shipowner who went into default.

CHAPTER SIXTEEN
MARKET SIZE

One way in which the development of Eurocredit lending exactly resembled that of other international credit market sectors is that the development went largely unnoticed for several years from its beginnings, which in this case can be dated at about 1965. The first regular press reports on Eurocredit lending began to appear only from the start of 1971 (in *Euromoney*). The World Bank began making rough estimates of market size in 1971 and 1972 but, like the Organization for Economic Cooperation and Development, has published comprehensive estimates going back only to 1973. Morgan Guaranty is the most authoritative private source of market estimates,[1] but it began publishing these only in 1975 and it was only in March 1978 that it attempted the first consistent estimates going back to 1970.

The lack of information about the market's early years is irritating for historians but not otherwise very important, except in helping to explain the apparently large jump in market size in 1973. This jump was almost certainly due in part to a growing willingness of banks and their customers to publicize credits and the new diligence of statisticians in adding them up. Nor is there much significance in the difference between Morgan Guaranty's estimates of market size on the one hand and, on the other, those of OECD and the World Bank, who usually reconcile their revised estimates. The difference arises partly because Morgan includes credits when announced and the two official agencies only do so when the agreements have been completed. Morgan also includes certain credits which the official

---

[1] *World Financial Markets,* published monthly by the Morgan Guaranty Trust Company of New York. See Appendix 3 for a list of official and other sources of market information.

agencies omit, notably credits with maturities of less than a year and credits guaranteed by official agencies of the lending banks' governments. The difference between the two sets of estimates averaged a relatively unimportant $1 billion a year up to 1976 and became pronounced only in 1977, when Morgan's estimate of almost $42 billion of new Eurocredits was about $8 billion larger than that of the two official agencies. However, both sets of estimates show much the same trends for the volume of total lending and the proportions going to the main borrowers and classes of borrowing countries (industrialized, developing, oil exporting, and Communist). This book makes selective use of both sets of estimates.

More recently, the Bank for International Settlement (BIS) has attempted a regular maturity analysis of gross Western banking claims on 147 countries and territories to provide a better breakdown than previously available between routine short-term trade financing and medium-term facilities which may need to be renewed, sometimes in an awkwardly bunched way. A pilot analysis was privately circulated in 1977 showing 47 percent of total claims as being for up to one year (i.e., normal trade financing), 9 percent for one to two years, 37 percent for longer than two years, and a residual 7 percent not positively identified. Regular publication of these analyses began in 1978.

Finally, the World Bank's Debt Tables regularly provide data on the public debt of 84 developing countries to official and private lenders, including statistics on commitments, disbursements, payments of principal and interest, and the ratios of debt service to the current income and national output of the debtor countries. The information is derived partly from the debtor countries and partly from the 17 donor countries of the Development Assistance Committee (the DAC) of the OECD as well as from the Commission of the European Economic Community. Virtually identical information is published in the annual reports of the World Bank and the DAC but, because of the difficulties of obtaining prompt information from many developing countries, the data are often about two years out of date.[2] This contrasts with the promptness of Morgan Guaranty's estimates of new Eurocredit commitments, published monthly for the preceding month, OECD's published every three months for the preceding quarter, and the BIS data which are usually no more than three to six months out of date.

An important point is that all market estimates refer only to publicized Eurocredits, which are merely commitments to lend, and not

---

[2]Another defect is that the data usually exclude external debt for military purchases, which is often considerable.

loans actually made.[3] The Bank for International Settlements has informally and tentatively estimated the volume of unpublicized Eurocredits (largely those of single banks to single customers) as equivalent to approximately another 30 percent of publicized Eurocredits in 1977. However, since the BIS has also estimated, more precisely, that 22 percent of medium-term credits in 1977 were undrawn, the two qualifications cancel out almost exactly (i.e., 78 percent of 130 equals 101).

While OECD, the World Bank, and Morgan Guaranty provide the best available estimates of Eurocredit commitments, the Bank for International Settlements provides the fullest estimates of the total exposure, gross and net, of the Western banking system to 147 countries and territories, an exposure of which Eurocredit financing is only a part. These estimates are published quarterly and in the annual report of the BIS, appearing each June.

---

[3]By contrast, published information on international bond issues is far more exact, and borrowers immediately receive the full amount of the issues made.

CHAPTER SEVENTEEN
EUROCREDIT BORROWERS

The pattern of borrowing in the Eurocredits market emerges from Tables 8 through 12 and Figure 9. These show that the industrial countries took the lion's share of almost two-thirds of publicized credits in 1974, but that the proportion then dropped to between 30 percent and 40 percent during the three following years. The oil-importing developing countries were crowded out of the market in 1974, during the first scramble for funds after the oil crisis, and obtained only one-quarter of all publicized Eurocredits in that year. But in the three years following, their Eurocredit borrowing approximated that of the industrial countries in volume and as a proportion of total Eurocredit borrowing. The oil-exporting countries borrowed hardly anything in their first flush of prosperity, but after 1975 borrowing, mainly by the more populous oil exporters to finance development, averaged about 15 percent of all publicized Eurocredit financing. The volume of publicized credits going to the U.S.S.R. and Eastern Europe rose rapidly from 1972 to 1975 but more slowly thereafter, averaging about 10 percent of all publicized Eurocredits during the three years to the end of 1977. As a generalization, there has been hardly any worry about the level of lending to industrial and oil-exporting countries; there has been some greater caution but no deep concern about lending to the U.S.S.R. and Eastern Europe; and concern about lending to oil-importing developing countries has tended to be concentrated on some rather than all.

TABLE 8
**FOUR MAJOR EUROPEAN DEFICIT COUNTRIES
(FRANCE, ITALY, SPAIN, AND UNITED KINGDOM)
EXTERNAL FINANCING REQUIREMENTS AND
SOURCES OF FINANCE**
($ billion)

	1973	1974	1975	1976	1977	Total 1973/77
Current balance*	−4.41	−25.04	−7.74	−15.62	−2.05	−54.86
Reserve change	+1.45	+1.00	−0.31	−3.02	+23.56	+22.68
Total requirement	+5.86	+26.04	+7.43	+12.60	+25.61	+77.54
Financed by:						
Eurocredits	+8.42	+12.44	+2.04	+4.38	+5.78	+33.06
International bonds	+1.01	+0.48	+2.52	+4.25	+3.61	+11.87
Total international capital market	+9.43	+12.92	+4.56	+8.63	+9.39	+44.93
IMF	+0.15	+1.78	+1.54	+1.91	+1.25	+6.63
Other flows†	−3.72	+11.34	+1.33	+2.06	+14.97	+25.98
Total financing	+5.86	+26.04	+7.43	+12.60	+25.61	+77.54
International capital market finance as percent of total financing	161	49½	61¼	68½	36¾	58

*Includes official and private transfers.
†Includes direct and portfolio investment and unidentified financial flows.
Note: In 1973, the four countries attracted more capital than they needed to finance their combined current deficits and were thus able to reexport capital.
SOURCE: International Monetary Fund and OECD.

THE INDUSTRIAL COUNTRIES

After the 1973 oil crisis, the biggest borrowers among the industrialized nations were the principal deficit countries, Great Britain, Italy, and France, vainly hoping that the world's strongest economies would maintain their domestic demand so that the weaker economies could keep up export-led growth and thus avoid a painful "adjustment" to the oil price increase by a reduction of output and employment in their own countries. "Borrowing is more sensible in human and economic terms than trying to cut imports by massive deflation," said the British Chancellor of the Exchequer, Mr. Denis Healey, when he announced

TABLE 9
EXTERNAL FINANCING REQUIREMENT AND SOURCES OF FINANCE, UNITED KINGDOM
($ billion)

	1973	1974	1975	1976	1977	Total 1973/77
Current balance*	−1.80	−7.83	−3.72	−2.50	+0.30	−15.55
Reserve change	+0.83	+0.46	−1.48	−1.22	+16.83	+15.42
Total requirement	+2.63	+8.29	+2.24	+1.28	+16.53	+30.97
Financed by:						
Eurocredits	+3.17	+5.72	+0.18	+1.72	+1.84	+12.63
International bonds	+0.89	+0.09	+0.51	+1.19	+1.38	+4.06
Total international capital market	+4.06	+5.81	+0.69	+2.91	+3.22	+16.69
IMF	+0.07	−0.10	−0.14	+2.32	+2.12	+4.27
Other flows†	−1.50	+2.58	+1.69	−3.95	+11.19	+10.01
Total financing	+2.63	+8.29	+2.24	+1.28	+16.53	+30.97
International capital market finance as percent of total financing	154½	70	30¾	127½	19½	53¾

*Includes official and private transfers.
†Includes direct and portfolio investment and unidentified financial flows.
Note: In 1973 and 1976, the U.K. attracted more market capital than it needed to finance its current deficits and was thus able to reexport capital.
SOURCE: International Monetary Fund and OECD.

TABLE 10

**EXTERNAL FINANCING REQUIREMENTS AND
SOURCES OF FINANCE, FRANCE**

($ billion)

	1973	1974	1975	1976	1977	Total 1973/77
Current balance*	−0.69	−5.94		−6.03	−3.25	−15.91
Reserve change	−1.49	+0.32	+3.74	−2.87	+0.47	+0.17
Total requirement	−0.80	+6.26	+3.74	+3.16	+3.72	+16.08
Financed by:						
Eurocredits	+0.05	+3.22	+0.72	+0.59	+2.33	+6.91
International bonds	+0.09	+0.39	+1.83	+2.72	+1.66	+6.69
Total international capital market	+0.14	+3.61	+2.55	+3.31	+3.99	+13.60
IMF	+0.08	−0.06	−0.22	−0.25	+0.01	−0.44
Other flows†	−1.02	+2.71	+1.41	+0.10	−0.28	+2.92
Total financing	−0.80	+6.26	+3.74	+3.16	+3.72	+16.08
International capital market finance as percent of total financing		57¾	68	104¾	107¼	84½

*Includes official and private transfers.

†Includes direct and portfolio investment and unidentified financial flows.

Note: In 1976 and 1977, France attracted more market capital than needed to finance its current deficits and was thus able to reexport capital.

SOURCE: International Monetary Fund and OECD.

Britain's record $2½ billion Eurocredit borrowing in his budget of March 1974.

During the five years prior to the end of 1977, the four main European borrowers, Britain, Italy, France, and Spain, covered nearly 60 percent of their external financing requirements by borrowing in the international capital market. Indeed, in some years they raised more than they needed to finance their current external deficits plus changes in their national reserves of gold and foreign exchange. This meant they were importing sufficient market capital on the one hand to be able to go on exporting capital to other countries by way of official aid and private outflows.

The case of Spain was slightly different from that of Britain, Italy, and France. This was because the Spanish authorities were borrowing in the market not only to avoid a recession but also to finance continuing investment for long-term growth, as in the case of market borrowing by advanced developing countries like Brazil and Mexico.

TABLE 11

**EXTERNAL FINANCING REQUIREMENTS AND
SOURCES OF FINANCE, ITALY**

($ billion)

	1973	1974	1975	1976	1977	Total 1973/77
Current balance*	−2.51	−9.04	−0.53	−2.86	−12.11	−11.83
Reserve change	+0.35	+0.51	−2.17	+1.88	+4.95	+5.52
Total requirement	+2.86	+8.55	−1.64	+4.74	+2.84	+17.35
Financed by: Eurocredits	+4.71	+2.39	+0.12	+0.20	+0.58	+8.00
International bonds	——	——	+0.06	+0.09	+0.28	+0.43
Total international capital market	+4.71	+2.39	+0.18	+0.29	+0.86	+8.43
IMF		+0.94	+1.18	−0.24	−0.92	+1.96
Other flows†	−1.85	+4.22	−3.00	+4.69	+2.90	+6.96
Total financing	+2.86	+8.55	−1.64	+4.74	+2.84	+17.35
International capital market finance as percent of total financing	164½	28		6	30¼	48½

*Includes official and private transfers.

†Includes direct and portfolio investment and unidentified financial flows.

Note: In 1973, Italy attracted more market capital than needed to finance its current deficit plus an increase in its reserves, and was thus able to reexport capital.

SOURCE: International Monetary Fund and OECD.

TABLE 12
EXTERNAL FINANCING REQUIREMENTS AND SOURCES OF FINANCE, SPAIN
($ billion)

	1973	1974	1975	1976	1977	Total 1973/77
Current balance*	+0.59	−3.23	−3.49	−4.23	−1.21	−11.57
Reserve change	+1.76	−0.29	−0.40	−0.81	+1.31	+1.57
Total requirement	+1.17	+2.94	+3.09	+3.42	+2.52	+13.14
Financed by:						
Eurocredits	+0.49	+1.11	+1.02	+1.87	+1.03	+5.52
International bonds	+0.03	____	+0.12	+0.25	+0.29	+0.69
Total international capital market	+0.52	+1.11	+1.14	+2.12	+1.32	+6.21
IMF			+0.72	+0.08	+0.04	+0.84
Other flows†	+0.65	+1.83	+1.23	+1.22	+1.16	+6.09
Total financing	+1.17	+2.94	+3.09	+3.42	+2.52	+13.14
International capital market finance as percent of total financing	44½	37¾	37	62	52½	47¼

*Includes official and private transfers.
†Includes direct and portfolio investment and unidentified financial flows.
SOURCE: International Monetary Fund and OECD.

The case of the United States, the fifth largest Eurocredit borrower among the industrial countries, was different yet again. All American Eurocredit borrowing was by private companies forced to borrow in external markets to finance their foreign investment until the lifting of American capital export controls at the beginning of 1974 made it possible for them to use the American domestic capital market once again.

The concentration of Eurocredit borrowing by a handful of industrial countries was strongest until 1976. Thereafter, borrowing became more widely diffused among the member countries of the Organization for Economic Cooperation and Development, with a greater share going to the smaller industrial countries, notably the Scandinavian countries. And from 1977, a substantial share went to Canada, which had partly exhausted its ability to go on financing large current account deficits on the fixed-interest international bond markets.

The weaker economies were ultimately disappointed in their hope that the stronger countries would save them from recession. On the contrary, the strongest countries were precisely those which were quickest to retrench, believing that restoration of price stability would provide the best hope for an eventual resumption of sustainable economic growth.

This made its impact on the pattern of Eurocredit lending. International bankers remained relatively confident that even the weakest industrial countries would be able to go on servicing their external debt. But they did not believe that those borrowers could go on doing so without ultimately dampening domestic demand to reduce imports and release resources for exports. Their willingness to go on providing Eurocredits was not, therefore, unlimited in the absence of some correction by the borrowers.

Italy was the first of the major industrial countries forced out of the

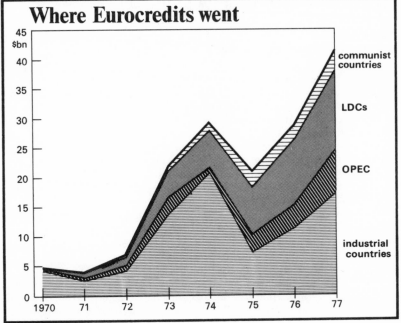

Where Eurocredits went

Sources: OECD, Morgan Guaranty

FIGURE 9

Eurocredits market. In 1974, it had to be rescued by an emergency loan of $2 billion provided by West Germany, its strongest European partner, against the collateral of gold.[1] Then, in 1976, $1.1 billion were raised in the international bond markets by the European Community for on-lending to Italy and Ireland. Britain likewise found that it could not go on depending on the Eurocredits market indefinitely and unconditionally. The collapse of sterling's exchange rate in 1976 forced the British government to seek a $5.3 billion standby from foreign central banks, reluctantly provided on the strict understanding that it would be available for no longer than six months and that medium-term financing would then have to be obtained (as it duly was) under strict conditions from the International Monetary Fund.

EASTERN EUROPE

Excluding a small number of isolated loans, Eurocredit lending to Eastern Europe began in 1972. The value of such lending then rose more than sixfold and from 3 percent to 12 percent of total Eurocredit financing during the three years through 1975. Thereafter, Western bankers and the East European authorities became more cautious. Eurocredit lending to the area continued to expand, but it did so more slowly, with the proportion falling to about $10\frac{1}{2}$ percent of total publicized Eurocredit financing by 1977 and less than $5\frac{1}{2}$ percent by 1979.

Borrowing from Western banks by Comecon, or the East European common market, predated 1972; it was only Eurocredit financing which became important from that year.[2] As long ago as the mid-1960s,

---

[1]The gold, valued for collateral at $120 an ounce (when the market price was around $150), represented the injection of a spurious commercial element into an act of foreign policy. Had need arisen, West Germany could not have realized the gold without breaking the market price; nor would West Germany have derived any benefit from adding still further to its own gold stocks, the world's second biggest after America's and unusable for exactly that reason. The economic necessity which forces the world's two biggest producers, South Africa and the U.S.S.R., to market newly mined gold limits the ability of large official holders to sell gold in a world having 80 years of supply above the ground, most of it in readily marketable forms.

[2]Officially known as the Council for Mutual Economic Assistance (CMEA). Marshall Aid was offered by the United States for the recovery of all Europe in 1947, but Stalin declined to accept. On the contrary, Stalin viewed the reconstruction of Western Europe (and particularly West Germany) as a threat. His response was the blockade of Berlin from 1948 to 1949 and the creation of the CMEA in the latter year. The members, ranked in order of economic size, are the U.S.S.R., Poland, the German Democratic Republic, Czechoslovakia, Rumania, Hungary, Bulgaria, and the Mongolian People's Republic. Cuba joined in 1972 and Vietnam in 1978. Albania withdrew, without formally resigning, in 1962.

a rapid expansion of Eastern Europe's trade with the outside world had come to depend increasingly on Western finance to cover Comecon's growing deficits with Western industrial countries (which were only partly offset by Comecon trade surpluses with developing countries).

However, for many years, financing consisted mostly of fixed-interest credits from Western European suppliers and banks (mostly guaranteed by official agencies of the exporting countries), of drawings by Communists banks on their credit lines with Western correspondent banks, and on the rediscounting of trade bills. It was the very much faster growth of Eastern European trade deficits (see Figure 10) and the expansion of Eurocredit facilities which combined to make Eurocredit financing a more important factor for East-West trade during the 1970s. But its importance should not be exaggerated; even by the end of 1978, outstanding publicized Eurocredits accounted for less than one-third of Eastern Europe's gross debt to Western banks.

The political aspects of East-West trade are outside the scope of this book and need be mentioned only briefly. The liberal view in the West (held also by some in the East) is that a more open development of the area's economy may contribute to internal political liberalization as well as improved international relations. It is precisely such implica-

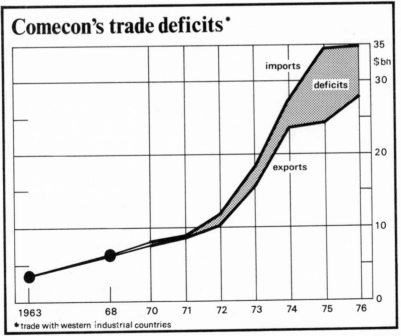

Comecon's trade deficits*

*trade with western industrial countries

Source: GATT

FIGURE 10

tions which make orthodox Marxists distrust growing dependence on Western technology and finance; rectitude prevailed for a long time in China and still does in Albania, as well as some of the newer Asian Communist countries which try to balance their external current accounts year by year to avoid the need for Western finance.[3] At the same time, there are Western critics who fear the export of technology to countries which they regard as implacably hostile.[4] For their part, the Comecon authorities have shown a clear desire for Western imports and finance, while at the same time attempting a close control over political liberalization in their countries.

Leaving political considerations aside, East-West trade has considerable economic attractions for both sides and its financing appears to carry little risk. The value of Comecon's trade with the outside world remains small, despite its rapid growth, amounting to less than 5 percent of world trade according to GATT estimates.[5] But the inefficiencies of Russian agriculture have left the U.S.S.R. heavily dependent on Western grain imports, while the whole of Comecon has become increasingly dependent on imports of Western technology. The value of Comecon's imports from Western industrial countries doubled during the 1960s and then approximately quadrupled to about $34 billion during the seven years through 1977.[6]

From the Western view, Russia provides a valuable outlet for periodic excesses of American, Canadian, and Australian grain production. Some Western capital goods industries have become highly dependent on exports to Comecon. An example is West Germany's machine tool industry, which was exporting about a quarter of its output to Eastern Europe by 1977. Technological exports have also taken the different form of joint ventures in Eastern Europe, with Western firms supplying equipment and expertise, the host countries supplying tightly disciplined labor, and shipments of output from the joint ventures to the Western investors providing partial payment.

---

[3]The first signs of Chinese willingness to bend the rules came in 1978, when the Bank of China indicated that it might be ready to accept long-term deposits from Western banks; this was intended to get around the awkwardness of having to call such financing Western "loans." However, even such pretences were quickly dropped when China finally moved into the international bank credits market with a rush in December 1978, borrowing more than $10 billion in four months to help finance the economic modernization on which the new Chinese leadership had decided.

[4]Including Dr. Henry Kissinger, the former U.S. Secretary of State, who said in June 1978: "There cannot be a free market in our relations with the Communists. The governments of the industrial democracies must act to apply political criteria to their international lending."

[5]*International Trade 1977/78*, GATT, Geneva, 1978.

[6]Ibid.

Despite some concern about the very rapid growth of Eurocredit lending to Eastern Europe during the 1970s, Comecon's debt and debt service remain small in relation to the area's resources. The community has an untarnished repayments record, an imperative to keep that record unblemished, and the means to do so. On the admittedly imperfect guesstimates available, Comecon's hard currency debt may have been something over $50 billion gross and around $40 billion net in 1977, or less than 5 percent of the area's output of more than $1,000 billion, while debt service seems to have been about 10 percent of hard-currency export earnings and less than that in relation to total export earnings.[7]

As well as the indications that Comecon's debt and debt service were kept within manageable proportions even during the fast rise in borrowing during the 1970s, there are Russia's large though unknown gold reserves. Consolidated Gold Fields has estimated Soviet output at more than 400 tons a year, second only to South Africa's annual production of about 700 tons, and it has estimated Soviet reserves at about 2,700 tons, which would be the world's fourth largest after those of the U.S., West Germany, and France. Although the Soviet authorities have said they regard gold as their last-line reserve, they sold almost 4,500 tons on Western markets during the 25 years to the end of 1977.

Far more important is the Soviet Union's interest in ensuring that none of the Comecon countries runs into default for the sake of the area as a whole and it has the means to avoid such a thing happening. The Kremlin is a tougher cookie than the IMF or, in the diplomatic language of international public servants: "The market took a favorable view of the Comecon countries' ability, in case of need, to manage their external position and to correct swiftly foreign trade imbalances as a consequence of a comprehensive system of controls and the political ability to make full use of them."[8] Which indeed they did between 1975 and 1977, when Comecon reduced its trade deficit with Western industrial countries from over $9 billion to less than $6 billion.

Apart from such assuring aspects, Western bankers also have positive

---

[7]Guesstimates of Comecon output are taken from the *World Bank Atlas of Population, Per Capita Product and Growth Rates, 1977*. Data on Comecon trade are taken from *International Trade, 1976/77*, GATT, Geneva, 1977. Recorded Comecon debt to Western banks at the end of 1977 was $33 billion gross and $25 billion net, according to the quarterly report of the Bank for International Settlements, May 1978. Estimates of Comecon's total gross hard currency debt have been made by Lawrence J. Brainard of Bankers Trust and by Chase Manhattan Bank. Estimates of the area's total net hard currency indebtedness were made by OECD Financial Market Trends, December 1977. The paragraph to which this footnote applies has attempted a compression of these assorted guesstimates.

[8]*Financial Market Trends*, OECD, December 1977.

inducements to lend to Comecon. It has not only proved profitable in itself but, given the very fast growth of East-West trade, Eurocredit lending has generated to an even greater extent than it usually does other banking business with the borrowers and with exporters to the borrowing countries.

Yet when all that has been said, Western bankers regard Eurocredit lending to Comecon as third-best after lending to Western industrial countries and oil exporters, nor has Eurocredit lending to Comecon risen indiscriminately at all times. During the year up to mid-1977 there was a pause when the value of new Eurocredit lending to Comecon fell by 30 percent below that of the preceding 12 months. Distinctions are made between borrowers, with the U.S.S.R. ranked the most credit worthy because of its resources and relatively small external debt. Hungary is ranked second, partly because of its exceptional willingness to provide fairly comprehensive information about its balance of payments and reserves (more, in fact, than Rumania, the only Comecon country which belongs to the IMF, but the only IMF member which does not provide information for publication). At the other extreme, Poland as the largest Eurocredit borrower in Comecon up to 1976 but also the one with the biggest trade deficits, found its access to the market sharply reduced in 1977, as did Czechoslovakia (although Poland was then readmitted in 1978). A feature from 1975 onward was the increase in borrowing for the area as a whole through Comecon's two regional banks, the International Bank for Economic Cooperation (IBEC), correspondingly roughly to the IMF, and the International Investment Bank (IIB), corresponding roughly to the World Bank.

The difficulties of getting adequate information about Comecon borrowers is one of the main concerns of Western bankers and even when information and assurances are supplied, they are not always reliable. A $600 million Eurocredit was provided to the IIB in 1977 by a Western banking group led by Chase Manhattan to finance part of the Orenburg gas pipeline and detailed feasibility studies were carried out on that assumption. But later, asked by a visiting journalist how the money was being used, a senior Comecon official said he had "no idea".[9] The difficulties of getting sufficient information often prolong and sometimes abort Eurocredit negotiations and they also have the effect of bumping up unpublicized fees, which Comecon borrowers prefer to the implied stigma of high and publicized lending margins.

In summary, Eurocredit lending to Comecon grew very rapidly up to 1975, but more slowly thereafter. Caution has been justified and

---

[9]Nora Beloff, "The Comecon Bumble-Bee," *The Banker*, London, May 1978.

used, but it is difficult to find any cause for alarm. Such lending is likely to continue its expansion, partly because there seems little prospect of an early move to balance or surplus in Comecon's trade with the West and the area's credit needs could increase considerably if Soviet oil resources start running down in the 1980s, as some experts believe. Thanks to Soviet oil, Comecon remained in approximate trade balance with OPEC up to the late 1970s, but that would clearly change if a need for large oil imports arises in the next decade.

OIL EXPORTERS

Eurocredit borrowing by OPEC countries began building up steadily from 1970 with a pause only in 1974, immediately after the quantum rise in world oil prices. During the three years from 1975 through 1977, when OPEC borrowers returned to the market, they obtained $13 billion of Eurocredits according to OECD and $14 billion according to Morgan Guaranty. However, more than 80 percent of the total on either reckoning went to five borrowers: Algeria, Indonesia, Iran, the United Arab Emirates, and Venezuela. With the exception of the United Arab Emirates, these are countries with relatively large populations or, in Venezuela's case, limited oil reserves, but in any event with a need to use their oil revenues, for economic development. Their imports therefore rose very rapidly and after 1975 their current payments surpluses either narrowed, as in the case of Iran and Venezuela, or returned to deficit, as in Algeria or Indonesia, following no more than temporary swing into surplus immediately after the 1973 oil price increase.

These countries could have financed new and higher levels of imports by the use of their reserves. Instead they chose to build up their reserves while at the same time building up experience and a reputation as borrowers in the international capital market. The returns earned from the investment of foreign exchange reserves offset at least a part of market borrowing costs and in some cases investment earnings may have exceeded borrowing costs, making it cheaper to borrow than to use reserves.

Among the major OPEC borrowers, the United Arab Emirates are a special case. Nearly all of the UAE's borrowing has been by Dubai, the second biggest of the emirates but a historic trading center rather than an important oil producer. Dubai therefore has a special inducement to industrialize and to borrow for that purpose on the implied credit standing of the UAE as a whole.

Most OPEC borrowing has been by governments and their agencies, predominantly for infrastructure such as airports, aircraft, harbors, roads, and telecommunications, and for new industries, especially those based on oil, like petrochemicals and electric power generation. However, there has also been fairly substantial Eurocredit borrowing by private companies in oil exporting countries, particularly in Saudi Arabia, Kuwait, and Bahrain.

DEVELOPING COUNTRIES

Nothing in the evolution of the international capital market during the 1970s caused greater controversy and confusion than Eurocredit lending to non-oil developing countries. Dr. Arthur Burns, then Chairman of the Federal Reserve Board, said in 1977 that he had spoken in "strident terms" to some American banks about their lending to foreign countries. A less strident view was expressed a year later on behalf of the major Western governments by an official French study which said that the debt problem of developing countries was "neither general nor unmanageable."[10]

As in the case of other countries, Eurocredit borrowing by non-oil developing countries predated the oil crisis and has been highly concentrated. During the four years prior to the end of 1973 the non-oil LDCs received about $7 billion of Eurocredits and in the succeeding four years they received another almost $40 billion. But about one-half the latter amount went to Brazil and Mexico and 70 percent to six countries, the others being the Philippines, South Korea, Argentina, and Peru. The remainder of about $12 billion was divided among about 55 countries. If there is a problem about Eurocredit lending to the non-oil developing countries it may be manageable or otherwise, but it is not general.

Conceptual understanding has been positively impeded by an indiscriminate avalanche of data, apparently produced in the belief that if only enough statistics are piled on top of each other, a spontaneous combustion of illumination will occur.

In the case of the developing countries, most statistics are dated, partial, and provide guidance only of the crudest kind. Information about external debt is usually two years out-of-date and usually excludes military debt, which is often large. Quite fundamental data are sometimes madly wrong; the first census of the United Arab Emirates in 1975 disclosed a population 60 percent larger than supposed.

International agencies add to confusion by their disagreement about

---

[10]"The Debt Situation of Developing Countries," submitted by France on behalf of Western governments at an UNCTAD conference on debt relief in Geneva in January 1978. UNCTAD reference *TD/B/685/add.1.*

the classification of countries. Spain, Portugal, Turkey, and Greece are ranked as developing countries by the World Bank, but as industrialized countries by the OECD, to which they belong. Ireland is universally classified as an industrialized country and Argentina as a developing country, although Argentina's per capita income is half as big again as Ireland's.

But the worst muddle results from the failure of most studies, official and private, to draw a sufficiently clear distinction between the Eurocredit debt of a handful of advanced developing countries dependant on private capital for most of their external financing, and the very different questions posed by the generalized debt burden of developing countries as a whole. However, it has become easier to make this distinction following a more subtle grading of countries at different stages of economic advance.

Until 1973, the world was simplistically divided into industrialized and developing countries. But from 1974 an obvious line was drawn between oil-exporting and oil-importing developing countries and by 1977 international jargon had created an elaborate class structure of low, lower-middle, intermediate-middle, upper-middle, and high income countries, the latter overlapping with the poorer gentry.[11] The gentry themselves were then divided in 1978 into MICs (mature industrialized countries) and NICs (newer industrialized countries), the latter responsible for more than one-half the industrial output and about three-quarters of the exports of manufactured goods of what the World Bank confusingly persisted in calling the developing countries.[12]

During the 1970s the bulk of what was called Eurocredit lending to developing countries went, in fact, to a handful of NICs and higher income countries and a far clearer picture emerges by treating the subject under three headings.

Exactly half of what is usually included in generalizations about Western bank lending to developing countries consists of the special case of lending to Brazil and Mexico, about three-quarters of it by American commercial banks. It would be far more accurate to describe this as a new expression of a historic political and financial relationship, comparable to the relationship of northern Western Europe with countries like Italy and Spain.

---

[11]The IMF/World Bank classifications based on 1976 per capita GNP were: high income, over $2,500; upper middle, over $1,135; intermediate middle, over $550; lower middle, over $280; and low income, below $280.

[12]The 11 countries designated as NICs in 1978 were Spain, Portugal, Greece, Turkey, Yugoslavia, Mexico, Brazil, South Korea, Hong Kong (a British Crown colony), Singapore, and Taiwan.

Between them, Brazil and Mexico received not only one-half of all publicized Eurocredits but also one-half of total Western bank lending to developing countries during most of the 1970s. They were also among the first developing countries to graduate to the international bond market, in 1972 in Mexico's case and in 1976 in Brazil's. Both are at the stage where they have come to depend on international private capital for more than 80 percent of their external financing. From the early 1970s, both countries began to borrow heavily in order to build up reserves for future need and for continuing access to the private markets, on which they must depend in the absence of official aid on a scale sufficient to finance their pace of development.

Both countries have diversified and relatively fast-growing economies, with more than one-half of gross domestic product contributed by manufacturing, commerce, construction, transportations, communications, and utilities. They have advanced well beyond dependence on any single export commodity. Coffee remains Brazil's most important single export and Mexico is similarly dependent on exports of petroleum and gas. But both countries earn more from exports of manufactures like electrical equipment, engineering goods, machine tools, and chemicals; and Brazil has been designing new types of automobile engines for Volkswagen in Germany, not merely exporting them.

There can obviously be no guarantee of the economic and political future. But both economies have reached a stage where danger signals can usually be picked up fairly early and there is enough at stake for the countries and their creditors to suggest that determined efforts would be made to avoid serious difficulties. Indeed, Brazil began bringing its current external deficits under better control in 1975 and Mexico in 1976 (partly by devaluing the peso). Nor does Eurocredit lending continue unabated at all times, any more than it did to Italy and Britain. Eurocredit lending to Mexico was cut back in 1974 and 1976 and lending to Brazil in 1977. In summary, any threat to the solvency of the two countries would be critical for them and the American banking system as well as for the international banking system. It follows that very exceptional measures would probably be taken to avoid any such threat.

The second greatest concentration of Eurocredit lending to non-oil developing countries during the 1970s was to Argentina, Peru, the Philippines, and South Korea which, between them, received about one-fifth of such financing. The long political and economic relationship between Argentina and the United States is less close but still comparable to that of Brazil and Mexico. In some ways, Argentina is economically and financially better placed. Its per capita output is considerably higher than Brazil's and Mexico's, its economic growth has been slower since the 1960s, but its balance of payments and external debt have been kept under better control. There is almost certainly a connection between these factors. Of the others in this group, South Korea has been an extremely rapidly growing economy whose export income during the 1970s rose exactly twice as fast as debt service (despite heavy borrowing). The opposite was true of the Philippines, but in its case heavy foreign borrowing resulted in a marked acceleration of economic growth during the 1970s.

Nevertheless, this group of countries falls into the awkward category where the amounts of foreign credit are large but not critical for the international banking system, and where matters can go wrong and have done so. An example is found in the case of Peru, which was unable to maintain full service of its external debt in 1977 and 1978, and which found its access to the Eurocredits market severely curtailed in 1977 and the door shut in 1978, when it was reluctantly forced into new negotiations for conditional finance from the IMF.

The third category of non-oil developing countries in the Eurocredits market consists of about 55 countries who received a total of roughly $12 billion during the four years to the end of 1977. Morocco, Taiwan, Malaysia, Hong Kong, and Chile obtained between $1 billion and $1½ billion each so that Eurocredit lending to the other members of the group averaged well below a cumulative $200 million each during the four years. Not only was lending spread very widely among borrowers, but lending was also spread far more widely among banks than in the case of Eurocredit financing of the world's biggest borrowers, which was far more concentrated among a relatively small number of the world's biggest commercial banks.

In this group, several countries have run into difficulties and others will doubtless follow. But because the risks are so widely spread among countries and banks the damage should be limited, unless a large number of these countries all defaulted at the same time, which would be a symptom rather than a cause of international collapse if it ever happened.

Tables 13 through 23 provide an analysis of the payments deficits of the non-oil LDCs and show the part played by international market capital in financing those deficits while allowing the borrowers to build up reserves at the same time.

TABLE 13
ESTIMATES OF NON-OIL LDC
PAYMENTS DEFICITS AND TOTAL FINANCING
($ billion)

	1970	1971	1972	1973	1974	1975	1976	1977
Trade balance	−6	−9½	−6½	−7½	−23½	−38½	−23½	18½
Services and private transfers	−5	−5¼	−5	−6¾	−9¾	−12	−13¼	−15
Official transfers (ODA)	+4¼	+4¾	+5½	+6¼	+8¾	+10½	+10½	+11
Current balance	−6¾	−10	−6	−8	−24½	−40	−26¼	−22½
Changes in reserves	+2½	+1¾	+5¾	+7½	+2¾	−1¾	+11¾	+8
Financing requirement	+9¼	+11¾	+11¾	+15½	+27¼	+38¾	+38	+30½
Aid (ODA) and other official flows	+4	+4¾	+4¾	+6¾	+8¾	+12	+12½	+13
Direct investment	+1½	+1¾	+2¼	+3½	+4½	+5	+4	+4
Portfolio investment	+½	+½	+1¾	+3	+3½	+3¾	+5	+5
Other official financing	+¼	+¾	+1		+1¼	+1¾	+2	+½
Errors and omissions*	+2½	+3½	+¾	−2¼	+2	+8¾	+3½	−2
	+8¾	+11¼	+10½	+11	+20	+31¼	+27	+20½
Medium-term Euroborrowing	+½	+½	+1¼	+4½	+7¼	+7½	+11	+10
Total financing	+9¼	+11¾	+11¾	+15½	+27¼	+38¾	+38	+30½
Financing† of which	6¾	8¼	11	17¾	25¼	30	34½	32½
Official ($ billion)‡	4¼	5½	5¾	6¾	10	13¾	14½	13½
Private ($ billion)§	2½	2¾	5¼	11	15¼	16½	20	19
Official (%)‡	63	67	52	38	40	46	42	42
Private (%)§	37	33	48	62	60	54	58	58

*Includes trade credits and repayments on Euroborrowings.
†Net of Errors and Omissions included above.
‡Aid (ODA), other official flows and other official financing.
§Direct and Portfolio Investment and Medium Term Euroborrowings.
SOURCE: *Economic Outlook,* OECD, December 1977.

TABLE 14

FLOW OF FINANCIAL RESOURCES TO DEVELOPING COUNTRIES AND MULTILATERAL AGENCIES— DISBURSEMENTS

($ billion)

	1970	1971	1972	1973	1974	1975	1976	1977*
Official Development Assistance (ODA)	6.79	7.66	8.54	9.37	11.30	13.59	13.67	14.76
Other official	1.14	1.25	1.55	2.46	2.19	3.02	3.31	3.01
Total official	7.93	8.91	10.09	11.83	13.49	16.61	16.98	17.77
Private investment and lending	4.73	5.13	7.13	8.24	4.86	18.29	17.00	17.24
Private export credits	2.14	2.83	1.45	1.20	2.49	4.14	5.42	7.14
Total private	6.87	7.96	8.58	9.44	7.35	22.43	22.42	24.38
Total flow of resources†	15.66	17.79	19.69	22.63	22.06	40.38	40.74	43.70
of which:								
official (%)	51	50	51	52	61	41	42	41
private (%)	49	50	49	48	39	59	58	59

*Preliminary estimates.

†Includes grants by voluntary agencies.

SOURCE: Development Assistance Committee, OECD.

TABLE 15

ESTIMATES OF NON-OIL LDC
PAYMENTS DEFICITS AND MARKET FINANCING

($ billion)

	1970	1971	1972	1973	1974	1975	1976	1977
Financing requirement	9¼	11¾	11¾	15½	27¼	38¾	38	30½
Eurocredits	½	½	1½	4½	6¼	8¼	11	12
International bonds-direct			¼	¾	¾	¾	1¾	3½
International bonds-indirect*	¼	½	1	¾	¾	2¼	3½	3
Total market financing	¾	1	2¾	6	7¾	11¼	16¼	18½
Other financing	8½	10¾	9	9½	19½	27½	21¾	12
Total financing	9¼	11¾	11¾	15½	27¼	38¾	38	30½
Market financing as percent of total financing	8	8½	23	39	28	29	43	61

*Based on calculations that about 55 percent of international bonds issued by all international organizations have been issued by such development institutions as the World Bank and 45 percent by the international organizations of developed market economies.

SOURCE: OECD and Morgan Guaranty.

TABLE 16
**TOTAL ANNUAL DEBT SERVICING OF DEVELOPING
COUNTRIES BY TYPE OF DEBT**
($ billion)

	1970	1971	1972	1973	1974	1975	1976*
Bilateral ODA and IDA type	1.4	1.5	1.7	2.0	2.0	2.2	2.6
Other international organizations	0.8	0.9	1.1	1.2	1.4	1.6	1.7
Export credits	4.9	5.5	6.5	7.7	8.9	11.3	14.0
Other (market terms)	1.8	2.6	3.4	4.8	7.3	10.7	13.5
Unallocated	0.1	0.1	0.2	0.2	0.2	0.2	0.2
Total	9.0	10.6	12.9	15.9	19.8	26.0	32.0

*Provisional.
SOURCE: Development Assistance Committee, OECD.

TABLE 17
**84 DEVELOPING COUNTRIES—BANK CREDITS
AS PROPORTION OF TOTAL EXTERNAL PUBLIC DEBT
OUTSTANDING (INCLUDING UNDISBURSED) BY
REGION**
(percentage)

	1970	1971	1972	1973	1974	1975
Latin America/Caribbean	13.4	17.4	21.6	27.9	32.4	37.2
East Asia/Pacific	7.3	6.6	7.5	10.4	15.6	23.1
North Africa/Middle East	7.9	9.4	10.6	17.5	15.6	20.3
More advanced mediterranean countries	13.9	17.6	19.2	19.0	25.3	29.2
Africa (south of Sahara)	4.0	4.6	7.0	13.1	16.4	16.1
South Asia	0.9	0.8	0.6	0.5	0.7	0.8
Total	8.2	10.0	12.1	16.3	19.3	23.3

Excludes some minor items.
SOURCE: World Bank.

TABLE 18*(a)*

84 DEVELOPING COUNTRIES—EXTERNAL PUBLIC DEBT OUTSTANDING (INCLUDING UNDISBURSED) DUE TO BANKS BY REGION

($ billion)

	1970	1971	1972	1973	1974	1975
Latin America/Caribbean	2.83	4.28	6.38	10.04	14.82	19.81
East Asia/Pacific	0.65	0.74	1.03	1.75	3.75	6.83
North Africa/Middle East	0.81	1.19	1.54	3.30	3.40	6.00
More advanced Mediterranean countries	1.09	1.61	1.96	2.14	3.61	4.65
Africa (south of Sahara)	0.28	0.39	0.68	1.68	2.71	3.06
South Asia	0.15	0.15	0.12	0.11	0.19	0.21
Total	5.81	8.36	11.71	19.02	28.48	40.56

TABLE 18*(b)*

EXTERNAL PUBLIC DEBT OUTSTANDING

(percentage)

	1970	1971	1972	1973	1974	1975
Latin America/Caribbean	49	51	54	53	52	49
East Asia/Pacific	11	9	9	9	13	17
North Africa/Middle East	13	14	13	17	12	15
More advanced Mediterranean countries	19	19	17	11	13	11
Africa (south of Sahara)	5	5	6	9	9	7
South Asia	3	2	1	1	1	1
Total	100	100	100	100	100	100

Excludes some minor items.

SOURCE: World Bank.

TABLE 19
**FOUR MAJOR NON-OIL DEVELOPING COUNTRIES
(BRAZIL, KOREA, MEXICO, AND PHILIPPINES)
EXTERNAL FINANCING REQUIREMENTS
AND SOURCES OF FINANCE**

($ billion)

	1973	1974	1975	1976	1977	Total 1973/77
Current balance*	−3.42	−12.68	−13.90	−11.36	−6.60	−47.96
Reserve change	+3.26	−0.67	−0.76	+3.92	+2.42	+8.17
Total requirement	+6.68	+12.01	+13.14	+15.28	+9.02	+56.13
Financed by:						
Eurocredits	+2.73	+3.59	+5.17	+6.93	+7.48	+25.90
International bonds	+0.27	+0.10	+0.36	+1.15	+2.08	+3.96
IMF		+0.16	+0.13	+0.84	+0.19	+1.32
Other flows†	+3.68	+8.16	+7.48	+6.36	−0.73	+24.95
Total financing	+6.68	+12.01	+13.14	+15.28	+9.02	+56.13
International capital market finance as percent of total financing	44½	30¾	42	52¾	106	53¼

*Includes official and private transfers.

†Includes direct and portfolio investment and unidentified financial flows.

Note: In 1977, the four countries attracted more market capital than needed to finance their current deficits and an increase in their reserves, and they were thus able to reexport capital.

SOURCE: International Monetary Fund and Morgan Guaranty.

TABLE 20

**EXTERNAL FINANCING REQUIREMENT AND
SOURCES OF FINANCE, BRAZIL**

($ billion)

	1973	1974	1975	1976	1977	Total 1973/77
Current balance*	−2.16	−7.56	−7.05	−6.63	−3.95	−27.35
Reserve change	+2.23	−1.14	−1.24	+2.51	+0.72	+3.08
Total requirement	+4.39	+6.42	+5.81	+9.14	+4.67	+30.43
Financed by:						
Eurocredits	+0.74	+1.67	+2.15	+3.23	+2.81	+10.60
International bonds	+0.06	+0.03	+0.04	+0.27	+0.73	+1.13
IMF				+0.05		+0.05
Other flows†	+3.59	+4.72	+3.62	+5.59	+1.13	+18.65
Total financing	+4.39	+6.42	+5.81	+9.14	+4.67	+30.43
International capital market finance as percent of total financing	18	26½	37¾	41¼	75¾	38½

*Includes official and private transfers.

†Includes direct and portfolio investment and unidentified financial flows.

SOURCE: International Monetary Fund and Morgan Guaranty.

TABLE 21
EXTERNAL FINANCING REQUIREMENT AND
SOURCES OF FINANCE, MEXICO

($ billion)

	1973	1974	1975	1976	1977	Total 1973/77
Current balance*	−1.42	−2.88	−4.04	−3.31	−1.80	−13.45
Reserve change	+0.19	+0.04	+0.14	−0.28	+0.47	+0.56
Total requirement	+1.61	+2.92	+4.18	+3.03	+2.27	+14.01
Financed by:						
Eurocredits	+1.59	+0.95	+2.31	+1.99	+2.70	+9.54
International bonds	+0.18	+0.05	+0.29	+0.45	+1.16	+2.13
IMF				+0.48	+0.14	+0.62
Other flows†	−0.16	+1.92	+1.58	+0.11	−1.73	+1.72
Total financing	+1.61	+2.92	+4.18	+3.03	+2.27	+14.01
International capital market finance as percent of total financing	110	34¼	62¼	80½	170	83¼

*Includes official and private transfers.

†Includes direct and portfolio investment and unidentified financial flows.

Note: In 1973 and 1977, Mexico attracted more market capital than needed to finance its current deficits plus increases in its reserves, and was thus able to re-export capital.

SOURCE: International Monetary Fund and Morgan Guaranty.

TABLE 22
EXTERNAL FINANCING REQUIREMENT AND SOURCES OF FINANCE, PHILIPPINES
($ billion)

	1973	1974	1975	1976	1977	Total 1973/77
Current balance*	+0.47	−0.21	−0.92	−1.11	−0.86	−2.63
Reserve change	+0.49	+0.47	−0.15	+0.28	−0.12	+0.97
Total requirement	+0.02	+0.68	+0.77	+1.39	+0.74	+3.60
Financed by:						
Eurocredits	+0.19	+0.84	+0.36	+0.97	+0.70	+3.06
International bonds	+0.03	+0.02	+0.03	+0.37	+0.12	+0.57
IMF			+0.01	+0.21	+0.05	+0.27
Other flows†	−0.20	−0.18	+0.37	−0.16	−0.13	−0.30
Total financing	+0.02	+0.68	+0.77	+1.39	+0.74	+3.60
International capital market finance as percent of total financing	110	126½	50½	96½	110¾	100¾

*Includes official and private transfers.

†Includes direct and portfolio investment and unidentified financial flows.

Note: Throughout most of the period, the Philippines attracted more market capital than needed to finance current deficits plus reserve increases, and the country was thus able to reexport capital.

SOURCE: International Monetary Fund and Morgan Guaranty.

TABLE 23
**EXTERNAL FINANCING REQUIREMENT AND
SOURCES OF FINANCE, KOREA**

($ billion)

	1973	1974	1975	1976	1977	Total 1973/77
Current balance*	−0.31	−2.03	−1.89	−0.31	+0.01	−4.53
Reserve change	+0.35	−0.04	+0.49	+1.41	+1.35	+3.56
Total requirement	+0.66	+1.99	+2.38	+1.72	+1.34	+8.09
Financed by:						
Eurocredits	+0.21	+0.13	+0.35	+0.74	+1.27	+2.70
International bonds				+0.06	+0.07	+0.13
IMF		+0.16	+0.12	+0.10		+0.38
Other flows†	+0.45	+1.70	+1.91	+0.82	——	+4.88
Total financing	+0.66	+1.99	+2.38	+1.72	+1.34	+8.09
International capital market finance as per-cent of total financing	31¾	6½	14¾	46½	100	35

*Includes official and private transfers.
†Includes direct and portfolio investment and unidentified financial flows.
SOURCE: International Monetary Fund and Morgan Guaranty.

CHAPTER EIGHTEEN
BANKING PROTECTION

The main ways in which banks try to protect themselves from Euro-credit lending risk are by analysis of borrowers, legal agreements, and various forms of cooperation with international organizations. But the first two have limited value and the third is available only to a limited extent. In addition, banks seek protection from the discrimination of higher lending margins and fees to weaker borrowers, but this helps only to the extent that some of the higher returns are kept aside as provision against possible loss.

The time and care spent on country risk-analysis has become a favorite platform topic for many bankers, and some banks have created highly complicated computer models to forecast national economic trends and even to evaluate such unquantifiables as social and political stability. The Bank of America's computer system was explained at a London conference in 1978 by its director of economic policy research, Dr. John Oliver Wilson.[1] He said the computer had rated 66 countries as being on average 31 percent more stable in 1977 than in 1970, although he did not say whether this had made the Bank of America 31 percent happier.

A revealing study was made in 1976 by the U.S. Export-Import Bank of 37 American banks holding more than half the external assets of the entire American banking system. Five of these banks used no particular system of country risk-analysis; only one bank had gone backward to test its system and had found the results "poor"; sensibly, under the circumstances, none of the banks relied on its systems for more than preliminary guidance in evaluating loans and terms.

---

[1]The *Financial Times* World Banking Conference, London, 1978.

There is little, in fact, to suggest that computers represent any improvement on old Mr. Nathan Mayer Rothschild, trundling about in his carriage, receiving his intelligence by carrier pigeon, and getting his sovereign risk-analysis wonderfully right. In the modern Eurocredits market, the many bankers who lack this flair tend to rely on the few who have it and a bank's participation in a syndicated credit is often determined by that of other banks rather than by an assessment of the borrower alone.

Attempts to give Eurocredit lenders legal protection are made difficult by the fact that lenders and borrowers reside in several countries and that the credits are arranged outside the jurisdiction of any single authority. This raises questions about which law and jurisdiction will apply, about the willingness of courts in any one country to try the issues, and, more important, about their ability to enforce judgment on a nonresident borrower who may have no assets within their jurisdiction. A special complication is the legal status of governments and international organizations which borrow in the market, although the laws of many countries have been changed in recent years to waive sovereign immunity in commercial transactions. However, in the case of sovereign borrowers, difficulties are usually settled by political negotiation rather than litigation. The value of a well-drawn loan agreement is that it may help put a bank's claims on a par with those of other creditors in such a political settlement.

A third way in which banks try to improve the quality of their Eurocredit lending is by cooperation with official international organizations, notably the Bank for International Settlements, the Organization for Economic Cooperation and Development, the International Monetary Fund, and the World Bank group. Private bankers look to all of these for information about international financial flows and debtor countries. Countries running into difficulties may be persuaded to accept conditions for the management of their economies proposed by the IMF. The World Bank, the IMF, and the OECD usually participate in international debt renegotiations. There has also been a certain amount of cofinancings involving the joint participations of private banks and the World Bank or its affiliate, the International Finance Corporation.

However, aside from the hope that these organizations may provide a continually improving flow of information, the scope for cooperation with them is limited. The Eurocredits market grew to its present size precisely because official organizations did not have the funds needed to plug the financing gaps which widened during the 1960s and even more during the 1970s. Many countries have deliberately avoided drawing on the IMF not so much from reluctance to accept conditions for the management of their economies but to demonstrate that they do not need such conditions, rather like a man proclaiming his health by saying that he has never had to visit a doctor.

Besides, official financing often takes longer to arrange than private financing and is often limited in scope. The World Bank requires government guarantees while its affiliate, the International Finance Corporation, is confined to investment in the private sector of developing countries. This cuts out many quasi-governmental organizations in developing countries either because they do not qualify for government guarantees required by the World Bank or because they do not qualify for private enterprise financing from the IFC. Moreover, official aid is often limited to the foreign exchange component of investment projects and to their initial but not recurring costs.

In theory, such aid "gaps" suggest a case for more cofinancing by official agencies and commercial banks. Another argument for it was made by the IFC's annual report for 1977, which said that participation by official lenders in joint investment should not be seen as a guarantee against commercial risk, but should "provide confidence in order to maintain a continuing flow of external capital to developing countries."

However, in practice such cofinancings have been relatively small. The World Bank's first cofinancing consisted of a $95 million 15-year loan to the Companhia Siderurgica Nacional of Brazil in December 1975, supplemented by $55 million of Eurocredits arranged by the Bank of America. But in the two years that followed, there were only eight such cofinancings for a total of less than $900 million, partly explained by the fact that the time taken to arrange them was up to 11 months, compared with the six to eight weeks usually needed to arrange a Eurocredit. As for the IFC, it had made equity investments and loans totaling $1.7 billion by 1977, accompanied by about 7\frac{1}{4}$ billion of private financing. But this was over a space of 21 years from the IFC's foundation in 1956 and average IFC investments at around $6 million are extremely small.[2]

In addition, there is the protection which banks seek from the discrimination of higher lending margins and fees to weaker borrowers. A prime lending margin of 1$\frac{1}{2}$ percent above LIBOR to one borrower and 1$\frac{3}{4}$ percent to another at a given moment expresses a difference between perceived risk at the time, but not necessarily a permanent one. It is also partly an expression of supply and demand; more banks

---

[2]In these cofinancings, the World Bank and IFC make their own loans and investments. Private lenders have a separate relationship with the borrower, but rely extensively on the analyses of the official agencies and the commitment of those agencies to the investment.

may have reached their statutory or self-imposed lending limits to one country but not another. To the layperson, the nicety of a $\frac{1}{4}$ point or even a $\frac{1}{8}$ point differentiation between borrowers seems as arbitrary as attempted quantifications of happiness or stability. And arbitrary they inevitably are, to some extent. But the traditional and serious purpose of grading borrowers in bank lending of every kind is not an academic exercise in spuriously precise differentiation. The object is to obtain an additional return from weaker borrowers so that at least part of it can be set aside to provide for possible loss. How much Eurobanks actually do set aside for the contingency of defaults is another matter and any-one's guess. A further purpose served by the quotation of higher margins and fees is that it provides banks with a polite alternative to out-right refusal of credits they do not want to grant.

Finally, the latter 1970s were characterized by attempts to improve the evaluation of international bank lending by the authorities, particu-larly in the United States. This consisted partly of efforts at better coordination between the authorities responsible for bank supervision in the U.S., the Federal Reserve Board, the Comptroller of the Cur-rency, the Federal Deposit Insurance Corporation, and the state bank-ing agencies. It consisted partly, also, of attempts at a more refined assessment of the concentration and quality of international lending by American commercial banks, which are restricted by the National Banking Act 12 USC 84 of 1863 from lending more than 10 percent of their capital and unimpaired reserves to any single borrower.

There are some who believe that this law, designed for the conditions of an American domestic market as it existed more than a century ago, may no longer be suited to the very different circumstances of the contemporary world, although it has not in fact impeded the growth of international lending by American banks. This is partly because some international lending is done through foreign affiliates or partly owned international affiliates such as consortium banks. More important is that the restriction does not apply to lending to a country as a whole, but to each individual borrower in that country, so that countries have learned to spread their borrowing among the central government, state agen-cies, nationalized industries, and even municipalities.

Besides this, a reasonably large although unknown amount of inter-national financing officially classified as lending to a country is, in fact, lending to the foreign subsidiaries of multinational corporations, fully guaranteed by the parent. A credit indiscriminately ranked as a loan to Ruritania is often, for all practical purposes, a credit to a corporation like General Motors or Exxon.

The authorities, particularly in the United States, have increasingly taken note of such important distinctions and bank examiners have been instructed to take greater care about classifying the quality of loans merely on a generalized view of the borrowing country rather than of the borrowing entity. Mr. John G. Heimann, the U.S. Comptroller of the Currency, said soon after his appointment in 1977 that he was more concerned about concentrations of international bank lending to certain industries and commodities than concentration measured by geographical boundaries alone. He drew a distinction also between lending to foreign state agencies generating revenues of their own, particularly foreign exchange revenues, and other entities dependent entirely on their central governments.[3]

---

[3]During the 1970s, the British government secured balance of payments support partly by forcing into the Eurocredits market municipalities which never had or could generate a cent of foreign exchange, imposing an extremely costly burden on local residents.

CHAPTER NINETEEN
THE BALANCE OF ADVANTAGE

The rapid growth of the Eurocredits market during the 1970s was accompanied by an unending lament from bankers and borrowers complaining, like the two matrons in the Woody Allen joke, about the quality of food at their holiday resort "and such small portions too." These concluding observations on Eurocredit lending attempt a catalogue of advantages and drawbacks for the two parties.

The Borrowers: Advantages

1. The greatest single advantage is the availability of international capital in larger amounts and to a wider range of borrowers than in the international fixed-interest bond markets.

2. Capital is available more quickly, with fewer formalities, and often with fewer conditions about its use than from international agencies and other official donors. Apart from providing capital on a scale no longer obtainable from official donors during the 1970s, the Eurocredits market also fills official aid "gaps" by providing more general balance of payments financing; financing of the total rather than just the foreign exchange cost of development investments; and financing of the recurrent and not merely the initial costs of such investment. The fact that Eurocredits are usually provided without conditions about the management of the borrowing country's economy provides flexibility of policy for the borrower; whether this is an advantage or drawback over the long run can be debated.

3. Eurocredit lending gives borrowers a measure of flexibility to protect themselves against interest and exchange rate risk in the short term under agreements allowing them to choose different currencies at each roll-over and to select the length of succeeding roll-over periods.

4. Still greater flexibility is provided by the very many Eurocredits agreements allowing cancellation by the borrower without penalty at 30 or 60 days notice. This allows stronger borrowers to replace existing credits on better terms when market conditions change in their favor, or to switch from the credits to the fixed-interest international bond markets in the case of borrowers having access to both markets.

5. Competition among banks gives borrowers considerable power to shop around for the lowest lending margins available at any time.

6. The market enables countries to build up reserves and credit standing at times of easy availability for future need and continuing access to the market.

7. A good record in the Eurocredits market helps borrowers graduate to the international bond markets; during the 1970s such a partial transition was made by Brazil and Mexico and, to a lesser extent, by Singapore and Hungary.

8. The greater the debt incurred, the greater the bargaining power of borrowers over lenders, who are increasingly obliged to replace maturing credits with new ones so that debt service can be kept up.

9. Inflation works in the borrower's favor. The 1977 report of the IMF noted that the combined current account deficit of the non-oil developing countries in that year was similar to the 1967–1972 average despite a threefold nominal increase; and the U.N. Council on Trade and Development (UNCTAD) observed that the nominal increase in total LDC debt during the decade to 1976 looked "much less dramatic" after allowing for growth of real output, trade, and inflation.[1]

---

[1]UNCTAD ref. *TD/B/685 add.1.*

The Borrowers: Drawbacks

1. The greatest single drawback for Eurocredit borrowers is the floating and unpredictable cost of this form of international market capital, only partly mitigated by the possibilities for early redemption and replacement of credits, which tend to be available to stronger borrowers rather than to all.

2. Private international capital is more expensive than official aid and thus drives up the total cost of a fixed element in the balance of payments. While the net balance on external trade and services fluctuates with the world's economic cycle, this is less true of the net level of external debt outstanding and the level of debt service. However, these drawbacks are acute only for a relative handful of countries with very large Eurocredit debts.

The Lenders: Advantages

1. Predetermined lending margins and fees provide relatively assured and predictable returns.

2. Costs are relatively low and returns high on the very heavy volume of lending in a wholesale business. Prime lending margins during the five years through 1977 averaged just below 1 percent above LIBOR. But spreads are typically higher for the heaviest borrowers; in 1977, when prime spread was $\frac{5}{8}$ percent above LIBOR, spreads to the British, Spanish, Venezuelan, Mexican, Brazilian, and Argentinian governments ranged from $1\frac{1}{4}$ percent to 2 percent above LIBOR. Moreover, margins above LIBOR represent an indication rather than a true measure of the return to banks, especially the biggest. Not only are big banks often able to obtain funds below the LIBOR deemed to apply equally to all members of a lending syndicate, but they are also able to finance themselves from deposits obtained below LIBOR from business corporations, the central banks, and government agencies of developing countries, partly industrialized countries, and Communist countries, as well as from smaller commercial banks outside the inner ring of the Eurocurrencies market. Besides this, the biggest commercial banks dominating the market are able to draw partly on interest-free domestic deposits. The average cost of funds to the major banks doing the bulk of Eurocredit lending is well below LIBOR and their returns considerably above quoted Eurocredit lending margins. On top of that, there are fees, most of which go to the biggest banks. It is impossible to know the true return on the approximately $150 billion of Eurocredits outstand-

ing at the end of 1978, but a guesstimate of $3 billion a year seems cautious, with perhaps one-quarter of that amount going to 10 international banks and about one-third to 20 international banks.

3. Besides its direct returns, Eurocredit lending often brings other business and deposits from the borrowers and helps banks diversify their operations globally.

4. Eurocredit lending and international lending as a whole made immense contributions to the earnings of Western banks and particularly to some of the biggest American banks, whose combined international earnings rose about five times and from 17 percent to 50 percent of total earnings in the eight years through 1977, a period during which their domestic earnings virtually stagnated. By 1977, Citibank and Bankers Trust were earning four times as much abroad as in the United States, and Chase Manhattan twice as much.

5. While the past is no guide to the future, international lending proved less risky than domestic lending during most of the 1970s, at least for the seven U.S. banks with the largest international operations and for which a breakdown is available. During the five years through 1975, they lost three times as much on their domestic as on their international operations, namely just under $\frac{1}{8}$ cent on every dollar lent abroad compared with just under $\frac{3}{8}$ cent on every dollar lent at home.[2] Another measure is that out of approximately $300 billion of official and private lending to 77 developing countries during the 20 years through 1976, rescheduling on the part of 11 countries amounted to $9 billion. All of that consisted of official debt and suppliers' credits, a large part of the latter guaranteed by government agencies of the donor countries.[3] The only defaults (by Cuba after 1949 and Ghana after 1966) amounted to a mere $200 million, or about 0.07 percent of the total aid flows to LDCs during two decades (it is fair to add, however, that banks are extremely reluctant to declare coun-

---

[2]SOURCE: Salomon Brothers. The seven banks are Bank America, Citicorp, Chase Manhattan, J.P. Morgan, Manufacturers Hanover, Bankers Trust, and Chemical Bank. By 1977, the average for a larger group of banks had risen slightly to about $\frac{3}{16}$ of a cent of provision against every dollar of outstanding foreign loans.

[3]The 11 countries who rescheduled service of part of their official debt and suppliers' credits during the 20 years to 1976 were Argentina, Brazil, Chile, Cuba, Ghana, Indonesia, India, Pakistan, Peru, Turkey, and Zaire. Brazil and Argentina rescheduled in 1964–1965; India, Pakistan, Ghana, and Cuba have never been major debtors to private banks.

tries as being in default, because countries, unlike companies, cannot be wound up for their creditors).

Lenders: Drawbacks

1. The ability of many borrowers to replace outstanding credits on better terms when market conditions turn in favor of borrowers.

2. The erosion of earnings from fixed lending margins as a result of inflation; offset only sometimes and in part by prearranged increases in lending spreads during the latter years of some Eurocredits.

3. Lack of information about many borrowers, especially in developing and Communist countries.

4. Pressure on big banks to lend for political reasons, sometimes exerted more or less subtly by their own governments or by borrowing countries with which they have connections.

5. Pressure on smaller banks to lend for the sake of relationships with bigger banks.

6. For smaller banks, the average cost of funds is higher than for big banks. Their true return on Eurocredit lending is therefore smaller, especially if they act prudently and make adequate provisions against possible loss.

CHAPTER TWENTY
THE BALANCE OF POWER

Power in the Eurocredits market is delicately balanced, but extreme concentration of lending has an element of weakness while extreme concentration of borrowing has an element of strength. There is considerable pressure on banks to renew or replace expiring facilities and the pressure is strongest on those banks with the most at stake. While banks can periodically scale down or even withhold lending to industrialized and Communist countries which are relatively manageable in political and economic terms, they are caught more firmly in the classical lender's trap in their relationship with many developing countries. Indeed, this puts strong pressure on banks to tolerate delays or interruptions of debt service without formal declarations of default, because cross-default clauses in loan agreements make all of a borrower's loans due for immediate repayment if any one of them is proclaimed to be in default.

In this respect, the biggest banks are, to some extent, at the mercy not only of debtors but also of smaller banks with less at stake, and these have sometimes had to be bought out of lending syndicates to prevent them from proclaiming a default and thus jeopardizing informal negotiations with a borrower.

During the two years leading to mid-1978, at least five countries fell into arrears of debt service without being formally proclaimed as being in default. They were Peru, Zaire, Turkey, Zambia, and the Sudan. In each case special factors were blamed. The difficulties of Peru, Zaire, and Zambia were attributed to the weakness of world copper prices compounded by border wars in the two African countries and the over-fishing and depletion of Peru's valuable anchovy shoals. In Turkey's case, the flow of money sent home by Turkish workers abroad fell off after 1974 as a result of the recession in Germany and other northern Western European countries, while in the Sudan's case, the speed with which that country could be turned into a "bread basket" was apparently overestimated.

Most analysts have suggested that future defaults by other countries may similarly have special rather than general causes. But this will not be much consolation and two comments are worth quoting. One of them, by Thomas H. Hanley, of Salomon Brothers, New York, was: "Historically, losses on international bank lending have been so modest that severe difficulty with just a few large credits could significantly impact loss ratios."[1] This was presciently written in the spring of 1976, just before the five countries mentioned earlier ran into trouble, and the international net loss ratio of U.S. banks as a whole did indeed rise from 0.13 percent in 1975 to 0.16 percent in 1976 and 0.18 percent in 1977.

The other comment was made by the World Bank, which put the major blame for the difficulties experienced by some countries with their external debt on "persistent mismanagement." But it added: "In some cases the creditors were also to blame because their lending took place for political reasons in full awareness of the borrower's lack of credit-worthiness."[2]

For banks, the problem is partly one of lending margins. Although banks may feel compelled to keep up the flow of credit to many borrowers and reluctant to make formal proclamations of default, they can increase lending spreads to large borrowers even in a market generally favorable to borrowers, as noted earlier in this chapter. Whether lending margins are sufficient is a matter of dispute. In a London speech in May 1978, Mr. Henry Wallich, a governor of the Federal Reserve Board, echoed the familiar plaint of bankers that margins had been reduced to "dangerously" low levels in the competition of a borrowers' market. Not everyone agreed. The OECD said: "In spite of the narrowing of spreads, the high profitability of Eurocredit operations continues to account for a large proportion of international banks' overall profits. . . . The comfortable risk premium incorporated in such lending provides a cushion in the event of defaults."[3] On either view, the crux of the matter is the provision that Eurobanks actually make against possible losses.

---

[1]Thomas H. Hanley, *United States Multinational Banking: Current and Prospective Strategies,* Salomon Brothers, New York, June 1976.

[2]*The External Debt of Developing Countries: Report No. 1595,* International Bank for Reconstruction and Development, May 1977.

[3]*Financial Market Trends,* OECD, February 1978.

The question for borrowers is whether Eurocredit financing offers advantages over fixed-interest financing. That question is only partly answered by Figure 11, which shows that Eurocredit financing was considerably more expensive than international bond financing in 1973 and 1974, but cheaper during the three succeeding years. This means that Eurocredit financing does periodically have advantages for borrowers having access to both major sectors of the international capital market. However, much depends on the borrower's confidence in interest rate projections and also on the willingness of Eurobanks to go on incorporating options for early redemption without penalty into Eurocredit agreements. The 1978 report of the Bank for International Settlements implied that banks might no longer be so willing to offer this facility in the changed circumstances of a lenders' market, saying that cancellation clauses in the past "had been negotiated at a time when the banks had not foreseen the emergence of outright borrowers' markets." There is, however, one very strong argument that borrowers with a choice usually prefer the certainties of international fixed-interest financing to the uncertainties of Eurocredit cost: It is simply that

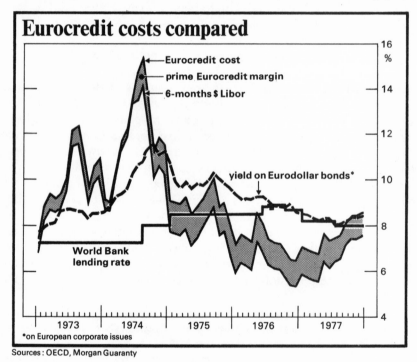

Eurocredit costs compared

Eurocredit cost
prime Eurocredit margin
6-months $ Libor

yield on Eurodollar bonds*

World Bank lending rate

1973   1974   1975   1976   1977
*on European corporate issues

Sources: OECD, Morgan Guaranty

FIGURE 11

borrowers having the option have mostly chosen the bond markets in practice. Canada is the prime example, having consistently financed itself in the international bond markets until sheer necessity drove it into the Eurocredits market on a significant scale for the first time in 1977. Austria, Australia, New Zealand, and Norway provide other examples of countries which have usually preferred the international bond markets because they had a borrowing choice which others lacked.

CHAPTER TWENTY-ONE
EUROBONDS: AN OVERVIEW

The birth of the Eurobond market is often traced to President Kennedy's Interest Equalization Tax, which took effect from the day of its announcement on July 18, 1963. And this was indeed the catalyst. By effectively closing New York to many foreign borrowers, the IET led to the issue of offshore bonds, or Eurobonds, on a regular basis. A further impulse came from the additional American capital controls imposed in 1965, which forced American corporations to finance a large part of their foreign direct investment by borrowing abroad. During the nine years of those controls, American corporations were the biggest borrowers on the Eurobond market, accounting for exactly one-third of the $27 billion borrowed.

But markets seldom spring into being overnight. The American authorities had been complaining since the start of the 1960s about the growing drain of capital out of the United States, blaming in part the inadequacy of European capital markets for the increase of European borrowing in New York. So although the form and timing of the IET caused surprise, some action to protect the capital account of the American balance of payments had been widely expected. Experimental issues of offshore dollar bonds had been made for several years and when the IET came into force the rudiments of a Eurobond market already existed for international borrowers crowded out of New York.

An OECD report in 1968 recorded more than $200 million of Eurobond issues between 1958 and 1962 and the World Bank has listed 22 public Eurobond issues and private placements totaling more than $500 million between 1957 and 1962, the borrowers including the World Bank itself, the Council of Europe, the European Coal and Steel Community, the Belgian national pension office, and Sabena, the Belgian national airline.[1] Indeed, the $15 million issue for Autostrade, the Italian state highway authority, supposed to have resulted from the market's "sudden" birth out of the IET, was offered on July 17, 1963, the day before the IET's announcement. The first Eurobond issue, as recorded by the World Bank, consisted of $5 million raised for 20 years in dollars in Europe in 1957 for Petrofina S.A., the Belgian petroleum company.

The Eurobond market has become one of the world's more exclusive clubs, conferring prestige on banks and borrowers alike. This helps explain the exceptional publicity given to the market and the presence in it of over 500 banks, although most of them seem to mill around the peripheries trying to look like members, while the big business and profits appear to be concentrated to an extreme degree among a handful numbering, at most, 30 banks at the center.[2]

The value of the Eurobond market is that it provides a supplementary channel for international capital beyond what is possible through traditional foreign bond issues on national markets, although it is mainly the Eurodollar bond market rather than the Eurobond market as a whole which performs this useful function. Some important national markets like London and Brussels are closed to foreign borrowers.[3] In nearly all the others where foreign bond issues are allowed, the volume of new foreign issues (like that of new domestic issues) is regulated to ensure a digestible flow. This is true of Germany, Switzerland, the Netherlands, Japan, and France. Only the American market is big enough to dispense with such regulation of issuing volume, but the need to comply with the disclosure requirements of the Securities and Exchange Commission deters many foreign borrowers. Besides, Canadian and World Bank issues remain the only ones with a relatively wide appeal to investors in the United States (as distinct from more sophisticated, internationally minded American investors buying foreign bonds in the U.S. or Eurobonds through offshore accounts).

But although the issue of foreign bonds in national markets is either forbidden, regulated, or effectively constrained (as by the SEC), the authorities raise far fewer barriers to investment in international issues

---

[1]OECD, III, *Functioning of Capital Markets,* 1968; *Chronological List of Foreign and International Bonds in Major Capital Markets 1946–69,* IBRD, April 1972.

[2]For convenience, the term bank is used throughout to embrace commercial, investment, and consortium banks as well as securities firms and all financial institutions which help to market international bonds.

[3]The Belgian authorities sometimes make an exception by opening their domestic market to issues by two entities of the European Community, the European Investment Bank and the European Coal and Steel Community.

by their residents. In Switzerland, France, Belgium, and the Netherlands, banks may not advertise Eurobond issues but they are allowed to sell them and to inform and advise their customers about them, so that the traffic carries on almost unimpeded. The sale of international issues in Japan is likewise allowed. Even in the United Kingdom investors can get official permission to take up international bonds by borrowing foreign currency rather than buying it at the often prohibitive investment currency premium.[4]

The disparity between the limitations imposed on the issue of foreign bonds in most national markets and the far greater freedom which exists for international investment is the gap which the Eurobond market bridges—providing an offshore market for international borrowers crowded out of national markets and a home (exempt from withholding for tax) for capital free to cross borders.

In practice, however, the issue of Eurobonds is almost completely free only in U.S. and Canadian dollars and in units of account (valued in terms of "baskets" of currencies). It is true that Eurobonds which do not have the seal of the Securities and Exchange Commission may not be offered or sold to residents of the United States (excepting for private placements among no more than 35 "large and knowledgeable" investors). Eurobonds may be sold to U.S. and Canadian residents only after they have been "seasoned" in the secondary market for at least 90 days. But that is a helpful protection for American and Canadian investors and no great impediment to the sale of Eurobonds. What really matters is that there is no restriction on the volume of new Eurodollar bond issues excepting the market's capacity to absorb them. The same is true of the far smaller volume of Eurobonds denominated in Canadian dollars and units of account. The important contrast is with the ban on Eurobond issues in Swiss and Belgian francs and the limitations imposed on the volume of new Euro-Deutschemark, Euro-guilder, Euro-yen, and Euro-French franc issues by the German, Dutch, Japanese, and French authorities as well as the limitations on the issue of traditional foreign bonds in the Swiss, German, Dutch, and Japanese markets.

That is the reason why this book has consistently preferred a narrow definition of Eurobonds as those issued without restriction outside the

---

[4]"Investment currency" consists of earnings or proceeds from the sale of approved U.K. investments abroad. It may be used for reinvestment overseas or sold for that purpose by one U.K. resident to another. Given the limited amount of such currency, it commands a premium. At mid-1978, "investment dollars" were being quoted in the U.K. at $1.22, representing a premium of 52 percent over the spot exchange rate of $1.85 at that time. As a result of this form of British capital control, it cost a U.K. investor £82 to buy $100 of dollars for foreign investment as against £54 for $100 used for current settlements such as import payments.

jurisdiction of any single national authority, by contrast with traditional or classical foreign bonds sold for a nonresident borrower in another country's domestic capital market under the laws and regulations of the country in which the issue is made. And, by that yardstick, the only true Eurobonds have been those in American and Canadian dollars and units of account.

But the market uses a broader definition of Eurobonds as those sold for international borrowers in several markets simultaneously by international groups of banks; and it defines traditional foreign bonds as those sold for a nonresident borrower in another country's domestic capital market by a selling group composed exclusively of banks in the market of issue. By this conventional definition, Deutschemark bonds sold for a foreign borrower by an exclusively German banking group are considered a traditional foreign bond issue, but when marketed by a syndicate including non-German banks the borrowing is classified as a DM Eurobond issue.

In the case of the Deutschemark, there is a very clear distinction between DM domestic bonds on the one hand and DM external bonds on the other. Investment in the former is effectively restricted to German residents alone, while investment in the latter is open to all. This produces marked differences in yields between DM domestic and external bonds. But there is virtually no distinction between the two classes of external DM bonds. The yields on DM Eurobonds and traditional DM foreign bonds are identical. Their combined issuing volume is regulated by an officially approved committee of German bankers. Outstanding issues of external DM bonds are traded on equal terms over the counter (by telephone between dealers) or on the German stock exchanges. And sales of both classes of DM external bonds are cleared equally through the *Auslandskassenverein* (foreign clearing system). The one and only distinction between the two classes of DM external bonds is the participation of non-German banks in DM Eurobond selling syndicates and the sale of DM foreign bonds by syndicates of German banks alone. See Figure 12.

"The institutional and other features of the Euro-DM bond market bring it closer to the markets for foreign issues in Switzerland or New York than to the Eurobond market proper," said the Secretariat of the OECD.[5] And much the same can be said of Eurobonds denominated in Dutch guilder (or florin), Japanese yen, French francs, and most other currencies.

To put the matter more graphically, the first "true" DM Eurobond

---

[5]*Financial Market Trends,* OECD, October 1977.

Why New York shut out foreign borrowers...
Government bond yields

...and why Germany shut out foreign investors
German reserves

COUPON TAX*

*25% tax on income on non-resident investment
in domestic DM securities

Source: IMF

FIGURE 12 In July 1963, the regular issue of Eurodollar bonds in Europe followed the American Interest Equalization Tax. The tax shut the New York market to many foreign borrowers who had been attracted to it by borrowing costs. The aim was to reduce flows of capital out of the United States to preserve the dollar's fixed exchange rate. In March 1964, Germany imposed a 25 percent coupon (or withholding) tax on nonresident income from German domestic securities (but not those issued by foreign borrowers in Deutschemarks). The aim was to reduce capital inflows, which had to be absorbed in the reserves in the absence of an upward valuation of the Deutschemark. The result was to stimulate the market in DM bonds by foreign borrowers.

will have been launched when an issue of Deutschemark bonds is made by a group of American, Canadian, and Japanese banks for an Australian borrower without anyone needing to ask or even inform the German authorities.[6] But until such a thing happens, the securities presently described as DM Eurobonds are in fact conventional DM foreign bonds, theoretically distributed more widely through their sale by an international rather than a purely German banking syndicate.

This is not mere quibbling. The extent to which the Eurobond market has provided an original supplementary channel for international capital depends greatly on how the market is defined. The argument for the "narrow" definition preferred by this book is that such a new and different channel for international capital has in fact been provided only by the unregulated part of the market consisting of the issue of Eurobonds denominated in American and Canadian dollars and units of account.

The argument for the "broader" definition preferred by the market itself, and based on the composition of bank selling groups, is that international syndication helps to distribute bonds more widely, with the virtuous effect of continually broadening the market by the attraction of ever more selling banks who, in their turn, rope in ever more borrowers and investors. But the validity of that claim is debatable. All the evidence suggests that foreign bonds issued in New York are distributed just as widely among international investors as Eurodollar bonds; that Swiss franc foreign bonds are likewise sold just as widely as Eurobonds, which Swiss banks play a large part in marketing; and that DM foreign bonds and DM Eurobonds are distributed equally widely among investors around the world. The participation of a minority of banks with an international clientele to whom bonds can be sold may add marginally to international distribution and market growth. But the unnecessary participation of hordes of other selling banks who do not have Eurobond customers of their own positively impedes the market's efficiency.

The statistical difference between the two definitions of Eurobonds is shown in Table 24. During the eight years up to the end of 1977, gross Eurobond and foreign bond issues totaled about $60 billion each, as conventionally measured. But on the narrower, unconventional definition, the volume of new Eurobond issues was only half the $80 billion of new foreign bonds sold during that period.

However, having made clear its reservations about the conventional

---

[6]The Deutsche Bundesbank could not legally stop such an issue because central banks do not have extraterritorial legal powers. But they usually have the means and influence to ensure that their wishes are not flaunted.

TABLE 24
INTERNATIONAL BONDS
cumulative total 1970–1977 ($ billion equivalent)

---

(1) CONVENTIONAL PRESENTATION:

Eurobonds in:		Foreign bonds in:	
$	35.8	New York	32.3
DM	13.1	Zurich	16.3
D.fl.	3.2	Frankfurt	6.0
C. $	2.7	Tokyo	2.3
F. fr.	1.0	Amsterdam	1.1
units	1.3	other	2.2
other	3.0		
Total	60.2		60.2

(2) UNCONVENTIONAL PRESENTATION:

"True" Eurobonds in:		Foreign bonds in:	
$	35.8	New York	32.3
C. $	2.7	Frankfurt	19.1
units	1.3	Zurich	16.3
Total	39.8	Amsterdam	4.3
		Tokyo	2.3
		other	6.2
		Total	80.5

Note: The total of international bonds on either tabulation was $120 billion, consisting of U.S. $57%, DM 16%, Swiss franc 14%, Dutch florin 4%, and all other denominations 9%. The total of Eurocredits during the period was $150 billion, of which 97% or about $215 billion was in U.S. $. The U.S. $ component of total international market capital of $270 billion during the period was thus 79%, the DM 7%, the Swiss franc 6%, and all other currencies 8%.

SOURCE: Morgan Guaranty; OECD; IBRD.

definition of Eurobonds, this book nevertheless goes on, rather reluctantly, to describe the Eurobond market in its own terms, partly because that is the way the market sees itself and the way in which nearly everyone else sees it, and partly because it is impossible to disentangle all of the existing data in a way which would allow a description of the Eurobond market on the narrower definition alone. But descriptions of the special characteristics of the Deutschemark, yen, and Dutch florin markets are included in Part Three of this book, devoted to foreign bond markets.

TABLE 25
CHARACTERISTICS OF INTERNATIONAL BOND MARKETS

Currency	Markets open/shut Foreign bonds	Eurobonds	Denomination of bonds	Type of bonds	Nonresident investors' tax status
US $	open	open	$1,000	Yankee bonds registered; Euro-$ bearer	exempt from withholding
Sw.fr. Swiss fr.*	open	shut	5,000 to 50,000	bearer	exempt from withholding
DM*	open	open	DM 1,000 to DM 10,000	bearer	exempt from withholding
Canadian $	unused	open	C. $1,000	bearer	exempt from withholding on investments over 5 years
Dutch Fl.*	open	open	D.fl. 1,000 to 10,000	bearer	exempt from withholding
Yen*	open	open	Y 100,000 Eurobonds; Y 500,000 foreign bonds	mostly bearer; some registered	exempt from withholding
units of account	none	open	EUA 1,000†	bearer	exempt from withholding
French Fr.*	unused	open	F.fr. 5,000	bearer	exempt from withholding
£*	shut	£/option bonds only	£500 to £1,000	bearer	exempt from withholding
Belgian franc	no nonresident issues allowed in B.fr. foreign or Eurobonds				

*Issuing volume controlled.

†European Units of Account valued at about $1.25 at mid-1978.

Guide to table: As an example, Swiss franc foreign bonds are permitted, but the volume of issues is regulated; Swiss franc Eurobonds are not allowed; Sw.fr. foreign bonds are issued in denominations of Sw.fr. 5,000 to Sw.fr. 50,000 in bearer form and income of nonresident investors from the bonds is exempt from Swiss withholding for tax.

Flotation costs (management fees, underwriting allowances, and selling concessions): ⅞ to 1% NY foreign bonds; 2% Yen foreign bonds; 1¾–2¼% DM foreign bonds; 2½% Dutch fl. foreign bonds; 4% Swiss franc foreign bonds; 2–2½% all Eurobonds excepting Dutch fl. privately placed notes, 1½%.

TABLE 26
INTERNATIONAL BOND ISSUES
by type, in millions of dollars

	1970	1971	1972	1973	1974	1975	1976	1977
Eurobonds, total	**2,966**	**3,642**	**6,335**	**4,193**	**2,134**	**8,567**	**14,328**	**17,735**
by category of borrower:								
U.S. companies	741	1,098	1,992	874	110	268	435	1,130
Foreign companies	1,065	1,119	1,759	1,309	640	2,903	5,323	7,284
State enterprises	594	848	1,170	947	542	3,123	4,138	4,707
Governments	351	479	1,019	659	482	1,658	2,239	2,936
International organizations	215	98	395	404	360	615	2,193	1,678
by currency of denomination:								
U.S. dollar	1,775	2,221	3,908	2,447	996	3,738	9,125	11,628
German mark	688	786	1,129	1,025	344	2,278	2,713	4,109
Dutch guilder	391	298	393	194	381	719	502	361
Canadian dollar	0	0	15	0	60	558	1,407	674
French franc	0	20	491	166	0	293	39	0
European unit of account	54	166	0	99	174	371	99	28
Other	58	151	398	262	179	610	443	935
Foreign bonds outside the United States, total	**378**	**1,538**	**2,060**	**2,626**	**1,432**	**4,884**	**7,586**	**7,185**
by category of borrower:								
U.S. companies	55	200	215	546	77	61	28	40
Foreign companies	83	212	345	396	455	1,386	1,654	1,158
State enterprises	16	163	249	446	568	1,314	2,439	1,909
Governments	53	254	177	297	138	765	1,307	1,834
International organizations	171	709	1,074	941	194	1,358	2,158	2,244
by currency of denomination:								
German mark	89	308	500	362	253	1,089	1,288	2,096
Swiss franc	193	669	815	1,526	911	3,297	5,359	3,463
Dutch guilder	17	17	31	0	4	182	597	211
Japanese yen	15	92	311	271	0	67	226	1,271
Other	64	452	403	467	264	248	116	144
Foreign bonds in the United States, total	**1,216**	**1,104**	**1,353**	**1,019**	**3,291**	**6,460**	**10,602**	**7,286**
by category of borrower:								
Canadian entities	904	635	986	925	1,962	3,074	6,138	2,946
International organizations	300	425	250	0	610	1,900	2,275	1,917
Other	12	44	117	94	719	1,486	2,189	2,423
Total	**4,560**	**6,284**	**9,748**	**7,838**	**6,857**	**19,911**	**32,516**	**32,206**

SOURCE: Morgan Guaranty, *World Financial Markets,* March 1978.

TABLE 27
INTERNATIONAL BOND ISSUES
by country of borrower, in millions of dollars

	1970	1971	1972	1973	1974	1975	1976	1977
Industrial countries	**3,800**	**4,930**	**7,415**	**5,829**	**5,390**	**15,214**	**24,200**	**22,554**
Australia	106	120	247	28	117	690	1,056	1,074
Austria	14	37	82	142	488	855	682	1,295
Belgium	2	0	25	135	20	31	134	277
Canada	1,046	849	1,501	1,195	2,080	4,499	9,336	5,229
Denmark	92	141	317	170	124	206	994	721
Finland	47	96	262	132	43	353	342	329
France	242	286	255	92	385	1,825	2,720	1,663
Germany	120	62	97	58	106	194	374	567
Greece	0	0	60	15	0	0	0	0
Ireland	42	100	30	95	134	70	20	86
Israel	0	0	20	0	300	2	119	111
Italy	340	149	110	77	50	106	85	312
Japan	120	121	106	77	237	1,739	2,084	1,935
Netherlands	261	279	235	206	467	686	486	533
New Zealand	11	92	64	0	33	467	413	567
Norway	94	100	111	97	76	944	1,406	1,649
South Africa	99	215	281	216	50	446	77	33
Spain	30	97	86	88	0	117	244	298
Sweden	65	87	225	171	75	1,000	1,111	1,500
Switzerland	0	52	35	0	49	152	301	135
United Kingdom	258	654	861	1,234	221	275	1,036	1,905
United States	796	1,298	2,207	1,420	187	329	463	1,289
Yugoslavia	0	0	0	30	0	0	71	120
Multinational companies	15	84	152	105	91	194	559	749
Other	0	10	47	46	56	32	87	177
Developing countries	**74**	**98**	**564**	**664**	**263**	**585**	**1,595**	**3,565**
Non-OPEC countries	74	98	479	565	201	517	1,456	2,752
Argentina	69	0	0	0	0	16	0	93
Brazil	0	6	116	63	25	35	268	732
Chile	0	0	0	0	0	53	0	0
Hong Kong	0	15	0	83	50	24	0	129
Ivory Coast	0	0	0	9	0	0	10	0
Korea	3	12	0	0	0	0	59	69
Malaysia	0	0	25	17	0	0	10	43
Mexico	0	47	207	176	50	293	448	1,159
Morocco	0	0	0	0	0	28	44	28
Peru	0	0	0	0	0	0	0	0
Philippines	0	0	0	25	17	30	367	118
Singapore	0	10	51	60	0	12	162	314
Taiwan	0	0	0	0	20	0	0	0
Other	2	8	80	133	39	25	87	67

OPEC countries	0	0	85	99	62	67	139	813
Algeria	0	0	25	71	60	35	109	239
Indonesia	0	0	0	0	0	17	0	0
Iran	0	0	20	21	0	0	30	81
United Arab Emirates	0	0	0	0	0	0	0	42
Venezuela	0	0	40	7	2	0	0	433
Other	0	0	0	0	0	15	0	18
Communist countries	0	25	50	0	40	239	96	248
Germany (East)	0	0	0	0	0	0	0	0
Hungary	0	25	50	0	40	102	25	174
Poland	0	0	0	0	0	21	71	74
Soviet Union	0	0	0	0	0	0	0	0
COMECON institutions	0	0	0	0	0	0	0	0
Other	0	0	0	0	0	117	0	0
International institutions	686	1,231	1,719	1,345	1,165	3,873	6,626	5,839
Total	4,560	6,284	9,748	7,838	6,857	19,911	32,516	32,206

SOURCE: Morgan Guaranty, *World Financial Markets*, March 1978.

CHAPTER TWENTY-TWO
EUROBOND INVESTMENT INSTRUMENTS

There are four main kinds of Eurobonds. These consist of:

1. Straight-debt Eurobonds carrying a fixed rate of interest.

2. Convertible bonds having a fixed rate of interest, but also giving investors the option of converting the bonds into common stock of the borrowing company.

3. Currency option bonds, giving investors the option of buying them in one currency while taking payments of interest and principal in another.

4. Floating rate notes, whose rate of return is adjusted at regular intervals, usually every six months, to reflect changes in short-term money market rates.

During the 15 years up to the end of 1977, nearly 85 percent of Eurobonds consisted of conventional straight debt; about 10 percent consisted of bonds convertible into equities; about 3 percent consisted of floating rate notes; and about 3 percent consisted of various currency option bonds, including units of account.[1]

Eurobonds have been issued in about a dozen currencies and denominations. But, between 1963 and 1977, about 60 percent were issued in U.S. dollars, about 22 percent in Deutschemark, and about 5 percent each in Canadian dollars and Dutch florin. The remaining 8

---

[1]The proportions throughout are in terms of the broad statistical definition preferred by the market itself, which classifies Eurobonds as bonds sold in several markets simultaneously by international groups of banks.

percent were issued in a variety of currencies, including just under 2 percent denominated in units of account (valued in terms of "baskets" of currencies). In summary, the Eurobond market is predominantly a market for straight-debt fixed-interest securities, mostly denominated in U.S. dollars and Deutschemark.

Straight-debt Eurobonds have the same technical characteristics as bonds everywhere. They are fixed-interest securities and thus differ from equities, on which dividends fluctuate with the borrower's profits. The fixed interest on the face value of bonds is paid at regular intervals (usually annually in the case of Eurobonds) until the bonds are redeemed at face value (or par) by the borrower on their maturity. However, many Eurobond issues, like other bond issues, have provisions allowing the borrower to redeem all or some of the bonds before maturity, usually by offering an *agio* (a premium over the issue price).

Technically, Eurobonds are more accurately described as debentures because nearly all of them are unsecured by any specific property of the borrower. This is in line with trends in national markets. In the United States, for instance, many railway bankruptcies have shown that a mortgage on the borrower's property lost a great deal of its value when the property stopped producing an income. Many investors in all markets have therefore come to prefer unsecured debentures issued by sound borrowers to the spurious security offered by the mortgage bonds of questionable borrowers. They argue, for instance, that a bond issued by a mining company to finance the development of a particular mine and secured by a mortgage on that mine is riskier than a bond issued on the name of the company and backed by its total assets and earnings record. The opposite view is that a mortgage bond gives investors undisputed title to the real asset which has been pledged, whereas debenture holders must share whatever assets are left with all the other creditors of a bankrupt borrower. But, however that may be, borrowing by debentures has become far more common than borrowing by mortgage bonds in most markets, and nearly all Eurobonds are debentures.

The greatest attraction of all types of Eurobonds for individual investors is that income on them is exempt from withholding for tax at source (which is true also of traditional foreign bonds held by nonresident investors). This does not exempt investors from reporting their income to their national authorities, but tax avoidance by legal means and tax evasion by illegal means are extremely widespread. A large proportion of investment in Eurobonds is by official institutions which are not liable for tax. Another large class of investors consists of private institutions which legally avoid tax by being based in tax havens. But the market estimates that almost one-half of all Eurobonds are held by individuals and tax evasion by individual investors is so widespread as to be almost universal. Most Eurobond investment by individuals is made anonymously through external accounts, such as those administered by Swiss banks. A minority of bonds is physically held by investors. Tax evasion is further facilitated by the fact that nearly all Eurobonds are sold in bearer form, providing no clue to the holder's identity. However, this creates a risk for investors choosing to keep bonds in their personal possession because, in case of loss, finders are keepers, the more so because the loss or theft of an undeclared asset makes it embarrassing for the investor to complain to the police.

But tax evasion is easy even when bonds are registered (as many traditional foreign bonds are) in cases where such bonds are held through external bank accounts. It is true that Swiss banks subscribed to an agreement in 1977 undertaking that they would not actively and systematically help their clients to break the laws of the clients' countries, but this does not oblige Swiss banks to make fussy inquiries as to whether their customers are reporting their income to their national authorities.

The considerable opportunities for tax avoidance and evasion afforded to investors almost certainly allow borrowers to issue both foreign and Eurobonds at yields below those they might otherwise have to concede. And that, in turn, helps to make possible a relatively high level of issuing costs in the Eurobond market. The borrowers are willing to concede such costs to selling banks in return for arranging finance which they might not otherwise be able to obtain, or which they might obtain elsewhere only at a higher total cost (despite lower issuing costs). Investors, on their side, are often willing to allow banks to take a relatively high distribution fee, regarding it as a small premium for obtaining what is effectively a tax-free investment.

Technically, Eurobonds are the same as other bonds in that the rate of return depends on the price of the bond. Fluctuations in the secondary market prices of bonds produce capital gains or losses, which investors may or may not realize, depending on whether they hang onto their bonds or sell them. But price fluctuations obviously influence the value of bonds as collateral when they have been bought on borrowed or partly borrowed money. And price fluctuations lead to a good deal of switching between bonds in the secondary market or between bonds and other investments, such as equities or short-term money market investments (like certificates of deposit issued by banks or commercial paper issued by business companies in the United States).

The main influences on bond prices are the level of short-term interest rates and the degree of liquidity in money market. When bond yields are above short-term interest rates, there is a positive yield differential. When bond yields dip below the cost of short-term money, there is a negative yield. When this materializes, as it sometimes does, it becomes extremely difficult for borrowers to raise new fixed-interest capital on the bond markets. Figure 13 shows how the volume of new Eurobond issues slumped by two-thirds when negative yield differentials materialized between 1972 and 1974, and how issuing volume subsequently boomed from 1975 through 1977, when very large yield curves once more opened up.[1]

The way this works can be illustrated by the example of a $1,000 Eurodollar bond (the normal denomination) carrying a fixed-interest coupon of 6 percent a year, payable annually. The annual coupons, worth $60 each, are literally detached from the bond when they fall due, and hence the folklore about rentiers who do nothing for a living except "clip coupons." The $60 is handed over to the investor when the coupon is presented by the investor or on his or her behalf to any of the several banks appointed as paying agents to an issue. In fact, coupons can be presented anonymously by bearers to many banks throughout the world, who will make instant payment less a small commission to

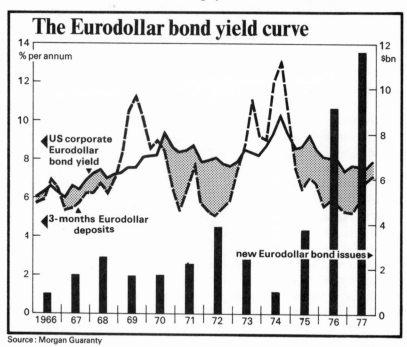

FIGURE 13

---

[1] Yield differentials measure yield difference over time; a yield curve measures the differences at any given moment.

recompense them for recouping the interest payment from one of the banks duly appointed as paying agents to the issue.

If the price of the bond falls in the secondary market, it does not directly affect the borrower, who merely goes on paying $60 a year on each $1,000 Eurodollar bond (although a fall in its value may influence the borrower's credit standing unless it is in line with a generalized fall in Eurodollar bond prices).

The holder of the bond has a capital loss on paper if it was bought at face value, or par. But the investor still gets 6 percent a year on the original investment and suffers an actual capital loss only when selling the bonds at a discount. However, the buyer of a bond sold at a discount receives a higher yield than the stated one. For instance, if a $1,000 Eurodollar bond with an interest coupon of 6 percent and eight years to maturity is bought at 92 percent of face value, the current or running yield of $60 on an investment of $920 becomes 6.52 percent and the yield to redemption or maturity is increased by an additional 1 percent per year of capital gain, to an annual 7.52 percent. In other words, the yield on Eurobonds, as on all fixed-interest securities, moves inversely to price; when the price falls the yield rises and when the price rises the yield falls.

The yield curve on bonds is measured in relation to short-term interest rates. In the case of Eurodollar bonds this is the London inter-bank offered rate (LIBOR) for three-month Eurodollar deposits. It is an imperfect yardstick because even banks which trade Eurodollar bonds actively as principals in the secondary market do not finance themselves exclusively or even mainly by means of Eurodollars borrowed for three months in the inter-bank market, instead obtaining their funds from a variety of sources. And nonbank investors hardly ever finance themselves at LIBOR, although they do look on U.S. commercial paper as an alternative investment, and yields on commercial paper usually move closely in line with LIBOR, although they are usually fractionally below LIBOR.

However, LIBOR is the most convenient yardstick available and it is the one conventionally used to measure the Eurobond yield curve, the basis being dollar LIBOR in the case of Eurodollar bonds, DM LIBOR in the case of Deutschemark bonds, and so on.

Short-term interest rates in all markets respond far more sensitively and quickly to an official tightening or easing of credit than do longer-term interest rates, and short-term interest rates also fluctuate more widely, longer-term rates usually catching up only partly and after a lag. The rule holds true in the Eurobond market. When the American authorities tighten credit, the rise in New York short-term interest rates pushes up Eurodollar LIBOR and the yield differential on Eurodollar bonds is narrowed and the yield curve flattens or, as from 1972 to 1974, turned into a negative yield (when Eurodollar bond yields fell below LIBOR). As soon as that happens, the secondary market prices of outstanding Eurodollar bonds fall. For instance, in June 1978, the price of $8\frac{1}{2}$ percent Eurodollar bonds issued for Ontario Hydro fell to $97\frac{1}{2}$ percent of face value in the secondary market following a rise in American short-term interest rates, thus pushing up the current yield on the bonds to 8.72 percent, while their yield to maturity (in 1985) was pushed up to just over 9 percent. This was not enough to reestablish a yield differential, but it did at least wipe out the negative yield by bringing the return on the Ontario Hydro bonds back into line with three-month dollar LIBOR following the rise which had just taken place in the latter.

Convertible Eurobonds, like their counterparts in domestic markets, are a hybrid of fixed-interest security and equity, giving the investor the option of converting from a fixed-interest security into the common stock of the borrowing company at a stipulated price and during a stipulated period. Normally, the conversion price is fixed at a premium above the market price of the common stock on the date of the bond issue. The investor is free to convert his or her fixed-interest security into common stock at any time during the conversion period, and the borrowing company is obliged to issue new stock for that purpose. But since the investor may convert only at the stipulated price, he or she will in fact do so only if the market price of the stock has risen above the conversion price. On the other hand, the interest attached to the fixed-interest security is lower than that on comparable straight-debt fixed interest bonds because of the hope held out to the investor of a profit resulting from a rise in the share price above the conversion price. The technique is best illustrated by an example.

In July 1978, $30 millions of 15-year convertible bonds were issued in the Eurobond market by Boots Co. Ltd., an English chain of retail chemists. The interest coupon was $6\frac{3}{4}$ percent, at a time when the coupon on a comparable straight-debt issue would have been above 9 percent.

However, investors were given the option to convert their bonds into common stock of Boots at any time between February 1, 1979, and July 1, 1993, at a price of £2.17 a share, then equivalent to about $4.05, representing a 10 percent premium over the share price of £1.97 or $3.68 on the date of the convertible bond issue.

Under this arrangement, investors could convert their bonds into common stock at any time after the start of February 1979, but only at a fixed £2.17 a share. In practice, they would naturally do so only if the share price rose above that level and, more particularly in the case of international investors, if the dollar price of the stock rose above the equivalent of $4.05.

The advantage of this technique is that it allows the borrower to obtain fixed-interest capital at a lower cost than otherwise available with the prospect of obtaining a wider spread of share ownership. The investor obtains what amounts to an equity investment with a floor; if the share price fails to rise or falls, a limit to the investor's risk is provided by the fixed rate of interest on the bond. But of course this insurance against risk is bought at the price of a lower fixed-interest return than could be obtained on a straight-debt bond.

Although about 10 percent of all Eurobonds sold during the 15 years to the end of 1977 consisted of convertibles, about one-half the $7 billion marketed during that period were sold in 1968, 1969, and 1972, nearly all of them in the form of dollar convertibles which were easily sold to investors during the American equities' boom (Figure 18, on page 181, shows that American share prices peaked in real terms as long ago as 1968, although they rose to new heights at current prices in 1972).

In 1978 there was a new and lesser boom in Eurobond convertibles, but the most successful of these were issued by Japanese companies, offering investors the bait not only of a rising Tokyo equities market but, perhaps more importantly, an opportunity of switching from bonds denominated in dollars or Deutschemark into equities denominated in the yen, which was then appreciating even faster than Germany's currency.

A variant of convertible Eurobonds are those issued with *warrants.* The warrants give the investor the option of conversion into equities at a stipulated price and during a stipulated period, as in the case of convertibles. But, whereas the investor in a convertible has the choice of exchanging a fixed-interest security for common stock, the holder of a warrant keeps the fixed-interest security and merely trades the warrant for common stock, the warrant being a part of the bond which the investor can literally detach and sell separately to other investors in the market.

The value of a warrant is always less than the price at which a borrowing company undertakes to issue new stock to warrant holders, so that investors wishing to exercise their right of conversion must either surrender some of their bonds or add cash to make up the share purchase price. The advantage for the borrowing company is that it may receive some cash for newly issued shares, instead of outstanding fixed-interest securities alone, as in the case of ordinary convertibles. The drawback, as in the case of all convertibles, is that a company receives less cash than it would from an ordinary issue of new stock at a time when its share price is high, but in return for that it will have received cheap fixed-interest funds during the period between the issue of convertibles and their conversion. The warrant holder has the advantage of two instruments which can be traded separately. But one of them, the warrant, becomes worthless if the borrowing company's shares fail to rise to a level making the exercise of the warrant option profitable.

Currency option bonds are issued in one currency, but with an option for the investor to take payment of interest and principal in a second currency. Nearly all currency option bonds have been issued in terms of sterling and another currency, usually the dollar or Deutschemark. It is such bonds which have often been referred to, loosely, as "sterling" Eurobonds. Actually, there have never been any sterling Eurobonds in the strict sense because the British authorities will not allow the use of sterling as the sole currency for the denomination and payment of international bonds.

The prohibition is part of the controls on outflows of sterling capital from the United Kingdom, which had existed for exactly 30 years in 1978 despite an undertaking to liberalize them within five years of Britain's joining the European Communities in January 1973. Access of foreign borrowers to the London capital market was restricted as long ago as 1938. The restrictions were reinforced by the Exchange Control Act of 1947 and by subsequent and even more restrictive Control of Borrowing Orders. The last sterling issue for a wholly foreign borrower in the London market was made in 1952 for Norway, and the last for a member of the Overseas Sterling Area in 1971 for New Zealand. In the following year, the sterling capital market was closed to all nonresident borrowers.

However, the use of sterling as an option currency for Eurobonds was allowed. The fact of the option made them foreign currency securities for the purposes of British exchange control, thus giving the British authorities control over their issuing volume and, more important, making them eligible for purchase by British investors only through "investment currency" or borrowed foreign currency, as in the case of all foreign currency securities.

Three varieties of such sterling option bonds were issued:

1. From 1964 to 1973, the equivalent of about $265 million of Eurobonds were sold denominated in sterling, but with options allowing holders to take payment of interest and principal in sterling or Deutschemark at a rate of exchange *fixed* for the full maturity of each issue at the time of its sale, initially at a sterling/Deutschemark exchange rate of DM 11 and in later years at around DM 8 to DM 7.

The *fixed* exchange rate option put the exchange risk firmly (and heavily) on the borrower and these issues were, in effect, disguised DM issues promoted mainly by some London merchant banks as a way of crashing the German issuing queue and management cartel.

The principle is easily demonstrated by the example of a bond issued at a fixed option rate of, say £1/DM 12. If the Deutschemark rises, say, to DM 4, investors will opt for payment in Deutschemark at a sterling cost to the borrower of £3 for every £1 borrowed. But if the Deutschemark weakens against sterling, investors will opt for payment in sterling and the borrower will derive no benefit from repaying £1 for every £1 borrowed. Real examples can be cited to show what actually happened.

For instance, in February 1967 New Zealand issued £7.2 million of such 15-year bonds with an option fixed at DM 11.11. Had the full principal still been outstanding at mid-1978, its value in terms of Deutschemark would have remained an unchanged DM 80 million. But New Zealand's sterling liability would have grown to more than £20 million, or almost three times its original size, because of sterling's depreciation to about DM 3.85. In fact, only a nominal £2.7 million remained outstanding. This represented a liability equivalent to £7.8 million to bondholders choosing to exercise their option of taking DM 11.11 for each pound sterling which New Zealand owed them, and surely no bondholder would have failed to exercise that option.[2]

Responsible for this particular international financing were S.G. Warburg, assisted by the Commerzbank, Kidder Peabody, and Brinckmann Wirtz. Sir Sigmund Warburg had been advocating fixed-rate option bonds since 1963, although in later years he stopped doing so. In the meantime, however, New Zealand masochistically repeated its doleful experiment in January 1968 with a 10-year Eurobond issue for £6 million at a fixed conversion option of DM 9.63.

2. From 1968 to 1974, there were 17 issues for a total of about £130 million of Eurobonds denominated in sterling with fixed, dollar option clauses plus rights of conversion into U.S. equities. These were mildly disguised Eurodollar convertibles and their introduction was neatly timed to coincide with the peak in real share prices which Wall Street had still not recovered ten years later.

---

[2]The arithmetic is £2.7 $\times$ 11.11 $\div$ 3.85.

3. In April 1972, a different kind of sterling Eurobond with a currency option was issued by Amoco, the American oil company, to help finance its Milford Haven refinery in England. This consisted of £10 million, then equivalent to $26.1 million, of 15-year bonds with an average life of 10.9 years. But in this case, the exchange rate for the option was not fixed for the life of the issue. Instead, it was a *floating* rate option. It was laid down that the option could be exercised only at the spot sterling/dollar exchange rate quoted in the markets three business days before each payment date for interest and principal.

The effect of this different arrangement was to put the exchange risk equally on the borrower and the investor. In this particular case, the investor suffered because the dollar value of the £500 bonds, which was $1,305 when they were issued at an exchange rate of $2.61, had fallen by mid-1978 to about $935 on an exchange rate of about $1.87, and the dollar value of the annual interest coupon of £40 had fallen from $104 to $75. But this happened only because sterling fell against the dollar during the five years through 1977. Had the opposite occurred and sterling risen, say, to $2.80, then the value of the £500 bonds would have risen to $1,400 and the value of the interest coupon to $112. In that case, the investor would have gained at the borrower's expense.

Sterling's depreciation against the dollar during the five years up to 1977 explains why no more issues like Amoco's were made until November 1977, when confidence in sterling had returned, at least temporarily. About $500 million of Amoco-type floating currency sterling option bonds were then announced in the winter and spring of 1977–1978. This gave some observers the misleading impression that the British authorities were quietly relaxing capital controls to permit a new type of "sterling Eurobond." In reality, nothing had happened except for a change in market conditions making sterling currency option bond issues possible once again for the first time in more than five years. Permission was given precisely because the impact of such issues on the capital account of the British balance of payments is hardly any different from that made by the issue of conventional Eurobonds or other foreign currency bonds.

The fact about Eurobonds with currency options is that they involve an exchange risk for the borrower on a *fixed option* while putting borrower and investor at equal risk on a *floating option*. This is not only true of the sterling option bonds, but also of Eurobonds denominated in units of account or in Middle Eastern currencies with options for payment in other currencies.

The borrower's risk on fixed-rate options during the dozen years to 1978 was particularly high. In the example described earlier, New Zealand's sterling liability increased because it had tied itself to a fixed sterling exchange rate against an appreciating Deutschemark, although it is true that New Zealand's liability rose only in terms of sterling, a currency with a falling purchasing power and real value. Had the opposite occurred by way of an appreciation of sterling against the Deutschemark, New Zealand would not have lost anything, nor gained anything either. The investor would not have lost in either event, but nor would he or she have gained beyond the preservation of his or her original investment in terms of whichever currency proved the stronger.

The more fundamental point is that the exchange risk on international currency option bonds, whether to the borrower or investor, is obviously increased by the extent of the potential disparity between the currencies used. When the prospect suggests no more than a limited disparity opening up between the option currencies, then the exchange rate opportunity may help to make floating option rate bonds more salable by offering investors a mild gamble with a limited risk. A case can therefore be made for options between currencies with approximately equal prospects, provided the option is not confined to two or more weak currencies. The high risk of options between weak and strong currencies has been driven home by experience.

The unit of account is the Graf Zeppelin of high finance, something which has hovered off the ground from time to time but never quite taken wing. The volume of unit of account Eurobonds issued during the 15 years up to the end of 1977 was about $1.3 billion, or a little less than 2 percent of all Eurobond issues in that period. It is claimed that they provide equality of currency risk to investors and borrowers, like the floating rate currency option bonds described above. In practice they are more useful for getting around new issue controls applying to all Eurobonds except those denominated in American and Canadian dollars and they are most widely regarded as disguised Deutschemark bonds.

Their basic weakness is a complicated structure bewildering not only to investors, but even to banks which specialize in issuing and trading them. Anyone who doubts this should try telephoning such banks. An inquirer who tried the experiment by asking five specialized banks for the dollar equivalent of a European Unit of Account (the most commonly used) found dealers at four of the banks completely unable to answer. The fifth bank was better informed. It was, at least, aware that the currency equivalents of the units are published daily in *The Financial Times* and was therefore able to read out the quotations printed in the morning newspaper (although, inevitably, the quotations applying to the previous day).

Several multicurrency units have been used to denominate Eurobonds. They include the EUA (European Unit of Account), originally based on the parities of the 17 member countries of the European Payments Union and later on the parities of the members of the joint European currency float (consisting, in 1978, of Germany, Belgium, Denmark, the Netherlands, and Norway). The ECU (or European Currency Unit) was at all times based on the parities of the active participants of the joint European currency float. The EURCO (European Composite Unit) is valued at the daily market rates of a group of European currencies and SDR units are valued in terms of the International Monetary Fund's Special Drawing Rights. Investors and borrowers may use any one of the currencies included in the "basket" being used; it does not matter which currency is chosen since the relationship of "basket" currencies to each other is fixed at any given moment. For instance, at mid-1978, the value of the European Unit of Account was DM 2.05, Y 202, Sw.fr. 1.81, and $1.87, which was the same as the exchange rates of the dollar at that time against the Deutschemark, yen, Swiss franc, and sterling.

Floating rate notes (FRN) are unique in being the only Eurobond asset which is not a fixed-interest security (the only other, partial exception, consisting of Eurobonds convertible into equities). Although floating rate notes accounted for about 3 percent of Eurobonds issued from 1963 to 1977, they began to be issued on an appreciable scale only from late 1975. During the $2\frac{1}{2}$ years leading to mid-1978, about $3 billion were issued, accounting for roughly $7\frac{1}{2}$ percent of all Eurobonds issued during that time.

Nearly all floating rate notes have been issued in dollars; indeed, one of their objects is to provide dollar capital for non-American banks, who have been the main borrowers by the issue of this instrument.

Floating rate notes are usually issued, like other Eurodollar bonds, in denominations of $1,000 each. They carry a spread, or margin, usually adjusted every six months, above six-month LIBOR, the London interbank offered rate for Eurodollar deposits. This spread is normally $\frac{1}{4}$ point, although it has been as little as the equivalent of $\frac{1}{8}$ percent at one extreme and as much as $1\frac{1}{2}$ percent at the other. In a majority of cases, there is a minimum interest rate and the usual maturity has been five to seven years, although a 15-year $100 million issue was made by the Midland Bank in July 1977.

In one sense, floating rate notes represent the retail equivalent of Eurocredits because the notes are a floating rate asset available to individual investors, by contrast with Eurocredits, which are provided by banks alone. But the degree of interest protection afforded to the investor in floating rate notes is not the same as that afforded to banks granting Eurocredits. The reason is that Eurocredits are always granted at a rate of interest above the average cost of money to the lending banks. But when a wide yield differential opens up between the cost of short-term funds and the return on straight debt, fixed-interest Eurobonds, then the return on floating rate notes falls below what is available to the investor in the fixed-interest market, and switching from floating rate notes to fixed-interest bonds in those circumstances becomes impossible without capital loss.

The reason why non-American banks have been the main borrowers by floating rate notes is that it allows them to obtain dollars without eating into their credit lines with other banks, as they do when they obtain dollars in the inter-bank market or by the issue of certificates of deposit sold to other banks. Moreover, funds secured in the inter-bank market or by the issue of certificates of deposit do not count as capital. But national authorities in some countries are willing to consider the proceeds of floating rate note issues made by a bank as an addition to the bank's capital (subordinated to deposit liabilities).

Another advantage for banks as borrowers is that they usually lend at floating rates of interest and it therefore makes sense for them to obtain funds on the same basis, whether in the form of deposits or capital. It is true that issuing costs of 2 percent to $2\frac{1}{2}$ percent in the Eurobond market marginally increase the total cost of funds to borrowers on floating rate notes above the stated $\frac{1}{4}$-point margin above LIBOR usually paid to investors. But that still leaves the cost of floating rate note finance to banks below the returns they earn as lenders in the Eurocredits market. Moreover, floating rate notes are by no means the only source of funds for banks lending in the Eurocredits market, and the average cost of their total funds is therefore increased only marginally. But the most useful aspect of floating rate notes for banks issuing them is that they represent an additional way of raising capital to provide an enlarged base for an expansion of the bank's business in those countries which allow banks to count the proceeds of FRN issues as additions to capital.

However, non-American banks are by no means the only borrowers on floating rate notes. In July 1978, Chase Manhattan raised $150 million of 15-year capital on the Eurobond market by means of a floating rate note issue. In the same month Citicorp imported the technique from abroad by issuing $250 million of 20-year floating rate notes on the U.S. domestic capital market. This provided investors with a return of not less than 100 basis points above that on six-month U.S. Treasury bills during the first ten years and not less than 75 basis points above during the final ten years.

Another innovation (in June 1978) was a $100 million issue of 8-year floating rate notes by the state-owned Offshore Mining Company of New Zealand, coinciding with a $350 million 9-year Eurocredit. In this way, the borrower was tapping the retail and wholesale sectors of the international capital market simultaneously.

This borrowing had a special interest. Like Canada, New Zealand was one of the relatively small group of prime borrowers traditionally able to exercise a preference for the greater certainties of fixed-interest international capital. In 1977 and even more so in 1978, Canada was forced into the floating rate Eurocredits market partly by having over-borrowed in the international fixed interest markets, particularly in the American foreign bond (or Yankee bond) market. But New Zealand shifted to the floating rate international market in 1978 out of strength, at a time when short-term interest rates were high and rising still further. The floating rate note issue and the Eurocredit raised by the Offshore Mining Company of New Zealand in mid-1978 both provided for repayment by the borrower in full and at short notice at any time. This left the way open for a return to the fixed-interest international market as soon as long-term borrowing costs fell once again.

The link between the return on floating rate notes and money market interest rates is intended to protect the investor against capital loss. But, unlike banks, which finance themselves in the money market to provide Eurocredits at floating rates of interest, non-bank investors in floating rate notes do not normally finance themselves in this way and look on fixed-interest securities as one alternative investment. The opening of a wide yield curve on Eurobonds could therefore tempt investors to switch out of floating rate notes which do not carry a sufficient minimum interest rate guarantee, so that floating rate notes are not in all cases an asset which is proof against capital loss. On the other hand, the guarantee of a minimum interest rate by banks borrowing against floating rate notes carries the risk that the banks might find themselves obliged to pay more for money than they earn on it. For instance, if LIBOR falls below the guaranteed minimum on an FRN, the average cost of funds to the borrowing bank is raised and the margin of return on its Eurocredit lending is eroded or wiped out.

While some banks borrow by means of floating rate notes, other banks buy the FRNs because of their resemblance to money market instruments which can be readily traded, and the same consideration makes these notes an attractive investment for company treasurers deploying temporarily idle funds.

CHAPTER TWENTY-THREE
EUROBOND REDEMPTION

Redemption of bonds by the borrower before their maturity is common practice in the Eurobond market and has, indeed, become more widespread in domestic capital markets too since the 1960s. One reason for it is that it gives the borrower flexibility by allowing the replacement of fixed-interest securities issued at a time of high interest rates with others at a time of lower interest rates. But, in certain circumstances, techniques for early retirement of bonds can provide, also, a measure of market support for investors.

There is, of course, nothing to stop a borrower buying back his own bonds in the open market at any time without any formal arrangement. An unusual example was provided by Tyco Laboratories, an American computer company, which issued $25 million of 5 percent 15-year bonds in 1969, convertible into common stock at $61.50. Over the years, Tyco repurchased some of these Eurobonds in the open market at prices ranging from 40 percent to 50 percent of face value (a rather stark illustration, in itself, of the extent of capital loss risked by investors in some Eurobond issues). Then, in May 1978, Tyco regurgitated just over $7 million of these bonds back onto the market at 75 percent of face value, having made a neat profit from trading in its own securities. But the redemption yield of 11 percent offered to investors at the discounted reoffering price allowed Tyco to unload, despite the fact that the opportunities for profitable conversion into common stock were no longer obvious at a share price of $16.

More common are three main kinds of formal arrangements for early redemption of Eurobond issues in whole or in part, and the borrower's intention to use such techniques is spelled out in the offering prospectus, except in the case of "bullets," the market's jargon for bond issues making no provision for any form of early retirement. As in the case of many bond issues on domestic capital markets, Eurobond issues may provide for:

1. A *purchase fund* which the borrower sets aside to repurchase some of his outstanding bonds in the open market up to a stipulated amount in any given year of the issue's life. This is essentially a support mechanism. The borrower is under no legal obligation to use the purchase fund and indeed the borrower is usually precluded from using the purchase fund to bid his bonds above par and thus reduce the return to others buying them in the secondary market. But the purchase fund may be used to buy bonds which have fallen to a discount. And, despite the absence of any legal obligation, a borrower often uses a purchase fund to support bonds in the secondary market for the sake of his credit standing and future borrowing. Indeed, the provision of a purchase fund gives a measure of assurance to investors in a new issue and thus allows the borrower to offer a lower interest coupon than might otherwise be necessary.

2. A *sinking fund* differs from a purchase fund in putting the borrower under a legal obligation to buy back a given amount of outstanding bonds during each year of its operation, but it is likewise a support mechanism. If the bonds have fallen to a discount, the borrower may fulfill his obligation by buying back the required amount in the secondary market. But, if the borrower has not been able to do this by the end of the year, he must buy back the required amount, or the amount he has not already bought back in the market, at par. This obviously gives the borrower an incentive to buy back the whole of his requirement in the secondary market when the price is at a discount, and that in turn helps support the price of the bonds. When a sinking fund has to buy back bonds at par at the end of a year, the bonds to be bought back are drawn by lot and the numbers of those drawn for redemption are advertised in the financial press. However, the operation of a sinking fund is not a one-way street. Investors whose bonds are drawn for early redemption at par when the secondary market price is at a premium obviously lose out. Moreover, sinking fund arrangements often allow the borrower to "double" or call at par twice as many bonds as are due for retirement in any particular year. The borrower will obviously choose to do this when a fall in bond yields allows him to buy back at par bonds whose price has risen to a premium and when such a fall in bond yields allows the

borrower to replace outstanding securities with a new issue at a lower borrowing cost.

3. *Early redemption* provisions in a Eurobond offering agreement give the borrower the option, but do not create any legal obligation, to call in the whole of an outstanding issue after a stipulated time or, more commonly, to call a given proportion of the outstanding issue annually after a stipulated period. Since the bonds will be called only if interest rates decline, investors will require the compensation of a higher issuing yield. Alternatively, and also more commonly in practice, are arrangements providing for early redemption at a premium which is reduced year by year. For instance, such early refunding provisions may give the borrower the option of calling all or part of the outstanding bonds from the third or fifth year of their life at, say, 104 percent of face value during the first year during which the option is exercisable, reducing by, say, $\frac{1}{2}$ point each year thereafter. If the agreement provides for calls from the fifth year, any bonds called in that year will be called at 104 percent of face value, any called in the sixth year will be called at $103\frac{1}{2}$ percent of face value, and so on. As in the case of sinking fund arrangements, bonds called for early redemption are drawn by lot and the numbers of those drawn are advertised. In the case of large blocks held for institutional investors in a clearing system, the managers of the clearing system select bonds for early retirement on a proportional basis. If, say, 10 percent of an outstanding issue is being called in a given year, the managers of the clearing system will provide to the borrower making the call one-tenth of the bonds held in the system by each large institutional investor holding more than a certain amount of the bonds, say 250 bonds equal to $250,000.

4. *Redemption of convertibles.* Eurobonds convertible into the borrower's common stock may be subject to early redemption in the same way as straight-debt bonds. For instance, the $30 million 15-year convertible by Boots, the British chemists, made in July 1978 and referred to earlier, gave the borrower the option of calling outstanding bonds from August 1981, at an initial 104 percent of face value, reducing by $\frac{1}{2}$ point in each succeeding year. In other cases, convertible bonds may be called if the share price rises very steeply, say to 150 percent above its market value at the time of the convertible bond issue. The borrower will clearly wish to call in such circumstances, because the company would be able to raise new capital more cheaply, whether by the issue of bonds or equities. However, in the case of convertible bonds, it is out-

standing bonds alone which can be called; once converted into common stock, the investor cannot be compelled to part with his or her asset although he or she may, of course, be tempted to do so by the market.

Two points remain to be explained. First, what happens to the investor who fails to receive formal notification that his bond has been called for early redemption and who misses the advertisements listing the numbers of such bonds? Usually, he is given at least five years and often longer during which he may still present his bond for the repayment of principal at the price at which the bond was called, although no interest will be payable for the period following its call.

Secondly, the various arrangements for early redemption explain the market's reference to, say, a 15-year Eurobond "with an average life of 10.9 years." This clearly does not mean that any individual bond will have an actual maturity of that duration, except by the rarest chance. What it means is that the issue as a whole will have an average life of that length as a result of sinking fund purchases or if a purchase fund is used in full.

A growing tendency by borrowers to include provisions for early redemption by one means or another during the 1970s reduced the average maturities of new Eurobond issues to an even greater extent than the contraction which took place in nominal maturities. According to Credit Suisse White Weld, the proportion of new Eurobonds issued for ten years or longer dropped from over 90 percent in 1965 to about 80 percent in 1973 and then to less than 10 percent in 1975 and 1976 before picking up again to about 25 percent in 1977. But the average life of new issues almost certainly contracted even more than that, although there are no reliable data to prove it.

The shortening of Eurobond maturities during the 1970s was a natural response by borrowers and investors to the uncertainties created by wide fluctuations in exchange and interest rates, making both sides wary of long-term commitments. But this shortening of maturities was the choice of a lesser evil by borrowers and investors, who gained a greater flexibility only at the cost of other disadvantages. Through no fault of the participants, the Eurobond market fell far short of the ideal of a capital market. From the point of borrowers, that ideal is a supply of funds at a relatively predictable and stable cost for long enough to allow an investment to pay for itself. But the shortening of Eurobond maturities combined with ever lengthening gestation periods before technological investments can pay off represented a double hardship for corporate borrowers. At the same time, the economic uncertainties of the 1970s made it impossible for the Eurobond or any other market to offer investors the stability which fixed-interest securities have traditionally been supposed to offer, by contrast with the greater risks and opportunities usually associated with equity investment.

The choice of currencies has been the most critical for investors and borrowers in the international bond market, a term deliberately used here to include not only the Eurobond market in its widest definition, but also the traditional foreign bond market in Swiss francs and the Japanese foreign bond market (which was opened on a significant scale only in 1977). During the dozen years through 1978, the impact of exchange rate changes far outweighed the lower costs paid by borrowers and the lower interest received by investors on international bonds issued in strong currencies. Figure 14 shows that yields (and hence nominal borrowing costs) on international dollar bonds were almost consistently higher than those on international Deutschemark bonds, and that yields on international Swiss franc bonds were invariably the lowest of all. But Figure 15 shows how very greatly this was overshadowed by the impact of exchange rate changes, by comparing the real return (and the real cost to borrowers) of two international bond issues made in 1967. Every $100 invested in a World Bank Swiss franc loan

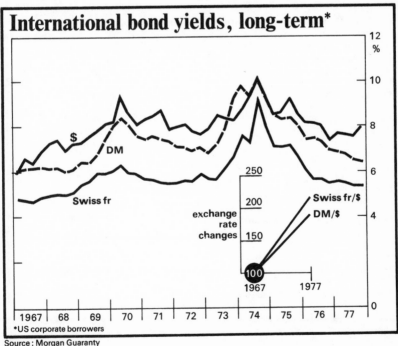

FIGURE 14

issued that year had a real value of $164 by 1978 in terms of capital appreciation, accrued interest, and after discounting inflation. On the other hand, every $100 invested in a Eurodollar bond issue made in 1967 by Autopistas, the Spanish highway authority, had a real value of only $80 by early 1978, although the Spanish dollar loan carried a 7 percent coupon while the World Bank's Swiss franc bonds carried a coupon of only 5 percent.

So long as currencies fluctuate widely against each other, as they do in a world of floating exchange rates, differing national inflation rates, and freedom for international movements of capital, then borrowers and investors in the international bond market face a common difficulty. It consists of trying to assess the extent to which borrowing costs (and hence yields) may be offset by exchange rate changes. To make any such forecast with confidence, let alone certainty, is plainly impossible, the more so because exchange relationships have tended to alter in a highly uneven way. Periods of relative stability have alternated with others of very wide fluctuation, and timing is therefore all-important. There were

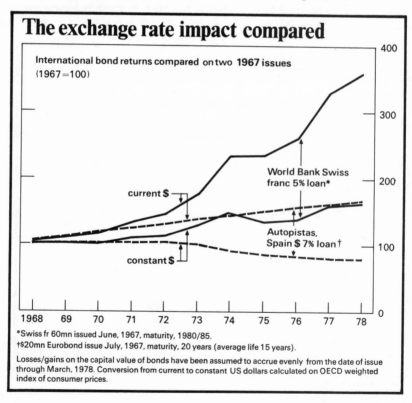

FIGURE 15

periods when higher coupons on international bonds denominated in fragile currencies actually did produce higher returns than the lower coupons usually attached to stronger-currency bonds. There were other times when they did not. Over the longer run from the latter 1960s onward, higher interest rates did not compensate for currency depreciations.

This situation has identical implications for borrowers and institutional investors in the international bond market. If they act in a cautious and orthodox way, then their objective is to match currency assets and liabilities. Many borrowers have been criticized for raising international capital in, say, Swiss francs, when it "would have been" cheaper to borrow dollars. But such a generalized criticism misses the point that it is wholly proper for an international borrower to borrow Swiss currency for a Swiss investment or one which promises to generate Swiss currency. Borrowing in a strong currency is "wrong" only for a borrower having no assets or prospects of income in the currency borrowed.

The same rule applies to institutional investors such as international pension funds or insurance companies. It is quite correct for them to eliminate exchange risk in a similar fashion by matching their currency assets and liabilities. For instance, an international pension fund which can foresee with considerable accuracy the amount of pensions it will have to pay over a given period in dollars and Deutschemark, for example, would be acting properly by investing proportionately in those currencies. A real problem is created by exchange rate fluctuations only for "performance oriented" institutional investors and individuals, and there is no help anyone can give them beyond describing the obvious risks and opportunities.

On the other hand, the difference between high interest rates on weak currencies and low interest rates on strong currencies provides an opportunity for profit without risk for investment banks and securities firms which actively trade Eurobonds as principals in the secondary market (and could do the same for any large institutional investor). At mid-1978, for instance, it was possible to borrow Swiss francs at just over 1 percent a year to finance holdings of Eurodollar bonds yielding $8\frac{1}{2}$ to 9 percent, while insuring against currency risk by buying Swiss francs forward in the foreign exchange market. It is true that the cost of forward cover tends to approximate interest differentials between currencies when the foreign exchanges are relatively stable; but when exchange rates fluctuate widely, opportunities for covered interest arbitrage can come into being.

CHAPTER TWENTY-FOUR
CURRENCY CHOICE

The choice of currencies available to borrowers and investors in the international bond market has already been referred to, but some remarks can be made about each of them.

The *U.S. dollar* was the currency of denomination and payment of 60 percent of Eurobond issues during the eight years up to the end of 1977 and of 57 percent of international bond issues during that period (Eurobonds plus traditional foreign bonds). What is significant is not the large but the relatively limited role played by the world's most important currency in the international bond market and the far greater choice of assets therefore offered by this market compared with others. Despite all the talk about "diversification" of official reserve holdings, the proportion of world reserves held in dollars remained at an unchanged 80 percent from 1970 to 1978, for the simple reason that there is not much else on the shelves and all countries other than the United States have actively tried to stop the use of their currencies as official reserve assets. The proportion of dollars in the Eurocurrencies market has likewise been at a consistent 80 percent and so has the dollar component of the international capital market as a whole (meaning international bonds and credits).

The dollar has therefore been the predominant currency of the international bond market to a far lesser extent than it has in other markets. It is the main currency of the Eurobond market only because the issue of international bonds in all other currencies is regulated by national authorities (excepting the Canadian dollar). The volume of international dollar bond issues is regulated by market forces alone, as shown during the dollar's weakness in the first half of 1978, when the proportion of new international dollar bonds fell to 45 percent, while the proportion in Deutschemark, Swiss franc, and yen rose to 45 percent (from 30 percent a year earlier).

The *Deutschemark, Swiss franc, yen,* and *Dutch florin* are discussed in greater detail in Part Three of this book, devoted to foreign bonds, but the regulation of their use for international bond issues by the national authorities has this in common: In all cases, the object of the national authorities is to reduce the balance of payments impact of foreign borrowing and investment in their currencies. Nonresident investment income is subject to withholding for tax (except in the Netherlands, which has no withholding for tax) in the case of domestic securities, but not in the case of securities issued by foreign borrowers, who are usually required to convert their proceeds out of the currency borrowed unless those proceeds are being used for investment in the country. The net effect is usually that of a turntable which spins foreign capital out almost as fast as it floods into these currencies.

The *Canadian dollar* became available as an international investment currency in June 1975, when income on nonresident investment in Canadian securities having a maturity of longer than five years was exempted from withholding for tax. The volume of Canadian Eurobond issues rose about tenfold to almost $600 million in 1975, rose further to nearly $1½ billion in 1976, but then dropped to less than $700 million in 1977 and zero in 1978. Soon after this market opened its durability was questioned by Mr. Philip M. Hubbard, a managing director of Orion Bank. Presciently, he wrote: "What many are now asking is whether the Canadian dollar market is a temporary phenomenon or whether a new and permanent sector of the Eurobond market has come into being."[1] Events provided the answer. Canadian dollars were attractive for international investors while the currency remained relatively strong, as it did through 1976, and Canadian dollar Eurobonds tended to yield more than those denominated in U.S. dollars. But for the borrowers, who were mostly Canadian, the cost of funds was still cheaper than in the domestic market (because of the bait for international investors of exemption from withholding for tax). It was also less complicated for Canadian borrowers than going to the U.S. foreign bond market and, in any case, Canadian Eurobonds offered an alternative. However, they stopped doing so when the currency weakened in 1977 and 1978 (though there was some revival of issuing in early 1979).

Of the other currencies, there is little to say. The number of *French franc* issues has been extremely small because of tight regulation by the French authorities. A few Eurobonds in *Luxembourg francs* have pro-

---

[1]Philip M. Hubbard, *Euromoney,* November 1975.

vided a disguised form of Belgian franc Eurobonds, which are forbidden, the value of the Belgian and Luxembourg currencies having been rigidly linked since 1947. A number of Eurobond issues were made also, from 1975, in Middle Eastern currencies, notably the *Saudi Arabian riyal* and the *Kuwaiti dinar,* both of which moved in approximate tandem, appreciating by 30 percent against the dollar between 1970 and the first half of 1978. The issuers have been either private Middle Eastern borrowers with a use for the two currencies or, more frequently, developing countries needing to offer investors a strong currency asset in order to obtain international bond financing. Nonresident investors have invariably had to buy or borrow the two currencies, while foreign borrowers have usually had to convert the proceeds into other currencies as a matter of practical necessity. In effect, the use of Middle Eastern currencies has therefore served as an index against foreign exchange alterations among the major Western currencies.

CHAPTER TWENTY-FIVE
BORROWERS AND INVESTORS

The identity of borrowers in the Eurobond market is public record, but that of investors remains the market's deepest mystery. This chapter starts with a brief description of the first before descending to speculation about the second.

During the first 15 years of regular Eurobond borrowing, to the end of 1977, slightly less than half was by companies and slightly more than half by governments, state agencies such as nationalized industries, and by international development banks (although the biggest of these, the World Bank, preferred the policy of borrowing by means of traditional foreign bond issues on the capital markets of member countries). The exact proportion of private and public borrowing was 48 percent and 52 percent.

In terms of status conferred on international borrowers, the Eurobond market is often regarded as one step up from the Eurocredits market to the ultimate prestige of acceptance in the world's main foreign bond markets, notably New York and Zurich. As a very rough rule, three successful issues in their domestic market are often required of borrowers before their first admission to the Eurobond market. Although borrowing by means of Eurodollar bonds became more costly than borrowing on Eurocredits as a result of falling money market rates between 1975 and 1977 (as shown in Figure 10) many borrowers with sufficient credit standing and needs of a size encompassable by the Eurobond market continued to prefer international fixed-interest financing to the greater unpredictability of floating rate Eurocredits.

Most borrowing in the Eurobond market has been by the governments, official agencies, and companies of the industrialized countries. Developing countries began to gain access only from 1972 and on an appreciable scale only in the period from 1976 to the first half of 1978, when borrowing on their part rose significantly from 10 percent to 20 percent of total Eurobond borrowing. But more than one-half of all Eurobond borrowing by developing countries up to mid-1978 was by Mexico and Brazil and most of the rest by other advanced LDCs which had similarly first established themselves as important borrowers in the Eurocredits market, notably Argentina, the Philippines, Taiwan, Singapore, and Hong Kong. Even then, the Eurobond market had become more important for the new credit standing it conferred on those countries than for the amounts of capital provided. On the other hand, Comecon borrowers had obtained only a nominal $700 million in the Eurobond market during the period to mid-1978, all of which went to Hungary, Poland, and the International Investment Bank (Comecon's approximate equivalent of the World Bank).

The most important generalization about nearly all borrowing in the Eurobond market is that it has been balance of payments borrowing, whether directly or indirectly, voluntary or otherwise. That is not contradicted by the fact that much borrowing even by governments and official agencies has been for directly productive purposes and, in some cases, even for investments promising to generate foreign exchange earnings. And borrowing by companies is nearly always for investments promising such earnings. Nevertheless, all foreign borrowing helps the national balance of payments of the borrower, at least in the short run, and is dictated by that consideration. Nothing drives home the point more forcibly than the pattern of Eurobond borrowing by American companies, who raised one-third of total Eurobond finance during the years of American capital controls from 1963 to the beginning of 1974, but less than 5 percent thereafter (as illustrated in Figure 16).

American companies used the international market when they were forced to finance their foreign investment by borrowing abroad (by their government, trying to protect its balance of payments). Thereafter, they once more financed themselves in the American domestic capital market, as they had done before controls. But deficit countries like Great Britain, France, and Italy continue to force their companies and nationalized industries to borrow abroad, in the Eurobond market among others. And, even when they are not positively forced to finance international investment by foreign borrowing, companies often choose to do so in order to match their foreign exchange assets and liabilities. American companies were an exception when they used their special opportunities (after 1974) to borrow a depreciating dollar for the acquisition of assets valued in appreciating currencies, notably in Western Europe.

The Eurobond investor is the least known person in the market.

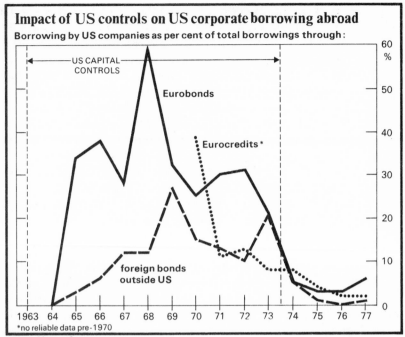

Impact of US controls on US corporate borrowing abroad

Borrowing by US companies as per cent of total borrowings through:

US CAPITAL CONTROLS

Eurobonds

Eurocredits*

foreign bonds outside US

1963 64 65 66 67 68 69 70 71 72 73 74 75 76 77

*no reliable data pre-1970

Source: Morgan Guaranty

FIGURE 16

Professional discretion, which prevents banks from discussing the business of their customers, is reinforced here by the fact that every bank in this competitive market jealously guards the identity of its investment clients from predatory raids by other banks. Even so, raids often take place, especially when personnel changes occur and investors follow trusted bankers from one bank to another in much the same way that advertising accounts often follow the move of executives from one advertising agency to a rival. Indeed, some banks are so nervous that they are reluctant to discuss even in general terms the kind of Eurobond investors they have. But most Eurobankers are not quite as edgy as that and their evidence makes it possible to piece together a rough, impressionistic picture of investors.

First, there is fairly widespread agreement that a majority of Eurobond investors are individuals, although their guesstimated holdings may have dropped from about 80 percent to around 60 percent of outstanding Eurobonds during the latter 1970s, when more institutional investors began coming into the market.

Most Eurobond investments by individuals are made through discretionary and advisory funds placed with banks for the purpose of investment in general, and not necessarily Eurobond investment alone. Discretionary funds are placed with banks by customers for investment by the banks for customers but at the bank's discretion. Advisory funds are entrusted to banks for investment on the customer's behalf, but only after consultation with the customer. However, customers' instructions vary in the latitude given to banks in the investment of advisory funds. Some customers specify precisely the particular securities they want, but many others are content to give only general instructions, such as that their money should be placed only in high-yielding issues, or alternatively only in Eurobond issues by particular classes of borrowers, such as blue-chip American corporations. Within those general instructions it is left to banks to invest the clients' funds as best possible.

Between them, such discretionary and advisory funds constitute the "in-house" placing power which is the most important strength of banks managing and selling new Eurobond issues and which has worked very heavily in favor of continental European banks, especially Swiss banks but also German and Belgian banks. It is impossible to know the amount of such funds administered by banks because, being neither assets nor liabilities of the banks themselves, they are not included in bank balance sheets and are often omitted even from banks' published reports. The difficulties are illustrated by the fact that the Zurich authorities were unable to guess the total of advisory funds handled by Swiss banks any more precisely than suggesting that they ranged between $60 billion and $140 billion in 1977, while the Bank for International Settlements privately opted for a guess in the middle of that range, at about $100 billion. But the amounts are huge by any reckoning and they represent a considerable factor in the Eurobond market even though only part of those funds are invested in Eurobonds.

However, such fiduciary funds are also a contentious factor, because their administration creates an awkward conflict of interest which the market has never fully faced. The conflict arises when banks managing and selling Eurobond issues place large amounts with more or less passive clients. Performance should provide some check on abuses, but it provides only an imperfect one in the case of many customers who are concerned with anonymity and tax evasion rather than with the finest investment returns available. Besides, many investors live in countries from which it is unhealthy to telephone or telex one's friendly banker in Zurich.

Who are these individual investors? They are by no means all small investors, defined by the market as those holding 10 to 15 Eurobonds, representing a stake of $10,000 to $15,000. Many have investments running to hundreds of thousands of dollars and a minority have Eurobond investments topping $1 million each. Indeed, there is a partly confusing overlap in market jargon because some bankers refer to individuals with stakes exceeding about $250,000 as "institutional" investors, while other bankers classify as "institutional" investment any private fortune large enough to be under professional administration.

The market puts individual investors into several categories, starting with the long-established Eurobond investors who have put part of their portfolios into the market since it started functioning on a regular basis. These prominently include Latin Americans and foreigners resident in Latin America, who have habitually shoveled large parts of their savings to havens abroad, into Eurobonds among other investments. Their main motive is flight from insecurity rather than taxes since, in the words of one prominent Eurobanker, the rich in Latin America seldom pay taxes anyway. A second category of long-established Eurobond investors consists of continental Europeans, notably French, Italian, and Belgian investors, who are likewise motivated by security although in their case opportunities for tax evasion are also an important consideration. In the case of Swiss, German, and Dutch individuals, the motive is almost exclusively tax evasion, given the relative security of their countries and currencies.

Besides all these, individuals who have long put part of their savings into Eurobonds include what one banker described privately as "the rich of no fixed abode," consisting mostly of entertainers, sports figures such as tennis stars, and similar persons who spend much of their time living in hotel rooms around the world while maintaining nothing more than tax-haven domiciles.

Around the mid-1970s, traditional Eurobond investors were joined in growing numbers by what might be called the "international new rich," consisting of individuals investing part of sudden fortunes made after the oil price explosion from trading, contracts, and kickbacks in the Middle East, the Far East, and, to a lesser extent, in other developing countries. Government officials of many countries are vaguely alluded to and mafia money is likewise said to make its contribution to the international recycling process.

The entry of new classes of individual investors into the market produced some shift in the channeling of funds. Some bankers estimated that the proportion of individual Eurobond investment through Swiss banks fell from almost 80 percent to less than 70 percent between the mid- and late-1970s, although that still implied an increase in the absolute amounts placed through Swiss banks in an expanding market. However, a relatively greater proportion of individual investment began to be placed through banks in London and Paris, especially by English- and French- speaking Middle Eastern and other investors from outside Europe having long cultural links with the two international cities, plus newer ones. They enjoy visiting Paris and London because of the greater pleasures available than in the relatively staid surroundings of Zurich, while London provides the delights of gambling as well as internationally renowned yet relatively cheap medical treatment in Harley Street, which has become crowded mostly with patients in flowing desert robes.

Other centers through which an increasing proportion of individual Eurobond investment began being channeled from the mid-1970s included offshore havens in the Caribbean and Singapore, the latter especially favored by those who had made fortunes in the Far East.

Institutional investment in Eurobonds, which is guesstimated to have risen from roughly 20 percent to 40 percent during the latter 1970s, increased mainly because of newcomers joining the ranks of international pension funds which had long included Eurobonds in their portfolios, including the pension funds of NATO, the OECD, and several United Nations agencies. The investment funds of many continental European banks, resembling mutual funds, have also traditionally invested part of their portfolios in Eurobonds.

The institutional newcomers prominently included marine and aviation insurance companies which had switched from doing business in sterling to doing it in dollars, even though the international business remained heavily centered in London. The newcomers included also PICs, or protection and indemnity clubs, set up as cooperative self-insurance pools by internatioanl shipowners and oil companies to insure their members against contingencies such as tanker collisions, accidents at offshore oil platforms, and the pollution claims arising as a result.

Another class of relatively new Eurobond investors are what the market calls "Arab funds," a term used to embrace official agencies in Middle Eastern countries and especially currency boards (the equivalent of central banks), particularly those of Saudi Arabia, Kuwait, and the United Arab Emirates. Although such agencies prefer to keep most of their assets liquid in the world's main money markets, the small proportion they put into Eurobonds makes a large contribution to the limited pool of funds in that market. At least one Eurobond salesman recalls selling no less than $40 million of a single new issue as a result of calling on SAMA, the Saudi Arabian Monetary Agency.

American investment in Eurobonds has been limited, although there always was a steady stream of it by individuals through external accounts. In addition, there has been a tradition of Eurobond investment by "captive" insurance subsidiaries set up in Bermuda and other offshore centers by U.S. corporations for self-insurance. Not being resident in the United States, such institutions were free to invest in Eurobonds without the penalty of the IET, nor are they affected by the Securities and Exchange Commission's prohibition against the investment in unregistered and "unseasoned" Eurobond issues. After the scrapping of the IET's penalty on U.S. resident investment in foreign securities at the beginning of 1974, a number of U.S.-resident institutions began to place some funds into Eurobonds which had either been registered with the SEC or "seasoned" in the secondary market for the requisite minimum of 90 days. It is true that official regulations and self-imposed restraints often limit the proportion of foreign securities, including Eurobonds, which U.S. institutions such as pension funds and insurance companies may include in their portfolios. The limitation is sometimes as little as 1 percent of total investments and hardly ever more than 5 percent. But, given the size of American institutional funds, even such limited amounts represent relatively substantial investments in terms of the Eurobond market's total.

However, the most contentious class of institutional Eurobond investors and probably the biggest category of institutional investors consists of banks in the issuing and secondary markets. No one can be sure, but if market guesstimates were right in putting institutional Eurobond investment at about 40 percent of the approximately $60 billion of Eurobonds outstanding at the end of 1977, then banks held more than half of that 40 percent or more than half of the roughly $25 billion which that represented. And there were times during the new issuing boom of 1975 through 1977 when they almost certainly held more, proportionately and absolutely. Most bankers testify to this, although it is, of course, always "other" banks which have allegedly excessive holdings. But there is also the circumstantial evidence of heavy turnover in the secondary market which suggests, among other things, the presence of banks which habitually trade their financial assets very actively and there was the persuasive evidence of 1973 and 1974 when Eurobond prices would surely have fallen even more than they did (thus incidentally correcting the inverse yield gap which appeared) if banks had not been supporting in the secondary market.

The presence of banks in the market is not wrong in all respects. Banks making a market in outstanding bonds must necessarily hold inventories and the shortening of Eurobond maturities already referred to provides assets similar to the five-year paper which banks normally deal actively in the American domestic short-term bond market and in the market for short-dated British "gilts" (government securities). Moreover, the wide yield differential on Eurobonds over the cost of short-term Eurodollar deposits from 1970 through 1972 and again from 1975 through 1977 made the holding and trading of Eurobonds highly profitable for banks (as for other investors) and sufficiently so to cushion some inevitable capital losses at times when the market turned.

But, aside from the legitimate need of secondary market-making banks to hold and trade inventories, the tendency of some banks to put their own assets at risk in the Eurobond market is open to question, even when it is temporarily profitable, but especially when banks become involuntary holders of new Eurobonds because their pretence of being able to place bonds with investors has proved greater than their ability to do so. The job of banks in the Eurobond market is to act as intermediaries between borrowers and investors and not to build up investments of their own. The involuntary holdings of some banks result from the zeal of specialized divisions and affiliates anxious to show the flag and striving for selling concessions even when it often involves having to take unsold portions of new issues onto their own shelves. It is a weakness of some banks, but not all. But where it exists, it suggests that boards of directors may not be watching their specialists as closely as they should.

CHAPTER TWENTY-SIX
INFLUENCES ON INVESTMENT DEMAND

The regular supply of Eurobonds from the early 1960s was created mainly by borrowers using this market, among others, to help finance national payments deficits, directly or indirectly. On the other hand, demand for Eurobonds by investors was one reflection of a growth in world savings plus the growing attractions of fixed-interest securities over other forms of investment, notably property and equities. Between them, these circumstances contributed to a structural and not merely cyclical growth of the Eurobond market. They allowed the market to become established; its expansion acquired a momentum of its own, the very fact of its existence attracting ever more borrowers, investors, and intermediating banks. Although new Eurobond issuing volume continued to rise and fall from year to year in response to conditions in the international capital market as a whole, each succeeding peak and trough in the volume of new Eurobond issues was higher than the preceding one.

One factor influencing the supply of funds available for investment everywhere was the substantial rise of savings in relation to national income in nearly all industrial countries, partly as a precaution against the inflation which began gathering momentum from the latter 1960s and partly as a result of it. For instance, the well-publicized increase in prices of residential property in most Western countries showed up, among other things, as an increase in the savings of homeowners.

The period from the late 1960s was characterized, also, by a progressive increase in the proportion of savings channeled into institutions, especially in the form of contractual savings. A growing tendency toward inflation indexation of pensions required a corresponding increase in pension fund contributions. The cost of life insurance also rose.

Last but far from least was the 1973 rise in oil prices, which transformed part of the spending power of consumers throughout the world into the savings of chronic surplus countries in the Middle East.

During the late 1960s and early 1970s, inflation had the initial effect of attracting excessive investment into celebrated "inflation hedges" such as real estate and gold. As a result, real estate prices in many countries were bidden to heights which reduced the yields or prospect of yields to unrewarding levels, except over a period too long for most investors to sit out. And an asset like gold, producing no income itself, was bidden to heights which made it too costly for most investors to go on holding in terms of income sacrificed. This led to a correction, in the form of a collapse in the real and to some extent even the nominal prices of assets such as real estate and gold toward the mid-1970s.

These developments did not amount to a blanket condemnation of real assets as a protection against inflation. They simply drove home the obvious point that the extent to which investors can afford asset protection is limited by the cost in terms of current income sacrificed.

The much vaunted "death" of the equities cult needs to be considered in the same framework. It is widely believed that investors buying equities are motivated exclusively by hopes of capital gains. Many investors actually do buy equities under this illusion and are sometimes rewarded. But the fundamental and rational motive for equity investment is the *prospect* of receiving a rising flow of dividend income over time. And that prospect is determined by the outlook for corporate profitability which is significantly determined by cyclical influences on economic output as a whole.

Figure 17 shows that the American equities boom peaked in real terms as long ago as 1968, although share prices expressed in nominal terms peaked out only four years later. The period after 1974 was characterized by a substantial fall in real share prices despite a renewed increase in their nominal price. But the "end" of the equities cult thus illustrated simply reflected the judgment that prospects for the real growth of output, profits, and dividends had become less favorable, as was duly confirmed.

The justified pessimism of investors made them increasingly unwilling from the late 1960s to go on paying large premiums for common shares in terms of a lower *immediate* return on equities than on fixed-interest securities. One result was a narrowing of the reverse yield gap between equities and fixed investment; Figure 18 shows that in the United States this became particularly pronounced in 1974 and 1977 when equity yields rose while bond yields fell, thus narrowing the gap between the traditionally lower yield on equities and the traditionally higher yield on bonds.

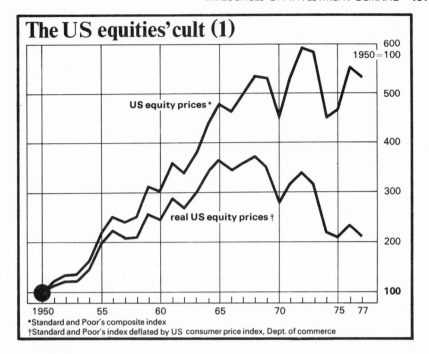

The US equities' cult (1)

600
1950＝100

US equity prices*

500

400

real US equity prices†

300

200

100

1950   55   60   65   70   75 77

*Standard and Poor's composite index
†Standard and Poor's index deflated by US consumer price index, Dept. of commerce

FIGURE 17

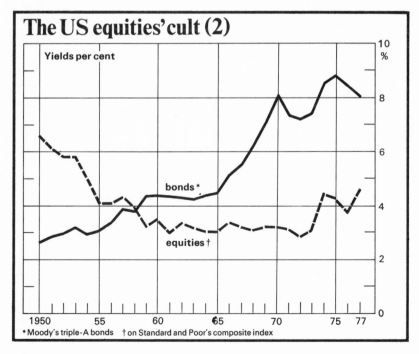

The US equities' cult (2)

Yields per cent

10
%

8

6

bonds*

4

equities†

2

1950   55   60   65   70   75 77

0

*Moody's triple-A bonds   † on Standard and Poor's composite index

FIGURE 18

Another consequence of experience during the decade up to 1978 was an increasing sensitivity of equity markets to the impact of monetary policy. This was shown by the rise in Wall Street prices during the spring of 1978 following a tightening of credit by the Federal Reserve Board and a suggestion by its chairman, Mr. William Miller, that proposed tax cuts should be postponed. A decade earlier, equity prices had still been rising on fears of inflation. But subsequent experience taught investors that the rise in the money value of their shares was offset by the decline in the real worth and earnings of corporations. In consequence, they had learned to bid up equities on the promise of price stability rather than the reverse.

In summary, the equities cult is by no means dead. A return to stable economic growth would bring it back to life (though not to fever pitch). But in a climate of slow economic growth and relatively high inflation, fixed-interest securities have proved the least bad investment. And fixed-interest investment in strong currencies, for which the international bond market provides an opportunity, was actually one of the few investments which proved profitable in real terms in the world climate of the late 1960s to the late 1970s.

It was that consideration which attracted a growing proportion of institutional investment into Eurobonds and other international bonds during the decade. And it did so without any special tax advantage for institutional investors, most of which are exempt from tax liability by their official status or offshore domicile. But in the case of individual investors, exemption from withholding for tax on the income from all classes of international bonds is an overriding consideration, far outweighing any other attractions. It should be noted that the alternatives for international investors are certain "moneylike" assets of several countries. For instance, there is no withholding for tax on income from non-resident investment in U.S. Treasury bills, certificates of deposit issued by banks, and commercial paper issued on a discounted basis by corporations. The proceeds of such investments may be subject to withholding on redemption, but not the proceeds of sale before redemption. International investors therefore often switch between international bonds and U.S. money market investments.

CHAPTER TWENTY-SEVEN
SELLING EUROBONDS

The method of issuing new Eurobonds is based largely on the model of the American domestic bond market, although that model has been followed in theory rather than practice in some important respects. As in the American domestic market, the borrower in the Eurobond market chooses a lead managing bank to arrange the issue. The lead managing bank is responsible for advising the borrower on the best size of the issue, terms, and timing, usually with the help of a small group of comanaging banks. The whole issue is underwritten by the managers plus a larger group of underwriting banks. In the American market, the underwriters enter into a binding contract to take onto their own books bonds which they cannot sell to investors at the agreed issuing price. In the Eurobond market this commitment is a pure fiction, underwriting banks simply dumping what they cannot sell. In addition to the managing and underwriting banks, Eurobond issues are launched with the help of still bigger groups of selling banks, which receive a commission for the bonds they sell.

The standard scale of fees, allowances, and commissions received by banks in the Eurobond issuing market ranges from 2 percent to $2\frac{1}{2}$ percent of the value of the issue, depending on its maturity. This compares with a scale of $\frac{7}{8}$ percent to 1 percent in the U.S. domestic and foreign bond markets at one extreme, and as much as 4 percent in the tightly knit Swiss franc foreign bond market. The standard scale of launching costs in nearly all sectors of the Eurobond market is most easily shown in Table 28.

The way this works is shown by the example of an issue of 9-year Eurodollar bonds (about the average maturity of those issued in 1976 and 1977), with the bonds having a customary denomination of $1,000

TABLE 28
LAUNCHING COSTS OF EUROBOND ISSUES
(percent of total issue)

Maturity	Management fee	Underwriting allowance	Selling concession	Total
Up to 5 years	⅜	⅜	1¼	2
5 to 8 years	⅜	⅜	1½	2¼
8 years and longer	½	½	1½	2½

each. If it has been agreed to sell the bonds to the public at face value, the lead manager buys the bonds from the borrower at 97½ percent (par minus 2½ percent), or $975 each. That represents the proceeds to the borrower. On an issue of $45 million (roughly the average size in 1976 and 1977), the borrower would thus receive $43,875,000, having paid $1,125,000 to get the issue launched. This obviously bumps up the cost to the borrower, a yield of, say, 9 percent a year to the investor costing the borrower almost 9¼ percent in the present example.

The lead manager holds onto the total management fee and underwriting allowances until they are subsequently shared with comanagers and underwriters on an agreed basis and after the deduction of expenses. But bonds to all members of the selling group (including managers, underwriters, and mere selling banks) are allocated at 98½ percent (par minus 1½ percent selling concession), or $985 each. Thereafter, everyone is on his own, by contrast with practice in the American domestic and foreign bond markets, where all members of a syndicate are contractually bound not to sell bonds to investors below the agreed issue price until the syndicate has been formally disbanded. The prime difference between the two systems is that investors in the New York markets receive their bonds on equal terms, while almost no two investors in the Eurobond market pay the same price for newly issued bonds. This is elaborated in Chapter 31. The lesson for Eurobond investors, privately conceded by many Eurobankers, is that investors are best off buying bonds in the secondary rather than in the primary, new issue market. The stipulation of the Securities and Exchange Commission that Eurobonds which have not been registered with the SEC may not be sold to U.S. residents until "seasoned" in the secondary market for at least 90 days, and the similar restraint applying to Canadian investors, is therefore positively helpful.

The high level of fees and commissions in the Eurobond market survived for a long time as an unjustified relic of the market's early days, when hunting up investors for a new kind of international bond really was a time-consuming and labor-intensive business. But that justification had worn very thin by the latter 1970s and in practice the fee and commission structure was greatly eroded although not formally abandoned. A growing number of stronger borrowers were able to whittle down the standard scale of charges outlined earlier in this chapter. Even more widespread was that issuing banks no longer collected their underwriting and selling concessions in full because of growing pressure to concede "reallowances" to any investor with enough sense and muscle to demand them. A market rule which had tried to limit "reallowances" to $\frac{1}{2}$ percentage point and to recognized securities dealers had been widely abandoned as unenforceable by 1976. By that time many banks were passing on to sufficiently powerful investors of any category as much as a full percentage point or even more of their $1\frac{1}{2}$ percent selling concessions. In other words, a selling bank receiving its bonds from the managers at the standard $1\frac{1}{2}$ percent discount, or $985 each, might pass on the bonds to investors for as little as $995 or even $990, thus making a mere $5 or $10 on the transaction.

It is easy enough to work out the approximate cost to borrowers of the 18\frac{1}{2}$ billion of new Eurobonds sold in 1977 (according to the OECD) in terms of the standard scale of charges. According to Credit Suisse White Weld, about 20 percent of new issues were for less than five years, about 55 percent for six to ten years, and the remainder for longer than ten years. The weighted average of standard launching fees and selling commissions paid by borrowers was therefore about 2.3 percent, or roughly $425 million. But it is impossible to know how much of that actually went to issuing banks or exactly how the 480 banks then belonging to the Association of International Bond Dealers shared whatever it was they actually got. However, the volume of Eurobond issues known to be managed by a relative handful of banks and the impressionistic evidence of bankers in the market suggest an extreme concentration of issuing business, with huge disparities between the incomes of a few managing banks at the top and the hordes of selling banks jostling for places at the lower end of "tombstones," the advertisements published by banks shortly after a new issue to record their part in its management and sale. Figures 19 and 20 are examples of these tombstones.

This extreme concentration of the market (discussed further in Chapter 28) suggests that most banks seem to be in the new issue business for prestige rather than money. Table 29, which is derived from market sources, indicates how the spoils were divided on a $45 million 9-year Eurobond issue in 1977 (the average size and maturity

This announcement appears as a matter of record only.

September 1976

ALCAN ALUMINIO DO BRASIL S.A.

U.S. $50,000,000

Eight Year Floating Rate Loan

Managed by

Orion Bank Limited

Bank of Montreal   Swiss Bank Corporation

The Royal Bank of Canada   Westdeutsche Landesbank
                                    Girozentrale

with

The Chase Manhattan Bank, N.A.   The Bank of Nova Scotia

The Toronto Dominion Bank

Agent Bank

Orion Bank Limited

FIGURE 19   A Eurobond "tombstone" advertisement placed by banks to record their part in managing an issue of floating rate notes. (*Courtesy of Orion Bank Ltd.*)

of new issues that year). It shows the lead manager getting almost $170,000, five comanagers getting nearly $80,000 each, but 80 to 100 banks in the selling group getting an average of only $1,350 to about $1,700 each. In fact, Table 29 understates the disparities which can occur in practice. The top banks sometimes get an even bigger share. At the other extreme, it is precisely the weakest and smallest banks at the bottom of a syndicate who come under the greatest pressure to sacrifice part of their selling commissions in order to get rid of bonds which they have sought in the hope of eventually building a pretense at placing power into reality. One Eurobank privately admitted selling as few as 300 new bonds a month for a gross return of less than $6,000. That admission came not from an obscure bank, but from the

London investment banking subsidiary of one of America's biggest commercial banks, helplessly seeking business which it was not qualified to handle.

The division of fees and underwriting allowances is a complicated, sometimes acrimonious, and always sensitive matter. The management fee is by no means always split evenly between the lead manager and comanagers, as shown in Table 29. Sometimes the lead manager takes 60 percent (or $135,000 in the example shown) while leaving the comanagers to share the remaining 40 percent (or $90,000) of the $\frac{1}{2}$-point managing fee. Underwriters suspected of not fulfilling their obligations are sometimes subtly "punished" by having rather large deductions for

This Advertisement complies with the requirements of the Council of The Stock Exchange in London.

August 25, 1977

AB Götaverken

(*Incorporated in Sweden with limited liability*)

U.S. $40,000,000 7⅝% Guaranteed Notes due 1982

Issue Price 100 per cent. less interest

U.S. $40,000,000 8⅛% Guaranteed Bonds due 1987

Issue Price 99½ per cent. less interest

Unconditionally guaranteed as to payments of principal, premium, if any, and interest by

the Swedish National Debt Office *on behalf of*

The Kingdom of Sweden

The following have agreed to subscribe or procure subscribers for the Notes and Bonds

Bank of America International Limited   **Orion Bank Limited**
Credit Suisse White Weld Limited
PKbanken
Skandinaviska Enskilda Banken
Svenska Handelsbanken
Westdeutsche Landesbank Girozentrale

The Notes and Bonds of U.S. $1,000 each constituting the above issue have been admitted to the Official List of The Stock Exchange in London. Interest is payable annually in arrears on September 15, the first such payment being due on September 15, 1978.

Particulars of the Notes and Bonds are available from Extel Statistical Services Ltd., and may be obtained during normal business hours on any weekday (Saturdays excepted) up to and including September 8, 1977, from

Bank of America International Limited		Orion Bank Limited		Strauss, Turnbull & Co.
St. Helen's, 1 Undershaft,	and	1 London Wall,	and	3 Moorgate Place,
London, EC3A 8HN		London, EC2Y 5JX		London, EC2R 6HR

FIGURE 20 A Eurobond "tombstone" advertisement placed by banks to record their part in managing (or arranging) the issue. (*Courtesy of Orion Bank Ltd.*)

TABLE 29
HOW FEES ARE SLICED . . .

$45 million 9-year Eurobond issue,* in dollars

Management fee (½% = $225,000):	
Lead manager	112,500
5 comanagers, $22,500 each	112,500
	225,000
Underwriting allowance (½% = $225,000):	
6 Managing banks underwriting 30% at average $11,250	67,500
50 major underwriters, underwriting 50% at average $2,250	112,500
40 minor underwriters, underwriting 20% at average $1,125	45,000
	225,000
Selling concession (1½% = $675,000):	
6 managers selling $18 mn at average $45,000	270,000
50 major underwriters selling $11¼ mn at average $3,375	168,750
40 minor underwriters selling $6¾ mn at average $2,530†	101,250
⁸⁰⁄₁₀₀ selling banks, selling $9 mn at average $1,687/$1,350†	135,000
	675,000
Total fees, allowances, and concessions, 2½% of $45 mn =	1,125,000

*Average size and maturity of Eurobond issues in 1977.
†Rounded

"expenses" made from their underwriting allowances, at least one case having been recorded of an underwriter receiving a check for $00.00, meaning literally zero, from a piqued lead managing bank.

The underwriting allowance, which is in the gift of the lead manager, is the most subtle part of the business. Because there is no true underwriting in the Eurobond market, in the sense of a legal obligation to take up and hold a commitment, the underwriters often get what many bankers call a "free ride." In practice, the underwriting allowance serves as a bribe to encourage banks to share in the distribution of a weak issue, or as a consolation for those who failed to get the allocations of new bonds they wanted in the case of a popular issue. Moreover, banks which have narrowly missed inclusion as comanagers of an issue are sometimes consoled by being put into a "special bracket" of large underwriters, meaning that they get big allocations of a new issue qualifying for a gratuitous $\frac{1}{2}$-point underwriting allowance, although

. . . AND WHO GETS WHAT

Lead manager:				
Management fee	112,500			
Underwriting allowance	11,250			
Selling concession	45,000			
	168,750	(× 1)	=	$168,750
5 comanagers, each:				
Management fee	22,500			
Underwriting allowance	11,250			
Selling concession	45,000			
	78,750	(× 5)	=	$393,750
50 major underwriters, each:				
Underwriting allowance	2,250			
Selling concession	3,375			
	5,625	(× 50)	=	$281,250
40 minor underwriters, each:				
Underwriting allowance	1,125			
Selling concession	2,530†			
	3,655†	(× 40)	=	$146,250
$^{80}/_{100}$ selling banks, each:				
Selling concession	1,350 to 1,687†	(×$^{80}/_{100}$)	+	$135,000
Total fees, allowances,				
and concessions	(2½% of $45 mn):			$1,125,000

†Rounded

without any real obligation for their sales to match their commitments.

In fact, there is no clear connection between underwriting commitments and the amounts which banks in a syndicate take up or sell to clients. The whole of any new issue is always underwritten by the managers, by "major" underwriters each underwriting an average of 1 percent of the issue, and by "minor" underwriters each assuming so-called responsibility for about ½-percent of the issue. However, in reality, about one-fifth or more of many Eurobond issues is sold by banks who are not underwriters but merely members of the selling group, entitled to sales commission alone. At the same time, the managers of an issue often take up or sell more than the amount they have underwritten, while underwriters often sell less than they have underwritten, although they still get their underwriting allowances, like the Marx Brothers' band which was paid more for not playing than playing.

During the "selling period" of one week to ten days between the announcement of an issue and its offer to the public, demand is assessed on the basis of the indicated size of the issue, the interest coupon, and the selling price, all of which are formally agreed by the managing banks and the borrower at the end of that period. A good deal of jockeying goes on. One of a manager's difficulties is determining when heavy demand represents ultimate demand from investors who will hold the bonds, or when it merely represents staging demand by underwriters who will make a quick profit by dumping the bonds in the market at any price above the discount at which they receive the securities (which, on the normal scale of allowances, could be at any price above $987.50 for a $1,000 Eurodollar bond being issued at par).

Dumping is extremely difficult to detect through the Eurobond clearing systems. The bonds are issued in bearer form, so that the ownership of individual bonds is not registered. Moreover, the clearing systems handle most bonds on a fungible basis, meaning that bonds are not individually earmarked as belonging to any particular holder, but that the clearing systems merely credit banks with a given number of bonds. And dumping is even more difficult to detect when members of an issuing syndicate use small continental European banks at a $\frac{1}{4}$-point fee for providing "cover."

However, banks which dump seem to cover their tracks for appearance rather than fear of dire consequences in the event of detection, because the intimacy of banking relationships over the whole spectrum of international operations (and not Eurobond business alone) makes it difficult for managing banks to strike miscreants from future syndication lists. Deducting "expenses" from unearned underwriting allowances seems to be about as far as managers usually dare to go. "We are all gutless in this business," said one banker. And another, having told a visitor that his bank "never" participated in selling an issue it did not like, went on to say that it never refused an invitation for fear of not being asked again. Indeed, banking relationships and the endorsement of big banking names dominate Eurobond issuing to such an extent that a certain vagueness is sometimes encountered about the borrowers. A Eurobanker who had just described a new issue as "going excellently" was nonplussed when asked about the borrower's business. "What do they *do?*" he said. "Oh, chemicals, or something like that, I think."

When heavy demand during the selling period is judged to represent ultimate investor demand, the lead manager may advise the borrower to increase the size of the issue, if that is what the borrower wants, or to cut the interest coupon. When the matter is not so clear the lead manager may, with the agreement of the syndicate, "overallocate," say, $5 million of a $45 million issue. Immediately after the issue is made, the lead manager will then buy back up to $5 million in the secondary market for the account and at the expense of all underwriters, *pro rata*. But this will prove necessary only to the extent that an issue really has been oversubscribed by the investment public.

On the other hand, when the response to a new issue proves weak, the issuing price can be reduced, say, to $99\frac{1}{2}$ percent of face value or less. Alternatively, if the borrower is strong enough, the managers may have to take much of the issue onto their own books and then gradually dribble it onto the market. That is exactly what happened when Société Générale and its comanagers were obliged to take onto their own books $24 million of a $30 million issue for the Industrial and Mining Development Bank of Iran in 1976. In the case of a weaker borrower, an issue meeting with indications of insufficient demand may be cancelled or, more politely, "postponed."

Last but by no means least is the delicate matter of "protection," by which managers promise allocations of new bonds to syndicate members during the selling period, before the bonds are offered to the public. When a new issue is in heavy demand, this is a favor on the part of the manager to valued underwriters needing large allocations for important institutional clients. But there is also an inducement for managers to scatter offers of protection when they are unsure about demand and particularly when they have reason to fear that initial demand for an issue may evaporate during the selling period, as it sometimes does when competing new issues overlap in an awkward way. Yet managers have to be careful not to protect too much for fear of the market sniffing a weak issue. There is, of course, a ploy for that contingency too, which consists of ostentatiously scaling down all allocations to give an impression of strong demand. Nor is such bluff always called, because demand does often pick up towards the end of a selling period, particularly from large commercial banks which need time to assess investor interest at their numerous branches.

CHAPTER TWENTY-EIGHT
ISSUING BANKS AND MARKET MAKERS

The Association of International Bond Dealers was founded in 1969 for the voluntary establishment of uniform practices in an unregulated market. By 1978, it had grown to 480 member banks in 27 countries, including 139 listed as lead managers and 108 as market makers, which are banks willing to make a secondary market in outstanding Eurobonds and performing a similar function to that of specialists on the New York Stock Exchange or jobbers on the London Stock Exchange.

But Table 30 gives some idea of the concentration of the business. It lists the top 20 banks in the new issues market, ranked by Credit Suisse First Boston (known as Credit Suisse White Weld until 1978) according to the amounts of new Eurobond financing they helped to arrange in 1977 as lead managers or comanagers. Each of the top five banks participated in the arrangement of between 30 and 40 percent of that year's approximately $18 billion of Eurobond issues, while each of the next five banks participated in the management of between 20 and 25 percent of the year's new issues.[1]

There is no way of ranking secondary market makers, but the alphabetical list of 25 exceptionally active banks in this sector, as selected by a number of market sources, and shown in Table 30, reinforces the impression of market concentration. In this list, 15 of the top 20 issuing banks overlap or are connected in some way with the 25 banks in the

---

[1]The Credit Suisse First Boston list shows each of the top five banks having participated in the management of between $5.4 billion and $7.7 billion of Eurobond issues in 1977 and each of the next five as having participated in the management of between $3.3 billion and $4.6 billion. There is no indication of the amounts of new bonds actually placed with investors by each of the banks.

TABLE 30
LEADING EUROBANKS

Lead managers and co-managers*	Secondary market makers†
Deutsche Bank	Banca Commerciale Italiana
Credit Suisse First Boston	Banque Internationale à
Union Bank of Switzerland	Luxembourg
(Securities) Ltd.	Banque Nationale de Paris
Swiss Bank Corporation	Bontrade
(Overseas) Ltd.	Commerzbank
Westdeutsche Landesbank	Crédit Lyonnais
Dresdner Bank	Deutsche Bank
Amsterdam–Rotterdam Bank	Dresdner Bank
S.G. Warburg	European Banking Company
Commerzbank	First Boston Corp.
Kredietbank S.A.,	First Chicago Ltd.
Luxembourgeoise	Istituto Bancario San Paolo
Banque Nationale de Paris	di Torino
Banque de Paris et des	Kidder Peabody Securities Ltd.
Pays-Bas	Kredietbank S.A., Luxembourgeoise
Société Générale de Banque	Merrill Lynch (London)
Algemene Bank Nederland	Samuel Montagu
Crédit Lyonnais	Morgan Stanley International
Société Générale	Salomon Bros. International
Morgan Stanley International	Scandinavian Bank Ltd.
Salomon Bros. International	Skandinaviska Enskilda Banken
Orion Bank	Swiss Bank Corp. (Luxembourg)
Banca Commerciale Italiana	Strauss, Turnbull & Co.
	Westdeutsche Landesbank
	White Weld Securities
	Wood Gundy Ltd.

*SOURCE: Credit Suisse First Boston, London. The rankings are by the total amounts of internationally syndicated Eurobond issues managed and comanaged in 1977.
†Some of the most active market makers in the Eurobond secondary market, as selected by several market sources.

list of active market makers. The connection in some cases is through consortium banks, like Orion (which includes Westdeutsche Landesbank among its owners) and the European Banking Company (whose shareholders include Amsterdam-Rotterdam Bank and Société Générale).

The composition of leading new issue banks changed considerably during the decade up to the late 1970s, mainly in favor of Swiss and other continental European banks at the expense of British and American banks. The shift reflected the fact that the power to place bonds with investors had come to weigh ever more heavily than connections with borrowers allowing banks to bring customers to market. But the rankings were influenced also by the insistence of the German authorities that German banks should manage internationally syndicated Deutschemark issues and the insistence of the Swiss authorities that Swiss banks should participate in the selling groups of international bonds sold in Switzerland.

In 1968, the top 20 issuing banks included six American banks (who were then busy bringing to the Eurobond market American clients shut out of New York by American capital export controls) and two British banks, S.G. Warburg and N.M. Rothschild. At that time, the top 20 did not include any Swiss banks. But once placing power had come to outweigh connections with borrowers, the three major Swiss banks moved to the top of the list (one in partnership with White Weld) and so did German, Dutch, French, and Belgian banks. By 1977, only two purely American investment banks remained among the top 20 in the issuing market, Morgan Stanley International and Salomon Brothers International (in seventeenth and eighteenth places). And S.G. Warburg remained the only British survivor, but in eighth place, down from third place in 1968.

Placing power, roughly defined as the ability to place at least $500,-000 of a new issue, had become so important by the middle 1970s that a bank leading an issue because of having a borrower as a customer often took a smaller slice than comanagers with greater ability to place paper. As an example, Kredietbank Luxembourgeoise, not among the top 20 in 1968, had moved to tenth place in the issue league in 1977 mainly on its placing power, comanaging 60 issues that year but acting as lead manager only for three.

The secret of placing power consists of the in-house funds already referred to, meaning money entrusted to banks by clients for investment. Breaking into the charmed group of managing banks in the Eurobond market is like breaking into a vicious circle: Banks are invited into management groups because of their placing power. The large blocks of new bonds which they are allocated as comanagers help, in their turn, to reinforce placing power, because institutional investors usually require lots of $250,000 to $500,000 and will therefore deal only with banks which can deliver securities in such large amounts. Moreover, institutional investors expect their Eurobanks to be big enough to handle large transactions in the secondary market too.

However, the efficiency of the new issues market is often impaired when managing banks invite into selling groups banks with which they have or with whom they wish to cement relations, rather than banks with real ability to distribute new bonds to investors. Such traditional selling groups are often kept approximately unchanged. As a result, managers sometimes allocate large amounts of new bonds to group members who cannot place the bonds while starving outside banks which can. This helps favored group members when outsiders pay them over the odds for the surplus bonds which selling banks cannot dispose of themselves. But outsiders are able to drive a hard bargain when they relieve insiders of new issues which the insiders cannot place with investors.

The secondary market for Eurobonds used to be described accurately, if unkindly, as consisting of a broker telephoning himself. There is still an element of this. Banks making the after market (which consists of the trading of bonds immediately after their issue) and the secondary market (which trades outstanding bonds thereafter) jealously defended the system by which they negotiate prices among themselves and with large institutional investors. They resisted attempts to introduce brokers who would put buying and selling banks in touch with each other in the secondary market, in the way that brokers put banks in touch with each other in the foreign exchange and many other markets. And there is a telling difference between the smaller number of banks willing to feed Eurobond quotations into closed circuit television and the greater number of banks willing to receive information from their screens but unwilling to help supply it.

Nevertheless, there seemed to be some improvement in the efficiency of the secondary market during the mid- and late-1970s. This resulted partly from the entry into the Eurobond market of more institutional investors with the power to demand and get better service. It resulted partly, also, from the entry into the secondary market of a greater number of well-capitalized banks, notably including European affiliates of American commercial and investment banks and American securities firms as well as several Japanese investment banks.

Most Eurobonds are listed on stock exchanges—dollar bonds in London and Luxembourg, French franc Eurobonds in Luxembourg, and external Deutschemark bonds on German stock exchanges. But relatively little trading takes place on stock exchanges except in the case of external DM bonds. The main purposes of listing are to provide information, to give investors confidence, to allow exchanges to provide some barometer of approximate quotations, and to make Eurobonds eligible for the portfolios of many institutions which are restricted to investment in quoted securities. But in practice, most Eurobonds are traded over the counter by telephone by the AIBD's recognized secondary market makers. Although Table 30 lists 25 especially active market makers, some sources estimate that the largest part of the business is done by no more than about 15 banks, each trading up to $10 million a day and holding positions (long and short) of between $10 million and $15 million. London is by far the biggest center, with 41 AIBD market makers in 1978, compared with 12 in Amsterdam, the next largest center, and a mere 6 in Germany and Austria combined (although that reflects partly a greater concentration of business and a greater volume of stock exchange trading).

All market makers specialize in selections of stock. Although about $60 billion of Eurobonds consisting of more than 1,000 issues were outstanding in 1978, only about 300 to 350 of these were actively traded. Top market makers stand ready to deal in 200 to as many as 350 issues each and tend to specialize in about 150 to 200, but of these only 50 to 100 are being actively traded at any one time.

Market makers act both as brokers and principals. There is no system of commissions, the return consisting of the difference between the asking prices demanded by sellers and the bid prices offered by purchasers. A bank asked for securities by another at, say, 98 percent, will supply them only if it has them on its books or is able to acquire them at some price below that bid price.

Market spreads between bid and asked quotations are indications of risk and turnover, with the widest spreads on risky or inactive issues and the narrowest on outstanding bonds carrying the least risk or being very actively traded. The spreads on straight-debt bonds vary widely between $\frac{1}{8}$ point to a full percentage point and they widen to 2 percent or more on Eurobonds which are difficult to trade and on convertibles (which carry the additional uncertainty of fluctuations in the share price).

When a market maker is carrying a long position (meaning that he has an inventory of Eurobonds), he makes a return partly on the difference between the yield on the bonds and the cost of financing his stock with funds borrowed in the money market, provided money-market rates are lower than bond yields. He aims, also, to make a return on the difference between his acquisition and selling price. When he has a short position, meaning that he does not possess stock which he has undertaken to supply, he has to acquire it from another market maker and the difference between the bid and asked quotations are then divided between them. For instance, when an investor asks for stock being quoted at 100 percent of face value bid and 101 asked, the market maker will try to pick it up at, say $100\frac{1}{2}$, passing it on to the investor at 101. This provides a $\frac{1}{2}$-point return to each of the two market-making banks involved in the transaction. However, returns of between $\frac{1}{8}$ to $\frac{1}{4}$ percent to the market makers are more common.

Market makers deal only with each other or with large institutional clients and the average size of transactions approximately doubled to about $40,000 during the four years of increasingly active trading to 1978. Whereas a transaction of $100,000 and upward was considered large in the mid-1970s, blocks of $250,000 to $750,000 were sometimes being traded by the late 1970s.

Individual investors cannot deal with the secondary market directly, except for those big enough to be accorded the standing of institutional investors. Others have to pass their orders to the market through their own banks, which usually charge between $\frac{1}{4}$ and $\frac{1}{2}$ point for that service.

The secondary market will not normally deal in blocks of less than 10 Eurobonds (or $10,000), but market makers are obliged by their own rules to make their best efforts to fulfill orders for the trading of 25 bonds or more.

An imperfection of the secondary market is that there are often only two or three major specialists in any actively traded issue. "That is the beauty of specializing," said one such market maker. "You have a better chance of getting a fair proportion of the business in that part of the market and it is more profitable to take positions."

His defense of this system was that it differs little from practice on the New York and London stock exchanges, where most stocks are dealt through only a few specialists or jobbers (although under trading practices which are far more closely regulated than in the Eurobond secondary market). Two further justifications were added, namely that market makers take considerable risks in bad periods, as in 1974, and that they do not, in any case, enjoy any monopoly because "anyone can compete." But that last point was somewhat weakened by the subsequent observation that only a hard core of market makers have the resources and expertise needed for survival and that challengers "tend to come and go."

CHAPTER TWENTY-NINE
ADVANTAGES AND DRAWBACKS

The Eurobond market's advantages and drawbacks for borrowers and investors are best summarized as follows.

The Borrowers: Advantages

1. The market's provision of an alternative source of international capital.

2. The choice of currencies available, allowing borrowers to match foreign exchange assets and liabilities for an elimination of exchange rate risk.

3. The status conferred on borrowers by the market which gives them the opportunity of improving their credit standing in all international markets and of graduating to the prestigious New York and Zurich foreign bond markets.

4. The flexibility provided by the alternatives of straight fixed-interest debt, floating rate debt (through floating rate note issues), and convertibles, as well as the flexibility provided by the variety of methods by which bonds may be redeemed before maturity. This allows borrowers to switch from debt in one currency to debt in another, or from previously contracted fixed-interest debt at a higher cost to new debt at a lower cost; or from fixed-interest debt to Eurocredit financing, whenever there is a change in market conditions.

5. The chance given to corporate borrowers to obtain a wider spread of international investment in their companies, including wider share-ownership through convertibles.

The Borrowers: Drawbacks

1. Foreign exchange risk for those sufficiently unwise to borrow currencies in which they do not have matching assets or which they have no prospect of earning.

2. The relative shortness of Eurobond maturities complicates longer-term planning for borrowers.

3. Limitations of access to the nondollar sectors of the market. It is true that this helped borrowers by concentrating a lot of borrowing into a depreciating currency during the 1960s and 1970s but it would go on helping them in this way only as long as the dollar remains weak. If the dollar became a strong currency, it would be a disadvantage.

4. The relatively high issuing costs in the Eurobond market, the inefficiencies of new issue distribution and secondary market trading. Those inefficiencies probably have the effect of increasing borrowing costs further, because borrowers are often obliged to offer terms which will compensate investors for those market defects.

The Investors: Advantages

1. For individuals, the overriding advantage is the exemption from withholding for tax on the returns on Eurobond yields and redemptions and the opportunities for tax evasion thus provided.

2. In a climate of inflation and depressed economic growth, such as that during the decade up to 1978, fixed-interest securities of all kinds provided what was probably the least unsatisfactory investment while fixed-interest securities in strong currencies, as offered by the Eurobond market, provided one of the few genuinely profitable investment opportunities.

3. The flexibility provided by the market by its provision of a choice between fixed- and floating-rate securities and convertible issues.

The Investors: Drawbacks

1. The inefficiencies of new issue distribution, which mean that many investors receive new Eurobonds at different prices, according to their clout.

2. The "premium" which investors are often obliged to pay for an effectively tax-exempt investment when banks stuff the portfolios of clients whose investment funds they are administering with new Eurobonds which those same banks have helped to issue.

3. The "premium" likewise paid by investors for anonymity and the opportunity for tax evasion by the difficulties which many have in giving regular instructions to the banks to whom they have entrusted flight capital for investment. In fairness, "premiums" 2 and 3 above represent a small cost which investors seem willing to pay for the advantages they obtain.

4. The foreign exchange risk which investors take when they do not match their foreign currency assets and liabilities, which they often have less scope for doing than borrowers, partly because individual investors often do not have foreign currency liabilities, although institutional investors often do.

PART THREE

FOREIGN BOND MARKETS AND FINANCIAL CENTERS

CHAPTER THIRTY

NEW YORK AS AN INTERNATIONAL CAPITAL MARKET

Throughout history, international financial centers have usually sprung up wherever wealth has become concentrated. But this did not happen in the United States or not, at any rate, in the customary and obvious way. Although America became the world's biggest economy at the start of this century and the biggest capital exporter about 1914, New York has never become firmly established as the world's leading capital market for international borrowers. The United States has tended to export capital by way of foreign direct investment on the part of American industry and by official flows of aid, rather than by attracting foreign borrowers to its domestic capital market.

It is easy to draw historical contrasts. Venice became an international financial center in the twelfth century, Amsterdam in the seventeenth and eighteenth, and London in the nineteenth because of extensive overseas trade, especially with colonies and dependencies. Such trade created not only wealth and banking skills, but also a world view making citizens willing to invest in foreign loans.

However, the development of the United States as a continental power was very differently based on the conquest of a huge land mass, the exploitation of its natural resources, and the growth of domestic commerce. While this development was taking place, the political isolation enshrined in the Monroe Doctrine was matched by a large degree of economic isolation. Foreign trade played a relatively small part in the economy, mainly because of America's exceptional self-sufficiency in raw materials, a situation which changed only very recently with a growing need for imported oil.

But there was another explanation too, namely that when American industry had grown sufficiently powerful to move into world markets, it did so by expanding its manufacturing abroad rather than by exporting goods. The pattern was set by President Theodore Roosevelt's "trust busting" early this century,[1] which caused the biggest American corporations to start looking outside the United States for opportunities denied at home; and it was reinforced after the Second World War by the tax advantages and the attractions of cheaper labor abroad. Moreover, Europe and Japan did not have the means to import American goods on any large scale for some years after 1945 and the only way American industry could expand abroad during that time was by foreign direct investment, which was financed almost entirely in the American domestic capital market.

An erroneous conclusion sometimes drawn from this difference of historical experience is that the international capital market remains so largely centered in Europe because of a legacy of financial skills and an international outlook which failed to develop in the United States. It is a thesis with obvious appeal for Europeans and even for many American bankers who enjoy being stationed in the Old World, but it is not true.

What is true is that New York, Chicago, and San Francisco necessarily developed as continental financial centers. But the problems of mobilizing the financial resources of a continent were at least as great as those faced elsewhere; for instance, the skills needed to sell a loan for Alabama on the New York market at the turn of this century were very similar to those required for selling a South Africa issue in London at that time.

In some respects, indeed, American bankers faced special difficulties. Correspondent banking has therefore developed more extensively in the United States than in any other country because of the fragmentation of the banking system, which obliges large money center banks to compete for the interest-free deposits of literally thousands of smaller banks in return for services, including participation in loans beyond the resources of regional banks. The major American city banks also compete keenly for the deposits of large American corporations, whose business is too big to be handled by their hometown banks or by any bank on its own, particularly since American law does not allow any bank to lend the equivalent of more than 10 percent of its capital and

---

[1]Thwarted in his attempt to secure new and more comprehensive antitrust legislation from the Congress, President Theodore Roosevelt dug up the almost forgotten Sherman Anti-Trust Act of 1890, which forbade the formation of "combinations or conspiracies in restraint of trade." In 1902, Roosevelt used this act against the Northern Securities Company, a railway combine created by J.P. Morgan, John D. Rockefeller, Edward H. Harriman, and James Hill. In the following seven years, Roosevelt brought suit against 43 other major corporations under the Sherman Act.

reserves to any single customer. It is therefore customary for large American corporations to have several bankers, by contrast with British and European companies, who usually have close ties only with a single bank. Similarly, investment banks and securities firms in the U.S. were forced by the sheer size of the American market to develop techniques for spreading underwriting risks and to create networks for the distribution and trading of securities on a nationwide scale.

All of these continental financial skills have proved highly adaptable to international use. Indeed, the techniques for issuing Eurobonds, for trading them in the secondary market, and for syndicating Eurocredits owe more to American practice than to any other. Moreover, New York did in fact become the world's leading center during the 1920s, the only time between the two world wars when an international capital market functioned on any significant scale. It is true that this period was characterized by the irresponsible marketing of many foreign loans which subsequently went into default, leaving American investors with a suspicion of foreign issues which has not been completely dispelled to the present day. But this legacy of suspicion was not strong enough to stop New York from reemerging as the world's leading center during the late 1950s and early 1960s, until controls were imposed on the outflow of capital from the United States for the sake of preserving the dollar at the center of a fixed exchange-rate system. Those controls contributed more than any other factor to the evolution of offshore international capital markets in Eurobonds and Eurocredits. And those markets had become so well established by the time American capital controls were lifted at the beginning of 1974, that only some of the business driven out of New York returned.

In summary, there are no deeply rooted historical reasons why New York did not become the main center of the international capital market. It was stopped from consolidating this natural role by American controls which created powerful competition from offshore capital markets. The point can be amplified, if it needs to be, by looking back to the First World War, when the United States first became the world's biggest capital exporter, and then dividing the years since that time into eight periods. Those periods are:

1. World War I, when the international capital market went into hibernation.

2. The 1920s, when the market revived and its center shifted, for the first time, to New York.

3. The 1930s Depression, when international capital flows virtually dried up.

4. World War II, when nearly all international capital movements were in the form of official flows.

5. About a dozen years after 1945 when official flows continued to dominate, along with foreign direct investment, leaving the international market no more than a residual role.

6. A brief period from about 1958 to 1963, when market flows revived and their center again shifted to New York.

7. The years from 1963 to 1974 when U.S. controls shut the New York market to many foreign borrowers (as well as many American borrowers), thus promoting the growth of offshore international capital markets.

8. The period after 1974, when New York was once more open to foreign borrowers, but nevertheless remained a residual center because of the entrenched competition of the newer offshore markets.

In short, New York dominated the international capital market whenever it was allowed to and whenever there was an international capital market to be dominated. And, even now, the international market remains an American market to a far larger extent than suggested merely by the volume of international financing arranged in the United States itself. The proportion of Eurobonds denominated in dollars has usually been close to two-thirds of the total, while the proportion of publicized international Eurocredits denominated in dollars has consistently been more than 95 percent of the total. The overseas offices of American investment banks and securities firms play a large part in helping to sell Eurobonds and making a secondary market for them, and American commercial banks dominate the Eurocredits market. In fact, the American financial controls of the 1960s had much the same unintended result as the antitrust action of 60 years before; American banks moved a large part of their international operations to foreign centers just as American industry had started manufacturing abroad as an alternative to exports at an earlier period.

As a result of this process, there are now two markets for international dollar debt, one of them offshore and the other in the United States. This chapter is concerned with the latter.

Although it had been planned to lift American capital export controls from the end of 1974, they were still being refined as late as July 1973, when restrictions on lending to nonresidents by banks in the U.S. were finally extended also to foreign banks in the U.S. But in the wake of the oil crisis at the end of 1973, the dismantling of controls was brought forward to January 29, 1974, so that the U.S. banking system could play its part in the recycling of oil exporting countries' newly enlarged surplus earnings. The immediate effect was dramatic. In 1974, banks in the U.S. recycled in the form of short-term loans to nonresidents about $18 billion of the $25 billion which had poured into them in the form of new short-term deposits from foreigners (mainly oil exporters). They then recycled a further $11 billion in this way in 1975 and $19 billion in 1976, but only another $3 billion in 1977, by which time the current account of the American balance of payments had moved into record deficit, with an accompanying decline of the dollar's exchange rate.

However, the lifting of American controls had a less dramatic effect on the New York foreign bond market than on international lending by banks in the U.S. Issues by previously debarred borrowers on the New York foreign bond market rose from almost nothing to over $2 billion in the three years through 1976, but the volume then struck at about that level in 1977. Moreover, the total of just under $7 billion raised by formerly debarred borrowers in the four years after the IET was lifted was small beer by any standard, representing less than one-quarter of all foreign bonds issued in New York (although one-third in 1977 itself), less than 15 percent of financing on the Eurobond market and a mere 7 percent of all international bonds sold in all markets between 1974 and 1977.

Put into historical perspective, the picture is little different. In the six years up to 1930, the heyday of New York as an international capital market, about 6\frac{1}{2}$ billion of international loans were raised there, compared with less than 3\frac{1}{2}$ billion in London, then the next biggest center. By 1930, outstanding international dollar bonds in New York totaled almost 7\frac{1}{2}$ billion, or the 1978 equivalent of more than $30 billion.

There was, unsurprisingly, almost no international borrowing on the New York market between the end of 1929 and the end of World War II. Then, between 1946 and the IET in mid-1963, about $14 billions were raised, but more than one-half went to Canadian borrowers and the World Bank, both of whom were subsequently exempted from the IET for all practical purposes. If one is therefore comparing just over $6 billion raised on the New York foreign bond market by previously debarred borrowers in the four years after the end of the IET with similar sums which such borrowers raised between 1924 and 1929, and again between 1946 and 1963, it is obvious that the ending of American controls did less than unleash floodgates. And, a truer comparison of what such sums were able to finance is, of course, obtained by adjusting them, say, on the index of U.S. wholesale prices. That done, the $6.8 billions raised between 1974 and 1977 compares with about $10 billion provided between

1946 and mid-1963 and about $30 billion (in 1978 terms) between 1924 and 1929. See Figure 21.

In summary, international borrowers shut out by the IET returned with some initial rush after the tax was lifted, but the growth in such borrowing then slowed down. The amounts remained small compared with the total of foreign bonds sold in New York and all international bond markets and also by historical standards, particularly by comparison with the amounts raised during the 1920s boom. So, in discussing the New York foreign bond market, or the Yankee bond market as it is often called, one is referring mainly to its inherent importance and potential rather than its recent size. Moreover, one is concentrating mainly on its importance and potential for others than Canadian borrowers and the World Bank, whose issues have dominated the market during the past generation, even when other borrowers were not deliberately impeded.[2] Table 31 shows the New York foreign bond market in perspective of the international bond market.

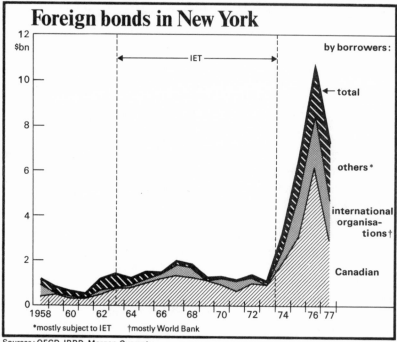

Sources: OECD, IBRD, Morgan Guaranty

FIGURE 21

---

[2]In a sense, the New York bond market has largely served as a neighborhood rather than an international market (for Canadian borrowers) and an international market only at one remove (for the World Bank, which then relends the proceeds to its member countries).

TABLE 31
NEW YORK COMPARED

$ million

	Foreign bonds in the U.S.	Foreign bonds in other centers	Eurobonds	Total
1958	1,139	302	82	1,522
1959	802	337	31	1,170
1960	637	393	29	1,058
1961	557	559	79	1,196
1962	1,186	430		1,605
1963	1,413	389	164	1,967
1964	1,191	264	719	2,174
1965	1,532	376	1,041	1,908
1966	1,435	578	1,142	3,155
1967	1,994	403	2,002	4,400
1968	1,840	1,135	3,573	6,548
1969	1,199	827	3,156	5,182
1970	1,217	378	2,966	4,561
1971	1,106	1,538	3,642	6,286
1972	1,392	2,060	6,335	9,756
1973	1,020	2,626	4,193	7,779
1974	3,291	1,432	2,134	6,857
1975	6,462	4,884	8,567	19,913
1976	10,604	7,586	14,328	32,518
1977	7,286	7,247	17,584	32,117

SOURCE: *Capital Markets Study*, OECD, for data to 1962; Morgan Guaranty for data for 1963 to 1977.

CHAPTER THIRTY-ONE
THE MECHANICS OF YANKEE BONDS

The importance of the Yankee bond market is that it is the most difficult of all markets to penetrate and the mere fact of having done so tends to raise a borrower's standing in all markets. Prestige is therefore one reason why some observers anticipate a steady if unspectacular growth in this market, through borrowers seeking the ultimate accolade of acceptance by it. For instance, the $350 million raised by the British government's first Yankee bond borrowing in April 1978 was trifling in terms of Britain's needs, or ability to obtain money elsewhere. Market prestige, rather than money alone, was what the British government wanted.

Another reason for anticipating growth is that the high entry costs are justified only for foreign borrowers intending to make continuing use of the market, once in. The disclosure documents required by the Securities and Exchange Commission are far larger and more detailed than the prospectuses provided in the Eurobond market. Preparing an SEC prospectus for the first time can therefore be very costly, especially when a foreign borrower has to adapt to U.S. accounting practices for that purpose. Moreover, Wall Street law fees tend to be high compared with those elsewhere.

Presentation costs remain comparatively high even for borrowers who have become established in the U.S. market, although they are then much lower than the exceptional costs of preparing an SEC prospectus for the first time. In the autumn of 1977, the New York Federal Reserve Bank estimated the routine legal, printing, and other costs "necessary to satisfy the registration requirements of the SEC" at about $\frac{1}{4}$ percent on issues of over $100 million, rising to 1 percent on those below $10 million. This range of $100,000 to more than $250,000 compares with costs which are reported to vary narrowly around $50,000 in the Eurobond market, irrespective of the size of an issue.

However, presentation costs are not an important obstacle. Except perhaps for borrowers incurring the special expenses of using the U.S. market for the first time, relatively high presentation costs are more than offset by significantly lower management fees and selling commissions than in other markets (see below). A far greater deterrent than cost is that many foreign borrowers are reluctant to make the disclosures the SEC requires, "particularly about directors' salaries and sales by lines of business," according to an unpublished study by the New York Federal Reserve Bank at the end of 1976.

It is true that foreign borrowers can, like U.S. borrowers, circumvent the need for SEC disclosures by private placement among no more than 35 "large and knowledgeable" investors who can reasonably be assumed to have access to the same kind of information which a registration statement would provide, and who can be assumed also to be able to fend for themselves. But such private placement obviously misses the prestige which goes with a public issue.

Whether the scrutiny of U.S. credit rating agencies such as Moody's or Standard and Poor's represents another daunting hurdle is a matter of some disagreement. The convention is that a rating by Moody's (Aaa, for example) precedes one by Standard and Poor's (AAA), as in a prime credit, rated Aaa/AAA. The first four categories, through Baa/BBB, are classified by both agencies as being of "investment grade," meaning that interest and principle are considered secure, although the last of these categories is said by Moody's to have "some speculative characteristics" and by Standard and Poor's as being on the "borderline" between sound investment and speculation. Moody's then goes all the way down to C, for highly speculative issues, some of which are in default, while Standard and Poor's goes down as far as DDD, DD, and D for bonds in default but with differences in salvage value.[1]

Foreign governments dislike the need for rating and foreign borrowers have been known to withdraw quietly rather than accept the stigma of anything less than a triple A. Nor are foreign borrowers generally acceptable to the New York market with less than the highest rating, except for familiar Canadian names which are acceptable at double A or even, in rare cases, a notch or two below. However, American rating agencies are commercial organizations anxious to secure business, and some European bankers claim to have the impression, whether rightly or wrongly, that the agencies have shown some willingness to make

---

[1]Burton Zwick, "The Market for Corporate Bonds," *Quarterly Review,* Federal Reserve Bank of New York, Autumn 1977.

distinctions, based on realistic differences, between the standards adopted toward U.S. and other borrowers. Rating is not, of course, legally compulsory and some borrowers have gone into the market unrated, Brazilian and Mexican borrowers among them. But they pay a considerable cost in having to concede returns of up to 200 basis points above those on prime Australian issues, 250 points above those on World Bank issues, and all of 350 basis points above U.S. Treasury bonds.

However, for those foreign borrowers able to clear the hurdles, there are considerable advantages provided by the breadth and depth of the U.S. capital market. As against an average size of about $40 million and an average maturity of less than ten years for new Eurobond issues in 1976 and 1977, maturities of up to 30 years are possible in New York, issues of $100 million are common, and very much larger issues are by no means exceptional. Aside from the World Bank, which has regularly secured 25-year money in the Yankee bond market, the European Investment Bank, the European Coal and Steel Community, and the Inter-American Development Bank have all done the same. European and Australasian borrowers have frequently secured 20-year funds in New York and even a relatively lesser known borrower like the Republic of Iceland sold a 15-year bond issue in New York in 1977, which is close to the longest maturity available to any borrower in the Eurobond market, and a rarity at that.

The greater breadth of New York is also particularly noticeable in the narrower spreads of the secondary market. Dealer spreads between "asked" prices demanded by sellers and "bid" prices offered by prospective buyers range from $\frac{1}{8}$ to $\frac{1}{2}$ point in the New York secondary market for bonds (and as little as $\frac{1}{16}$ point on the most actively traded U.S. government securities). By contrast, such spreads in the Eurobond market range from $\frac{1}{8}$ point on the most actively traded issues to as much as 2 full percentage points.

Besides the greater depth and breadth of the New York primary and secondary bond markets compared with the Eurobond market, there is also far stiffer competition among managers and underwriters of bond issues. As a result, management fees and commissions tend to be less than 1 percent compared with up to $2\frac{1}{2}$ percent in the Eurobond market and as much as 4 percent in the Zurich market. Moreover, American underwriters have a quaint habit of actually underwriting instead of collecting their fees without underwriting, as in the Eurobond market.

In the U.S. market the flotation cost, or the spread between the public price of newly issued bonds and the proceeds to the borrower, is normally about $\frac{7}{8}$ percent (0.875 percent) on highly graded new issues.

This comprises a fee of 0.175 percent to the investment banks and securities firms managing the issue (compared with management fees of 0.375 to 0.5 percent in the Eurobond market), plus underwriting fees of 0.2 percent (0.375 to 0.5 percent in the Eurobond market) and selling commissions of 0.5 percent (1.25 to 1.5 percent in the Eurobond market).

The way this works is illustrated by the example of an issue of $1,000 bonds which it has been agreed to sell to the public at face value, or par. The managers of the issue will buy these bonds from the borrower in some agreed proportion at $991.25 each (that is, at face value minus 0.875 percent for management, underwriting, and selling concessions). This $991.25 represents also the proceeds to the borrower. The managers will then sell some of their bonds to their own investment clients at $1,000 each; they will sell other bonds to underwriters at $993 (face value less 0.7 percent underwriting and selling concessions); and they will sell still others at $995 each (face value less 0.5 percent selling commission) to investment banks and securities firms who are members of the selling group, but who are not underwriters.

As long as the selling syndicate remains in being, managers, underwriters, and selling group members are under a contractual obligation to sell the new bonds to the investment public only at or above the agreed issuing price, in this case par. They may not get rid of bonds below this agreed price. Any member of the syndicate unable to sell his full allotment on the agreed terms returns his unsold bonds to the "pot" run by the managers for the syndicate as a whole, and those bonds are then sold by other syndicate members who do have customers for them. When the entire issue has been sold, or all except an irreducible minimum, the syndicate is disbanded, and syndicate members are released from their contractual obligation. Any bonds from the "pot" which are still left unsold are returned on a proportionate basis to syndicate members who did not sell their full allotments. At that stage, they are free to get rid of any remaining unsold bonds in the secondary market below issue price, if that proves necessary.

In theory the Eurobond market behaves in the same way, but in fact it does not. Underwriters and selling banks in the Eurobond market often dump bonds below issue price at the time of issue, their large underwriting fees and selling commissions allowing them to do this while still retaining some profit (a selling bank in the Eurobond market will get its bonds for as little as $985 each, compared with $995 in the New York market). In the New York market, smaller selling commissions leave less room for dumping, except at a loss. More important is that such delinquency can be traced in the New York market, where all bonds are registered, so that the managers can discover which selling banks have breached their contract by selling below the agreed issue price. Any selling banks doing this therefore face penalties for breach of contract and run a very real risk of not being invited into future syndicates.

In the Eurobond market, dumping is easy not only because of the much larger underwriting and selling concessions. It is also almost undetectable, because the bearer bonds do not carry the names of the sellers and holders. Moreover, the newly issued bonds pass through the clearing system in a way which makes it almost impossible to trace the sellers by the serial numbers on the bonds. And, even when delinquency is occasionally detected, or at least strongly suspected, it is usually passed over in pained silence for the sake of not disturbing friendly relations between banks.

Indeed, in the Eurobond market, clauses in syndication contracts stipulating minimum prices at which new issues might be sold to investors were abandoned in 1976 because they had proved unenforceable. The importance of this difference of practice is that issues are much more finely priced in New York than in the Eurobond market, where banks tend to cement cosy relations with each other at the expense of borrowers and investors. The borrower in New York is not embarrassed by seeing the price of a new issue drop significantly immediately on issue. Nor is a borrower annoyed by seeing it rise significantly above the agreed issue price (which means that the funds could have been raised more cheaply than the managing banks had advised).

The investor in New York may not have the occasional thrill of a large immediate rise in the price of his new security (although issues are often so priced as to give him the satisfaction of a modest rise in the after-market price). But neither does the investor in New York find himself with a security which has dropped sharply in price before he has even taken delivery, as often happens in the Eurobond market. Above all, practice in New York ensures that all subscribers to a new bond issue are treated equally, by contrast with the Eurobond market where investors receive new issues at widely varying prices, according to their muscle.

The only defense sometimes made of the practice in the Eurobond market is that higher fees and selling commissions to bank syndicates take the place of what might otherwise be higher interest coupons. Maybe, but the American practice seems more straightforward and fairer to borrowers and investors.

It is reasonable to add that while the American bond market is open to public issues only by the most highly rated foreign borrowers, even they usually have to concede slightly higher interest coupons than comparable American borrowers. This is partly because the American investment public remains chary of almost all international borrowers other than Canadian borrowers and the World Bank, on a mixture of inertia and lingering folk memories of the 1920s. Indeed, even the World Bank spent its first 20 years under the presidency of two highly orthodox American private bankers, Eugene Black and David Woods, painstakingly building up a reputation for respectability in the markets.

It is also true that foreign borrowers sometimes have to pay slightly more in the New York than the Eurobond market. But in such cases, it tends to be the apparent rather than the true cost which is higher, for the reasons argued above, namely that a lower interest coupon in the Eurobond market may be more than offset by the higher flotation costs.

Because of the wariness of American investors, large portions of foreign bond issues in New York continue to be taken up by international investors, as from 1946 to 1963, but by contrast with the roaring 1920s, when American investors were all agog to get into foreign bonds along with their plunge into Wall Street and Florida swampland. International investors are often ready enough to buy securities issued by their governments in foreign currencies and foreign markets, being reasonably sure that their governments will honor international debt and that their governments are, moreover, powerless to debase currencies other than their own.

All that said, a potential remains and not just because of the prestige conferred in all markets on those borrowers able to secure acceptance by the New York market. One reason given by those who foresee a growth in the Yankee bond market, though perhaps a gradual rather than dramatic one, is the prospect of an increasing shift into the United States and the dollar over the longer term, partly on political uncertainties elsewhere and partly because of the world's drift into protectionism, which provides an inducement for non-American international companies to move some or more of their manufacturing to the United States in a reversal of the pattern of the past generation, when foreign investment in America has been mainly portfolio investment while U.S. investment abroad has been mainly direct.

There are other reasons for anticipating such a change of trend, among them alterations in exchange relationships and relative labor costs since the late 1960s, which have made the United States more attractive for foreign direct investment (and vice versa). Moreover, companies in some northwestern European countries have begun running up against the limits of social tolerance for the import of foreign labor and have become readier to export capital instead. Moreover, they have tended to prefer direct investments in the world's biggest market, the United States, rather than in the uncertain fringe areas of Europe from which they have been drawing labor. The implication for the Yankee bond market is that if such developments continue, more international companies may wish to raise capital in New York to finance their entry into the United States and, thereafter, to emphasize their American presence and the American identity of their U.S. operations.

In closing, a summary can be attempted of some of the advantages and drawbacks of the Yankee bond market for borrowers and investors.

The Borrowers: Advantages

1. The ability to raise far larger amounts of fixed-interest capital for significantly longer maturities than in any other international market.

2. Finer pricing of new issues so that the borrower is less likely than in other markets to find himself paying a higher interest coupon than subsequent trading shows he need to have paid.

3. The prestige conferred by a public Yankee bond issue in all markets, which has the practical effect of reinforcing the borrower's credit standing in other markets and reducing the return he needs to offer in other markets.

4. The emphasizing of an American presence for foreign borrowers using the Yankee bond market to finance direct investment in the U.S.

The Borrowers: Drawbacks

1. The hurdles of SEC disclosure requirements and the scrutiny of the U.S. credit rating agencies (although clearing those hurdles brings the advantages cited above).

2. High costs of entering the U.S. market for first-time borrowers (although relatively higher presentation costs thereafter are more than offset by lower flotation costs in the form of management and underwriting fees and selling commissions to issuing syndicates).

The Investors: Advantages

1. By contrast with the 1920s, public issues for foreign borrowers in the U.S. are now confined to prime names, with the additional safeguard of SEC standards, which did not exist 50 years ago.

2. Besides the generally higher quality of international issues on the Yankee bond as compared with the Eurobond market, investors

in Yankee bonds are assured of receiving new issues on equal terms, unlike the Eurobond market, where favored investors pay less than others.

3. The secondary market in Yankee bonds is more efficient than that for Eurobonds; bigger trades can be affected more quickly and at narrower margins between buyers and sellers.

4. Income from investment in Yankee bonds by investors not resident in the United States is exempt from withholding for tax, in the same way as nonresident investment in all international bonds (Eurobonds and traditional foreign bonds sold in other centers). It is true that Yankee bonds held in the U.S. are registered, but they are usually registered in the name of the financial intermediary through which the investor has acquired them and through which he or she holds them. The investor's anonymity can therefore be preserved, and Yankee bonds held outside the U.S. in European clearing centers, are held in the form of bearer bonds providing no means of tracing the holders even indirectly. In other words, the opportunities offered for tax evasion by investors not resident in the United States are almost the same as those offered to international investors by any form of international bond (which includes U.S. resident investors in Eurobonds and foreign bonds issued in Europe).

5. Although Yankee bonds offer no special tax advantage for U.S. resident investors, they do benefit from the fact that returns are often higher than those on comparable U.S. domestic bonds because of the need for foreign borrowers to offer a special bait in the U.S. market.

The Investors: Drawbacks

1. Although the secondary market is better than that for Eurobonds, it is smaller and therefore less liquid than the secondary market for domestic U.S. bonds.

2. Regulatory restraints and self-imposed limitations curtail investment in nonresident securities by U.S. institutional investors to a range which is commonly between 1 percent and 5 percent of their total portfolios but, given the size of those portfolios, that still leaves considerable sums available for such investment.

CHAPTER THIRTY-TWO
THE SWISS TURNTABLE

The amount of international capital provided in Swiss francs is nothing short of astounding. During the five years through 1977 it totaled the equivalent of nearly $25 billion, or more than one-half the sum raised during that period in the distinct and separate Eurobond market (in which Swiss franc issues are not allowed by the Swiss authorities). Indeed, it has to be emphasized, at the cost of laboring the point, that this chapter deals exclusively with international capital mobilized in the form of Swiss francs, as distinct from the very large amounts marshaled in other currencies by the Swiss banking system.

In some years, Swiss franc capital exports have been the equivalent of almost 13 percent of Switzerland's gross national product, or proportionately more than five times as much as the dollar component of international capital market flows.[1] This obviously does not mean that Switzerland exported more than a one-seventh of national output as capital to the rest of the world. On the contrary, it means that the Swiss authorities had found ways of encouraging the reexporting of international capital almost as quickly as it flooded into their small and open economy. How this is done helps to explain the instruments and terms available to international borrowers and investors in the Swiss franc market, so the background is worth describing.

The problem posed by international capital flows for a country of

---

[1] In 1976, Swiss franc capital exports of Sw.fr. 19 billion were equivalent to 12.8 percent of Swiss GNP of Sw.fr. 148 billion. In the same year, international bonds and Eurocredits in dollars approximated $45 billion, or $2\frac{1}{2}$ percent of American GNP of $1,700 billion. In the American case, unlike the Swiss, most of this represented, at least indirectly, capital exports rather than reexports.

Switzerland's size and attractions grew so large during the 1960s and particularly during the 1970s, that it proved almost unmanageable. Switzerland became the first country to conquer the inflation which swept the world during the early- and mid-1970s, by getting annual consumer price increases back below 2 percent from 1976 onward. But this was achieved only at the cost of a rising exchange rate which put traditional exports at a growing disadvantage in world markets. There was also a tight monetary policy which created a deeper recession than experienced by any other industrial country (the *volume* of Switzerland's national output fell by no less than 9 percent between 1974 and 1976).

Anyone who asks why the Swiss authorities did not respond to the hot-money problem by simply stopping nonresidents from acquiring Swiss franc assets can be answered twice over: It was believed to be impossible for any duration, and, had it been possible, it might have damaged Switzerland's international banking business, on which the country depends very heavily for foreign income.

To start with the second and more academic of these points, it is perfectly true that Swiss banks carry on an extremely large international business in currencies other than their own. The trust funds which they administer, mostly for foreign customers in foreign currencies, had risen to well above $100 billion by 1977,[2] contributing to the formidable placing power of Swiss banks in the Eurobond market. Swiss banks are also very active in the Eurocurrencies market and, through their foreign branches, in the Eurocredits market. However, it is at least arguable that international investors might place less money with Swiss banks if they were stopped from putting any money into Swiss francs. Moreover, if Swiss banks were forced to conduct all their international business in foreign currencies alone, there might at least be a danger of turning Switzerland into an Alpine variant of the Cayman Islands.

In the last resort, an international financial center cannot wholly shut foreigners out of its currency if it is to remain more than a mail drop.

---

[2]Fiduciary funds placed by Swiss banks in the names of the banks for clients at the clients' risk totaled Sw.fr. 57 billion, then about $23 billion, at the end of 1976. In addition, Swiss banks administer advisory and discretionary funds which they invest for clients in the clients' names. The total of these is unknown, but very well placed estimates in Switzerland put them at anywhere between Sw.fr. 150 billion and Sw.fr. 350 billion in 1977, or between $60 billion and $140 billion. Trust funds are invested for clients in all of the world's major money and capital markets. They are not included in bank balance sheets because they are neither assets nor liabilities of the banks; they are funds administered by banks as agents for fees.

The British authorities, belatedly converted to active discouragement of the international asset use of sterling, still left the London domestic capital market open to nonresident investors (although they did reduce its attractions from 1977 by withdrawing certain tax exemptions for nonresidents). In similarly leaving nonresidents access to some Swiss franc assets the Swiss authorities have, among other things, left options open for an unpredictable future, because there have been times when Switzerland has needed to attract rather than to repel foreign funds. This was true during the Wall Street boom of the 1920s and again during the Cold War (when Latin American investors, in particular, measuring the distance between Moscow and Zurich, nervously shifted large sums to New York). Indeed, supervision of Swiss franc capital exports was introduced shortly after the First World War with the original aim of limiting such exports to ensure sufficient funds for the domestic economy, and no one can say for sure that this particular wheel will never turn again.

More practically relevant have been the difficulties of stopping nonresidents from acquiring some Swiss franc assets, although many attempts to limit such acquisitions were made. A negative interest levy on nonresident Swiss franc bank balances was introduced at an annual 12 percent in 1974 and increased to a punitive 40 percent the following year. It applied to any increase of such balances of more than Sw.fr. 100,000 above their level at October 31, 1974. But, from February 1978, it was applied to all nonresident balances of above Sw.fr. 5 million, including foreign official balances (which had the effect of forcing considerable disinvestment by official and other large nonresident holders).[3]

At various times, the Swiss authorities attempted also to limit nonresident investment in Swiss franc securities, as from 1972 to 1974. And, although this was not a great success, new limits were tried in February 1978 in sheer desperation at the currency's renewed appreciation (but these were relaxed within months).

On the whole, the Swiss authorities have taken the view that it is impossible to put a complete stop to nonresident acquisition of Swiss franc assets for any length of time. The more consistent policy has therefore been to foster special markets which can be controlled as an alternative to unregulated offshore markets (one of which does in fact exist in the form of Euro-Swiss francs, which accounted for about 5 percent of the gross foreign currency, or Eurocurrency assets, of European banks in the mid- and late-1970s).

---

[3]Up to February 1978, a nonresident balance of, say, Sw.fr. 10 million at October 31, 1974, was subject to the negative levy only above Sw.fr. 10.1 million.

In leaving some sectors of the Swiss franc capital market open to nonresident borrowers with favorable conditions for nonresident investors, the Swiss authorities acted in the tradition of city police condoning vice in designated areas where it can be kept under watch, rather than have it proliferate underground.

In the case of the Swiss franc, some areas are clearly marked "out of bounds" for nonresidents, such as bank balances, previously mentioned. In addition, the central bank, like the British and Belgian authorities, does not allow the use of its currency for Eurobond issues for fear of losing control over issuing volume, although the German authorities have found a way of allowing the use of their currency for Eurobond issues without losing this control (the only Swiss franc Eurobond issue ever to slip under the net was Sw.fr. 60 million, then about $14 million, for the City of Copenhagen in 1963).

In other areas, nonresident investment is formally restricted, as in property, and in still others it is effectively deterred, as by the 35 percent withholding for tax on nonresident income from Swiss franc domestic bonds. This applies also to nonresident dividend income from Swiss franc domestic equities, although that is probably a lesser deterrent given that foreign investors in Swiss equities rely mainly on capital and above all currency appreciation. Here, however, the size of the Swiss equities market provides its own limitation, although the authorities placed various restrictions on nonresident investment in Swiss domestic securities from 1972 to 1974 and again in 1978.

Three market sectors are open to nonresident borrowers and partly, on special terms, to nonresident investors. These are also the three market sectors in which the Swiss National Bank concentrates its management of the volume of net capital exports. They are Swiss franc foreign bonds issued for nonresident borrowers in the domestic market, Swiss franc notes privately placed for nonresident borrowers, and Swiss franc bank credits extended for more than one year to nonresident borrowers or to finance exports of Swiss capital goods.[4] Nonresident investors in these bonds and notes are exempt from Swiss withholding for tax and foreign banks may participate with Swiss banks in the granting of medium-term Swiss franc credits extended to nonresident borrowers.

These three market sectors will be described in detail presently, but they have certain features in common designed to allow the Swiss

[4]Official authorization is needed also for certain Swiss bank credits to nonresidents, even when provided in currencies other than the Swiss franc.

authorities to limit proliferation of the use of their franc as a volatile international asset currency and as an official reserve currency for other countries, and also to allow the Swiss central bank to regulate the volume of net capital flows.

Nonresident asset use is restricted firstly by the fact that Swiss franc foreign bonds have a face value of at least Sw.fr. 5,000 and up to Sw.fr. 50,000, the equivalent of $2,500 to $25,000 at early 1978 exchange rates, compared with the usual face value of $1,000 of Eurodollar bonds and DM 1,000, or about $500 on Deutschemark external bonds. The privately placed notes are required to be in units of at least Sw.fr. 50,000 and are usually sold only in large blocks.

The use of these securities and bank credits as volatile instruments is limited by the requirement that investors in notes and foreign banks participating in Swiss franc credits to nonresident borrowers hold their investments to maturity, while early repayment on the part of borrowers is allowed only in special circumstances. A general prohibition on the placing of notes with foreign banks and monetary authorities is designed to prevent their being used as international bank assets or as foreign official reserve holdings.

There are also conditions intended to give the Swiss central bank control over the volume of net capital flows. The basic principles, very simplified, are these:

1. When a nonresident borrows Swiss francs from a Swiss resident and converts the proceeds into foreign currency, there is a net outflow of funds from Switzerland.

2. When a nonresident borrows Swiss francs from another nonresident and converts the proceeds into foreign exchange, the net effect on the Swiss balance of payments is neutral.

3. When a nonresident borrows Swiss francs from a resident without converting into foreign exchange the effect is likewise neutral.

4. When a nonresident borrows Swiss francs from another nonresident without converting the proceeds, the net effect is an inflow of funds into Switzerland. Naturally the reverse occurs upon repayment, so the mechanism has some features of a treadmill built into it, with a need to encourage new issues to drain off liquidity as old issues are redeemed.

The authorities try to manage the volume of net capital flows partly by regulating new issuing volume of Swiss franc foreign bonds and, occasionally, of note placements. The proportion of proceeds which borrowers are obliged to convert into foreign currencies is varied periodically and so are the proportions of new foreign bonds and notes which must be allocated to resident and nonresident investors. By these means very large capital exports were induced to offset the hot money which poured into Switzerland when the Bretton Woods system collapsed in 1971 and again in the wake of sterling's weakness in 1976 and the dollar's in 1977. On the other hand, capital exports were reduced in the recession and balance of payments downturn of 1974 to ensure sufficient funds for Swiss domestic requirements.

Whether the Swiss central bank has found the means for managing capital flows in all circumstances is naturally open to argument. It is a sobering thought that the whole apparatus has worked largely on the masochistic willingness of foreign borrowers to acquire liabilities in the world's strongest currency to finance assets generating weaker currencies. Why they should have done this is not easily explained except by the surmise that they were repeatedly mistaken in believing that the Swiss franc had topped out.

Less open to debate than any means used to manage capital flows is the necessity of trying to manage them somehow, given Switzerland's exceptional exposure to such flows with their disruptive potential for domestic liquidity, price stability, and the exchange rate.

The difficulties posed generally by international capital flows are referred to elsewhere in this book and need be recapitulated here only briefly. When the current account of a country's balance of payments weakens, capital flight adds to the drain of liquidity and the depression of the exchange rate in the absence of offsetting measures. Conversely, when a country is in current surplus (which happens to be Switzerland's chronic situation), capital inflows add to domestic liquidity and upward pressure on the exchange rate, again assuming no counteraction. Up to a point, capital flows virtuously reinforce adjustment in depressing the domestic liquidity, domestic demand, and exchange rate of deficit countries while having the reverse effects on surplus countries. A problem arises only when capital flows exceed what is necessary for adjustment, as they often do, at least temporarily, once they have been triggered. When this results from fluctuations in balance of payments between countries passing through different stages of the business cycle, temporarily distorted capital flows can usually be left to market correction.

However, in Switzerland's case the problem is not cyclical but structural, meaning an enduring one, arising partly from the unbroken succession of current surpluses from 1966 onward but, to a far greater extent, from the strong pull exerted on international capital by a stable and neutral democracy, with special banking secrecy thrown in as a bonus. And that merits a brief digression.

Under Swiss law, breach of banking confidentiality is not merely a civil offense, as in most countries, but a criminal one. All customers are equally protected and few need the added safeguard of the famous numbered account, although many enjoy the mystique and supposed prestige of having one. The sole advantage of a numbered account is that the holder's identity is known only to a tiny circle of executives within a bank, with a reduced danger of leaks and blackmail for internationally known customers. Ordinary customers hardly need this special protection.

It was long possible at some Swiss banks to open an account in any name with any signature to match and no questions asked. But this glaring loophole for criminal and terrorist funds was closed under an agreement between the members of the Swiss Bankers' Association and the Swiss National Bank in 1977. The agreement also requires banks to refuse funds reasonably suspected of being the proceeds of crime, leaving much to the imagination. However, the definition of crime specifically excludes evasion of tax and foreign exchange controls of other countries. Swiss bankers are not expected to satisfy themselves that their customers have committed no such breaches and nor, in practice, do bankers in other countries. Banking secrecy applies equally to all accounts in Switzerland, whether in Swiss francs or foreign currencies, and it helps to attract both.

This international pull of the banking sector became a festering political issue during the 1974 recession and the economic stagnation which followed. The Swiss electorate welcomed the stabilization of prices, but resented the high exchange rate which had helped to bring down inflation. This was because of the rising exchange rate's depressing effect on traditional export industries such as tourism, machinery, chemicals, and textiles, and not least, on the watchmakers of the Jura, whose skills were being threatened also by the innovation of the electronic watch.

Although the impact on domestic employment was cushioned partly by the fact of a declining native population and partly by Switzerland's ability to send many foreign workers home, the economy's failure to start expanding again was widely blamed on the rising exchange rate which was, in its turn, blamed partly on the magnet for international capital provided by Switzerland's banking sector (see Table 32). Indeed, some modification of the growth of banking in relation to other eco-

TABLE 32
SWISS CAPITAL EXPORTS IN PERSPECTIVE

$ billion

	World market			Swiss capital exports
	International bonds	Eurocredits	Total	Total
1973	6.2	21.9	28.1	3.0
1974	5.9	29.3	29.3	1.9
1975	16.6	21.0	37.6	4.6
1976	27.2	28.9	56.1	7.6
1977	29.0	40.8	69.8	7.7
1978	28.6	70.2	98.8	12.2

*International bonds are Eurobonds plus all foreign bonds other than Swiss franc issues. Swiss capital exports are foreign bonds, notes, and bank credits in Swiss francs. Figures rounded. Swiss franc totals converted into dollars at average exchange rates for each year.
SOURCE: Swiss National Bank and Morgan Guaranty.

nomic sectors was advocated by none less than the president of the Swiss National Bank, Dr. Fritz Leutwiler.

The task of trying to stabilize the exchange rate is therefore politically and not merely economically important in Switzerland. The option of creating money (and inflation) to hold down the exchange rate is not a realistic one, leaving the deflection of capital flows as the only alternative. And, by inducing capital to move out almost as quickly as it flooded in, the Swiss National Bank was often able to finance most of its foreign exchange intervention. In other words, the central bank did not have to print Swiss francs in order to buy dollars and thus hold down the Swiss exchange rate (at least to the limits to which it was held down). Nearly all the money was provided by the obligation for foreign borrowers of Swiss francs to convert their proceeds into dollars as soon as they got them.

The transformation of capital inflows into capital exports for the sake of the exchange rate might be called the negative side of the management of capital flows, the warding off of unwelcome pressure in as far as it can be warded off. But there is also what might be called the positive use of capital exports as an instrument of domestic economic management, given the peculiar limitations on the use of fiscal and monetary policy in Switzerland.

The constraint on fiscal policy is that the Federation has few entrenched rights to raise revenue except for a national defense levy and customs duties. Most of the latter are quaintly based on the weight rather than the value of imports and have therefore produced a relatively declining revenue, but they cannot easily be changed without protests from Switzerland's trading partners and, more to the point, the approval of the Swiss electorate in a referendum. The Federation's very ability to raise other revenue, by means of a turnover or sales tax, is subject to periodic confirmation by referendum and the rate at which sales tax is levied is likewise subject to approval or veto by referendum. But although the electorate has often proved unwilling to vote funds, it still expects services from Berne, including the plugging of cantonal budgets which started moving into the red in the mid-1960s, followed by the Federal budget from the mid-1970s.

The limitations on fiscal policy make monetary policy doubly important, but this too is constrained. Switzerland's sacrosanct farm and house mortgage rates are linked to the cost of living index. Other interest rates cannot be allowed to move too far out of line. This makes it difficult to use interest rates for monetary policy. Control of the money supply by other means therefore remains as a principal instrument of economic management, and capital exports policy is a very important part of the control of the money supply.

The control of international capital flows, introduced shortly after the First World War to ensure sufficient funds for the domestic economy, was originally carried out under a gentlemen's agreement between Swiss banks and the central bank. It was given legal force by the Federal Law on Banks and Savings Banks of 1934, amended in 1971. The law lays down that the central bank's authorization is needed for all international Swiss franc transactions exceeding Sw.fr. 10 million and having maturities of more than one year and less than ten years. The law provides also for the safeguarding of Switzerland's "economic interests." When these are thought to be at stake approval has to be sought from the federal government in Berne which has, for example, turned down applications for Swiss franc loans to South Africa and to foreign companies thought to be in excessive international competition with Swiss companies.

The law itself does not apply to Swiss franc transactions of less than 12 months, so as not to impede financing of Switzerland's current trade. But the gap left here for hot-money flows is partly plugged by the negative interest levy on nonresident Swiss franc bank balances. Similarly, while the law itself does not apply to transactions involving less than Sw.fr. 10 million, the central bank has periodically declared "mini" nonresident borrowings below this ceiling to be "undesirable," effectively stopping them; and in the case of notes placed for nonresident borrowers authorization is required in practice for issues of Sw.fr. 3 million upward.

CHAPTER THIRTY-THREE
THE MECHANICS OF THE SWISS INTERNATIONAL MARKET

This chapter provides a more detailed description of Swiss franc foreign bonds, notes, and the external bank credits.

SWISS FRANC FOREIGN BONDS

The issuing volume of new Swiss franc bonds for nonresident borrowers is closely controlled to ensure a digestible flow fitting in with the requirements of the domestic capital market. A new issues calendar sets out every six months in advance the aggregate of foreign bond issues which will be allowed, the number of individual issues, and ceilings on individual issues. This close control of issuing volume is a disadvantage for borrowers, who often face long lines.

Authorization is required for all issues and is usually given only for those exceeding Sw.fr. 10 million. Eight-year maturities are occasionally allowed, but usually only those of ten years and longer. Issues of Sw.fr. 50 to 100 million and 15-year maturities are common. Early repayment is not allowed before the original maturity has run at least one-half its course and at earliest after six years. An exceptional circumstance in which earlier redemption is permitted is when a change of law in the borrower's country imposes withholding for tax on coupon interest.

The proportion of their proceeds which nonresident borrowers are required to convert out of Swiss francs upon receipt has been varied by the Swiss authorities according to their need to encourage the reexport of capital. When hot money was flooding into Switzerland in 1971 and again from the end of 1974 onward, borrowers were required to convert their proceeds in full. But for a time during 1974, when Switzerland wanted to secure foreign funds, the requirement to convert the proceeds of borrowing out of Swiss francs was suspended altogether. Between these extremes, borrowers were required to convert half their proceeds in 1972. Whatever the proportion, the conversion has to be made through the Swiss National Bank into dollars at the highest Swiss franc exchange rate against the dollar on the day the proceeds are received. It is then left to borrowers needing currencies other than the dollar to reconvert in the market, the Swiss objective of pushing them out of the Swiss franc having been achieved.

Issuing costs are described as a "confidential matter" by the Swiss banking cartel, but market reports put them as high as 4 percent, compared with management fees and selling commissions totaling at most $2\frac{1}{2}$ percent in the Eurobond market and as little as 0.875 percent on corporate bond issues in New York.

The return on foreign Swiss franc bonds is usually 75 to 100 basis point above that on Swiss domestic bonds, reflecting the lower credit rating given by the Swiss market even to the most highly rated non-Swiss borrowers. In the past, when this interest differential threatened to attract resident funds from domestic to foreign Swiss franc bonds, the authorities laid down maximum proportions of new foreign bond issues that might be placed with resident investors. However, since the bonds are traded on the Swiss stock exchanges, where any investor can pick them up in the secondary market, such quota restrictions on new issue placements did not appear very effective and they were abandoned after 1974 (although temporarily reintroduced in February 1978).

Most foreign Swiss franc bonds have been issued for Austrian, Scandinavian, and French borrowers, who are rated in the market in approximately that order. During most of the 1960s and 1970s the disadvantages to borrowers of being locked into the appreciating Swiss franc was almost never offset by Switzerland's relatively low interest rates and the prestige of acceptance as a borrower in the exclusive Swiss market was therefore bought at a high price. Yet the foothold gained in the Swiss market would not prove particularly useful for foreign borrowers if circumstances ever changed to make the Swiss franc less strong, or even weak, because in such circumstances the Swiss authorities would almost certainly put severe restrictions on foreign Swiss franc borrowing in order to limit capital outflows.

During all the years when borrowers were doing badly by running up liabilities in the world's hardest currency, investors were obviously doing very well in acquiring Swiss franc assets. Nor did investors suffer from Swtizerland's nominally low interest rates, which are relatively high in real terms, after allowing for Switzerland's traditionally low rate of inflation. Swiss franc foreign bonds, issued in bearer form, have the advantage of providing anonymity. Their main advantage, however, is that they are the only Swiss franc assets available to nonresidents which are exempt from Switzerland's relatively high 35 percent withholding tax and at the same time extremely liquid (because of the secondary market on the Swiss stock exchanges). A limitation, though not a severe one, is that not having been registered with the Securities and Exchange Commission, Swiss franc foreign bonds are eligible for sale to U.S. investors only after the bonds have been seasoned for at least three months in the secondary market.

SWISS FRANC NOTES

The private placement of Swiss franc notes for nonresident borrowers grew rapidly from 1968 onward and was encouraged by the Swiss National Bank as a turntable for the reexport of capital inflows. Issuing volume was therefore restricted only occasionally and, even then, less closely than the new issuing volume of Swiss franc foreign bonds. For instance, in 1974 the total of new note placements was limited to 75 percent of those placed during the preceding year and the size of individual placements was limited to Sw.fr. 100 million. However, at most times no limits have been placed on the total of new placements or the size of individual placements and at no time has there been a new issues calendar, as for Swiss franc foreign bonds.

In every other respect, note placements are subject to very strict conditions. The proportion allocated to resident and nonresident investors has been periodically varied, as in the case of bonds, and so has the proportion which borrowers are required to convert out of Swiss francs, again in the same way as they are required to convert the proceeds of Swiss franc bond issues. Early repayment, as in the case of bonds, may be allowed only in special circumstances, such as the imposition of withholding for tax by the borrower's government.

However, there are several other conditions, partly to ensure that the notes do not compete unduly for Swiss resident funds with the *Kassenobligationen* (roughly equivalent to stretched out certificates of deposit for three to eight years) which Swiss banks issue in the domestic market to help them finance Swiss export credits and mortgage loans. Hence, notes placed for nonresident borrowers must have a face value of at least Sw.fr. 50,000 each (and often have to be placed in very much larger blocks), compared with the usual Sw.fr. 5,000 face value of *Kassenobligationen*. To make doubly sure, the central bank insists that the notes may not be "split" into smaller units after placement. Also designed to protect the domestic market are rules requiring strict privacy in the placement of notes for nonresident borrowers. There may be no prospectuses, leaflets, newspaper announcements, advertisements, or publicity of any kind. This tight ban on publicity at the time of placement is a disadvantage for some borrowers, anxious to broadcast their acceptance by the Swiss market to raise their standing in all markets, but it is strictly enforced and Swiss banks have at times been rebuked for leaks by the central bank. However, details sometimes emerged unavoidably from debates in the legislatures of borrowers, such as New Zealand and the Canadian province of Manitoba. And the World Bank has started to list such placements as a matter or record after the event.

Still other restrictions are designed not only to insulate the domestic market, but also to prevent the use of the notes as an international financial and official reserve asset. Thus a maximum of ten banks is allowed in any one placing syndicate, and each of these is required to place the notes firmly on its own books or with no more than 20 customers with whom it has regular business relations. This limits the number of subscribers to any new issue to 200 at most, implying an average subscription of at least Sw.fr. 500,000 or roughly $250,000 to an issue of Sw.fr. 100 million, which is a fairly common size. Clearly not a market for the small investor. But not a market for large investors either, since the Swiss authorities specifically prohibit the placement of notes with foreign financial institutions and with foreign monetary authorities. The only exception here is that notes issued for international development institutions like the World Bank, the Asian Development Bank, the Inter-American Bank, and the European Investment Bank may be placed with the monetary authorities of the Organization of Petroleum Exporting Countries.

Investors are required to hold the notes to maturity and, to make sure that they do, title to the notes must be held on the investor's behalf by the selling bank in Switzerland; the title may not be transferred to the investor's own keeping or to another bank acting for the investor. In very exceptional circumstances, application can be made to the central bank for an investor to surrender notes before maturity, but if this is granted only the bank which sold the notes may take them back for its own portfolio or for replacement with another regular customer, and the investor getting out under such special circumstances will obviously lose something on price.

Authorization is required for all placements exceeding Sw.fr. 3 million, though the average size of new issues was about Sw.fr. 75 million by the late-1970s. The special provision permitting placement of its notes with OPEC authorities allowed the World Bank to make a single issue of Sw.fr. 500 million in 1976, but the Quebec Hydroelectric Authority was able to place an issue of Sw.fr. 300 million in the same year even without this concession.

The advantage for borrowers is that they can secure larger sums more quickly and more cheaply than through the issue of Swiss franc foreign bonds, the only drawback being that they do not get the publicity and prestige of a public issue. Because there are no prospectuses and disclosure statements, no publicity, and no more than a standard legal contract, borrowers can get their money in as little as three weeks after their first exploratory telephone call to the bank they have chosen to manage their issue, as against a waiting list that has sometimes stretched as long as two years for access to the Swiss franc foreign bond market. And issuing costs, at $1\frac{3}{4}$ percent plus 0.4 percent issuing tax are comparable to those on the Eurobond market, or about one-half those on the Swiss franc foreign bond market.

Nonresident investors in the notes are exempt from Swiss withholding for tax but, unlike holders of Swiss franc foreign bonds, the investors here do not have a liquid asset.

The stipulation that investors must put up the equivalent of $25,000 at the very least and usually much more; that they must hold the notes for between three and eight years; that selling banks may place notes only with a small circle of their own clients and that they may not generally place them with foreign banks and official holders—all these conditions make this a market for a strictly limited class of investor. Not surprisingly, hardly anything is known about the investors in this market. Given that such investors are rare birds, Swiss banks are reluctant to classify, let alone name them. Investors mentioned by the market include very rich individuals plus institutions having foreseeable cash flows and international status or offshore bases, like the pension funds of international organizations and the captive insurance companies of American and multinational corporations in the Bahamas. The return on notes is generally about 1 to $1\frac{1}{2}$ percent above those on domestic *Kassenbobligationen,* but borrowers are finely graded with some Canadian issuers having to pay more than 100 basis points above the rates conceded to prime Austrian names.

SWISS FRANC BANK CREDITS

Swiss franc credits extended by bank syndicates for over one year and in amounts of Sw.fr. 10 million upwards provide foreign banks with the opportunity to acquire Swiss franc assets which is denied to them in the notes market (see Table 33).

The credits are extended to finance exports of Swiss capital goods or

TABLE 33
SWISS FRANC CAPITAL EXPORTS

($ million)

	Bonds	Notes	Bank credits	Total
1968	235	109	284	628
1969	221	511	540	1,272
1970	187	410	524	1,121
1971	465	1,175	886	2,562
1972	761	869	814	2,444
1973	907	1,075	1,000	2,982
1974	339	929	629	1,897
1975	913	2,776	962	4,650
1976	1,368	4,193	2,067	7,628
1977	1,542	3,875	2,246	7,625
1978	2,460	5,034	4,754	12,248

SOURCE: Swiss National Bank. Original data converted into dollars at average exchange rates for each year. Bank credits include those granted to finance Swiss capital goods exports and those extended to nonresident borrowers, as well as a minority in currencies other than the Swiss franc.

to nonresident borrowers and, in the latter case, foreign banks may participate. As in the case of notes and bonds, the central bank varies the proportion of their proceeds which nonresident borrowers are required to convert out of Swiss francs on receipt, and early repayment is not generally allowed.

Unlike Swiss franc foreign bonds and notes, which are fixed interest instruments, the bank credits resemble publicized Eurocredits in usually being granted at a margin above the cost of short-term finance to the banks. This margin, fixed at the start for the full maturity, usually at 0.875 to 1 percent above the cost of six-month inter-bank offered rate for Euro-Swiss francs, is adjusted every six months to reflect changes in the Euro-Swiss franc interest rate.

Foreign banks participating in these credits must give a written undertaking to the Swiss National Bank that they will hold their participations to maturity. Yet another feature distinguishing this market from the market for Eurocredits is that the managing bank alone has a contractual relationship with the borrower, the relationship of the other participants being with the managing bank. This puts an additional responsibility on the managing bank, but provides an added attraction for other participants, because their claims are on the managing banks and are thus regarded as being sounder than claims on a non-bank borrower.

CHAPTER THIRTY-FOUR
INTERNATIONAL BONDS IN FRANKFURT

The Deutschemark is the second most important currency in the international bond market. Nearly one-fifth of all international bonds (Eurobonds and foreign bonds) were issued in German currency during the nine years through 1978. And in 1978 itself, the proportion rose to about one-quarter when the steep fall of the dollar caused a shift of international bond issuing to Frankfurt and Tokyo. However, some of the fundamentals of the international Deutschemark bond market have already been discussed in Chapter 21. This chapter thus presents only some of the technical aspects of DM foreign and DM Eurobonds.

The impetus to the regular issue of DM international bonds was given by the "coupon tax" introduced by the German authorities in the early 1960s to discourage excessive capital inflows into the Deutschemark. The tax had an immediate effect on the market when announced late in 1964, although it became law only in March 1965. It is not, in fact, a tax in the conventional meaning of the word. It is a withholding for tax of part of the income of nonresident investors in DM domestic bonds; it was and remains a basic 25 percent although surcharges have periodically pushed it close to 30 percent. However, nonresident investment in the DM bonds of nonresident borrowers is exempted from the coupon tax. The effect is therefore to bar many nonresident investors from the DM domestic bond market, confining them to the external sector alone. German resident investors can switch between domestic and external DM bonds whenever sufficient yield differentials open in one over the other, but most foreign investors cannot. The exceptions are foreign institutional investors with tax-exempt status or domiciled in tax havens.

German capital controls are less extensive than those in many other countries and those applying to nonresident investors are, in any case, often evaded. For one thing, the coupon tax was not immediately applied, owing to an oversight, to global certificates covering multiple holdings by nonresidents of German domestic bonds. German banks therefore issued such certificates to large foreign investors in considerable volume until a gentlemen's agreement to stop doing so was reached under the prodding of the Deutsche Bundesbank. However, when nonresident investment in German domestic bonds was temporarily stopped during the early 1970s, a *Koffergeschäft* (suitcase business) sprang up in the smuggling of DM domestic bonds out of the country for sale to nonresidents. And such smuggling continued through most of the 1970s in domestic DM bonds with maturities of less than four years, whose legal sale to nonresidents was banned.

For international borrowers, a major distinction of German regulations is that they do not require nonresident issuers to convert the proceeds of DM bond borrowing out of Deutschemark, in the way that the Swiss, Dutch, and Japanese authorities require nonresident borrowers to convert out of their currencies. That opens the German market to a wider range of international borrowers, such as those wishing to use their proceeds for direct investment in Germany. By being able to match their currency assets and liabilities, such borrowers do not run the same exchange rate risks as many international borrowers in the Swiss, Dutch, and Japanese markets.

Another distinction is that the German authorities and issuing banks are less strict than their counterparts in some other countries in limiting their market only to the most highly rated international blue-chip borrowers. Lesser borrowers are admitted, though at a price. The very rapid expansion of borrowing on the German external bond market from 1977 was caused partly by the entry of borrowers from developing countries taking on the double burden of liabilities in an appreciating currency plus exceptionally high borrowing costs, amounting in some cases to 200 or even 250 basis points above the average of external DM bond yields. But many new borrowers were willing to pay such extremely high premiums as the price of graduating from the Eurocredits market to the greater prestige of the international bond market and for the opportunity of thus enhancing their credit standing in all markets. Moreover, their borrowing in the DM external bond market represented only a small part of their total international borrowing, so that the average of their total external debt service rose only marginally. However, despite the dual benefit of acquiring assets in an appreciating currency with very high yields, investor demand for securities of first-time borrowers in the external DM market was still limited.

As already mentioned in Chapter 21, the only important distinction between classical or traditional DM foreign bonds and DM Eurobonds is the inclusion of non-German banks in the issuing syndicates of the latter. Since the latter part of 1969, the volume of new international bond issues on the German market has been regulated to ensure a digestible flow. This control is exercised by a capital issues subcommittee on which five German banks are represented: the Deutsche Bank, the Dresdner, the Commerzbank, the Westdeutsche Landesbank, and the Bayerische Vereinsbank. German bankers make great play of this subcommittee's independence, alleging that the central bank had a "great struggle" to obtain even observer status. But bankers outside Germany are somewhat sceptical about such claims of total independence and their scepticism is supported by the admission of German bankers that "we would, of course, do nothing of which the central bank disapproves."[1]

The capital issues subcommittee works in an informal and even idiosyncratic way. Strictly speaking, it is composed not of the five banks listed above, but of mutually approved individual representatives of each of the banks; if one of them is on vacation or ill when the committee meets, his bank is not represented at that meeting.

The committee meets once or twice a month and sometimes only every second month, according to circumstances, and decides on the total volume of new international issues which it believes the market can absorb in the period ahead. It then allocates a share of that total to each of the five banks represented, which have their own queues of foreign borrowers. However, banks which do not need the whole of their allocation often trade part of it to another of the five banks with a borrowing queue in excess of its allocation. A cosy arrangement in its way, but it can help cut the waiting time for foreign borrowers, which sometimes stretches to as much as a year. The only international borrowers exempt from the subcommittee's control of issuing volume are the World Bank and some of the European agencies like the European Investment Bank and the European Coal and Steel Community. Their issues are timed in consultation with the German authorities and banks outside the framework of the capital issues subcommittee; they are usually given priority; and they are the main borrowers on the traditional DM foreign bond market (as distinct from the DM Eurobond market). Indeed, they are classified as being "almost" domestic German borrowers.

Issuing costs are on the high side, ranging from about $2\frac{3}{4}$ percent to more than $3\frac{1}{4}$ percent as against the range of 2 percent to $2\frac{1}{2}$ percent in the Eurodollar bond market. The cost to the borrower in the case of DM external issues with a maturity of less than seven years consists of managing and underwriting commissions of $\frac{3}{8}$ percent each, selling concessions of $1\frac{1}{4}$ percent, listing costs of $\frac{1}{2}$ percent, and fixed presenta-

---

[1]"Eurofinance," *American Banker,* September 1, 1978.

tion costs of 0.2 percent to 0.3 per cent. However, the costs for private placements are considerably less, as in other markets. Because permission of the German economics ministry is required for bond issues inside Germany, DM foreign and Eurobonds are technically issued externally, in centers like Stockholm, although they are listed on the German exchanges (mostly in Frankfurt and Dusseldorf, but in some cases also in Hamburg, Munich, Hanover, Berlin, and Bremen). However, the volume of over the counter trading outside Germany and between German banks and foreign centers is considerable and transactions must pass through the Frankfurt clearing system for external bonds (the *Auslandskassenverein*).

Most DM foreign and Eurobonds are issued in denominations of DM 1,000 each (about $540 at early 1979 exchange rates), but some are issued in denominations of DM 5,000 or DM 10,000 (about $2,700 or $5,400) each, and secondary market transactions are usually in multiples of DM 10,000.

Excepting at times of special arbitraging opportunities, investment by German residents in international DM bonds tends to be limited to the voluntary (and sometimes involuntary) holdings of German banks; investment by individuals for tax evasion; and legitimate investment by individuals in the convertibles issued on the German external market by Japanese companies to spread their share ownership internationally.

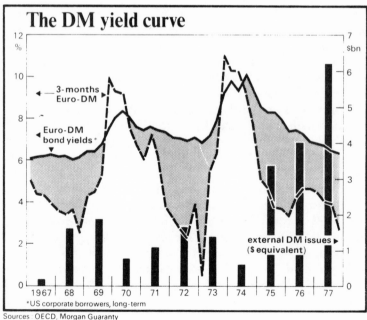

Sources: OECD, Morgan Guaranty

FIGURE 22

According to German data and the OECD, nonresidents have taken up more than two-thirds of net issues of external DM bonds in most years and more than 80 percent in some years.[2] Nonresident investment differs in kind as between countries. British and Dutch institutions tend to trade DM international bonds very actively rather than hang onto them. A large amount of investment comes from Belgium and France and from the mid-1970s there was a growing flow also from individual investors in Arab countries as well as some investment by Arab institutions. In addition, there is the usual flow of funds into the market through Swiss banks, but not necessarily from Swiss residents.

Unlike regulation of international borrowing in the Swiss, Dutch, and Japanese markets, German regulation seems concerned to a lesser extent with protection for the balance of payments and exchange rate. The main emphasis seems to be, rather, on regulation of the volume of international borrowing to fit in with that of domestic borrowing on the bond market (with an incidental regard for the cartel interests of the German banks). The usual advantages and drawbacks for international borrowers and investors are mitigated to some extent; borrowers have greater scope for matching DM liabilities with assets, while investors have a somewhat greater liquidity in the external DM market because it is bigger than many other international markets.

TABLE 34
INTERNATIONAL BOND ISSUES BY CURRENCY

($ billion equivalent)

	U.S. $	DM	Sw.fr.	D.fl.	Y	Total*
1970	3.0	0.8	0.1	0.4	0.0	4.6
1971	3.3	1.1	0.7	0.3	0.1	6.3
1972	5.3	1.6	0.8	0.4	0.3	9.7
1973	3.5	1.4	1.5	0.2	0.3	7.8
1974	4.3	0.6	0.9	0.4	0.0	6.9
1975	10.2	3.4	3.3	0.9	0.1	19.9
1976	19.7	4.0	5.4	1.1	0.3	32.5
1977	19.1	6.3	5.0	0.7	1.3	34.0
1978	13.1	9.0	5.7	0.8	3.8	34.3

	Percent of total					
	U.S. $	DM	Sw.fr.	D.fl.	Y	Total*
1970/78	52	18	15	3	4	100
1978	38	26	17	2	11	100

*Totals include international bonds in Canadian dollars, units of account, and other denominations. Figures rounded. Eurobonds plus foreign bonds.
SOURCE: Morgan Guaranty.

[2]*Financial Market Trends,* OECD, October 1977, p. 79.

CHAPTER THIRTY-FIVE
SAMURAI BONDS IN TOKYO

Although Tokyo was opened to international borrowers in 1970, it did not become a significant center for the issue of foreign bonds until 1977. The volume of new international yen issues then rose steeply in 1978, but the expansion of that year was regarded as exceptional by outsiders as well as the Japanese themselves. Although Tokyo may have the potential for becoming an increasingly important international capital market, its growth in the future could go on being as uneven as it was during the 1970s.

The Japanese authorities moved very cautiously in opening their capital market to foreign borrowers for two main reasons. Firstly, they were by no means as confident about their balance of payments surpluses as the rest of the world thought they should have been. Secondly, the Japanese authorities were concerned to preserve (or at least modify only carefully) the special character of their domestic bond market; they were therefore unwilling to risk disruption of their domestic market by allowing uncontrolled bursts of foreign borrowing in it.

It is true that the detailed regulation of Japan's financial sector is notoriously complicated. In the words of an exquisitely polite Japanese official, "It is impossible for foreigners to understand our rules, but the effort is appreciated."[1] Fortunately, however, the essentials are not quite so elusive.

Despite growing international complaints about Japan's large and seemingly chronic trade surpluses during the 1970s, the Japanese took a different view. They remembered that their current account had

---

[1]Robin Pringle, "Report from Tokyo," *The Banker,* London, March 1979.

swung very widely during the 1960s and that it had been in deficit during half of that decade. They were acutely aware, also, that their current balance had suddenly plunged into a very large deficit in 1974 and that it had taken a severe recession to bring it back into surplus after 1976. The 1973 oil crisis was traumatic for Japan, which is more dependent on imported energy than any other industrialized country; indeed, it reawakened memories of the threat to Japan's oil supplies in 1940 and 1941 and created a determination to guard against future emergencies, at the least by building up substantial reserves of foreign exchange.

At the same time, the Japanese were concerned by growing trade competition from Taiwan, Singapore, Korea, Hong Kong, and Brazil, to mention only some of their rivals. The Japanese did not, therefore, take it for granted that their trade surpluses would last forever. At the same time, they worried about their chronic and growing deficits on "invisible" trade in services such as shipping, insurance, and travel. On that view of the possibly temporary nature of their current surpluses, the Japanese continued to give priority during the 1970s to the export of capital in the form of direct investment abroad, with its promise of generating foreign exchange income in the future. The export of capital through yen-dominated international bonds and yen-dominated bank loans to foreign borrowers was regarded as less important.

Aside from external considerations, the Japanese authorities were careful about opening their bond market to foreign borrowers. They were concerned about controlling the volume of demand on their market and also any modifications which international borrowing might help to cause for the market's structure and practices.

Japan's bond market is the world's second largest, after the United States', ranked by the volume of gross new issues.[2] Its extremely rapid growth in the 1970s was caused mainly by the financing demands of the government, whose budget deficits rose from the equivalent of less than 1 percent of gross national product in 1971 to about 8 percent by 1978 (compared with a peak of 5 percent in the U.S. in 1975). As a result, public sector offerings and private placements rose from one-third to well over one-half of new domestic issues on the Tokyo market during the 1970s, with a corresponding decline in the proportion of new issues made by the six specialized Japanese banks which use the bond market to obtain the long-term capital which they, in turn, advance to Japanese industry.[3]

---

[2]*Financial Market Trends,* OECD, May 1978, p. 104.

[3]The six banks are the Industrial Bank of Japan, the Long-Term Credit Bank of Japan,

Access of domestic borrowers to the Tokyo bond market is confined almost exclusively to the Japanese central government and local governments and to the six specialized banks referred to previously. Between them, they have usually accounted for about 95 percent of new bond issues in Tokyo. The only other domestic borrowers generally allowed to tap the Tokyo bond market were Japan's nine electric power companies and Japan Air Lines (which is partly government-owned). Japanese corporate borrowers were effectively shut out of the domestic bond market from the time of the financial collapse of 1933, in being allowed to issue bonds only against mortgage collateral or bank guarantees. In those circumstances, it was usually more advantageous for them to raise capital by equity issues, bank borrowing, or borrowing in foreign bond markets.

The close control of access to the Tokyo bond market even of domestic borrowers helps explain the very cautious way in which the Japanese authorities opened that market to foreign borrowers. During the four years up to the end of 1973, when international borrowers were first admitted, only 20 public issues and private placements were sanctioned. Following the oil crisis, the Tokyo market was then shut to international public issues for the 20 months to July 1975, and it was reopened to private placements for international borrowers only after an interval of more than three years, in June 1977. Then, during the exchange rate crisis in the autumn of 1978, the Tokyo market was again shut to international borrowers for three months. Meanwhile, even in that record year of 1978, issues for international borrowers amounted only to about 5 percent of gross new issues on the Tokyo bond market.

The Tokyo market provides international capital in four main ways:

1. By the issue of traditional or classical foreign bonds for international borrowers, denominated in yen and known informally as *Samurai bonds.*

2. Private placements in yen, made for foreign borrowers, usually with Japanese institutional investors.[4]

3. Euro-yen bonds for foreign borrowers marketed worldwide by international bank syndicates.

4. Medium-and long-term yen credits provided to international borrowers by Japanese banks.

---

the Nippon Credit Bank, the Bank of Tokyo, the Central Bank for Commercial and Industrial Cooperatives, and the Norin Chukin Bank.

[4]International data on foreign bond issues in Tokyo usually include private placements.

The volume of Samurai bonds and private placements is regulated by Japan's Ministry of Finance to ensure a digestible flow and Ministry of Finance consent is needed also for Euro-yen bond issues. The Samurai bond market was at first opened only to two international organizations of which Japan is a member, the World Bank and the Asian Development Bank. But foreign governments were admitted as borrowers from 1972 and the agencies of foreign governments from 1977. However, the first Samurai for a foreign corporate borrower was allowed only in March 1979, for Sears Roebuck, the American retail firm which has extensive connections in Japan. That issue showed how internationalization of the Tokyo market could help change the rules for domestic borrowers as well, and in that way it also helped explain the cautious attitude of the Japanese authorities toward the opening of their market to the world. Sears was allowed to make an unsecured bond offering, which created a precedent for the first such issues by Japanese as well as foreign corporations after a ban which had lasted for 46 years. Even then, the Tokyo bond market was opened to unsecured borrowing only by very large, strongly capitalized, and highly rated Japanese and foreign companies.

Most Samurai bond issues have been for Y 15 billion to Y 30 billion (or about $75 million to $150 million at early 1979 exchange rates), but in July 1978, an issue of Y 75 billion, or $375 million, was floated for the World Bank. Private placements for foreign borrowers have usually been Y 10 billion, or about $50 million each. Samurai bonds are usually issued in denominations of Y 100,000, or about $500 each, but some bond certificates are issued in amounts of Y 1 million, or about $5,000.

The management of Samurai bond issues is solidly concentrated in four Japanese securities firms: Nomura, which was responsible for the lead management of 40 percent of all Samurai issues between 1970 and 1978, and Nikko, Daiwa, and Yamaichi, which were each responsible for the lead management of 20 percent during that time. Foreign underwriters were admitted to Samurai syndicates only in April 1978, and limited to the underwriting of 5 percent of a new issue.

International borrowers are required to convert the proceeds of Samurai bonds and private placements in the Tokyo market into foreign currency. But the net outflow out of yen is limited because of the loose control of foreign investment in Samurai bonds. Although the proportion of Samurai bonds which might be sold to nonresident investors was limited to 25 percent at issue, no limit was placed on nonresident purchases in the secondary market. Many Japanese investors therefore made a habit of taking up new Samurai bonds for resale to nonresidents, who were generally estimated to hold between 40 and 50 percent of all outstanding Samurai bonds by early 1979.

As in the case of other countries requiring foreign borrowers to convert their proceeds into foreign exchange (i.e., Switzerland and the Netherlands), there is a net outflow of capital only to the extent that residents buy the bonds of nonresident borrowers, while the balance of payments effect is neutral to the extent that nonresidents buy the obligations of other nonresidents. In Japan's case, therefore, the net outflow of capital through the Samurai bond market is only about half of the amount raised in it. This is not true, however, in the case of private placements on behalf of international borrowers in the yen market, which are taken up mostly by Japanese institutional investors such as pension funds and insurance companies. And, in addition to Samurai bonds and publicized private placements, the equivalent of about $2 billion of "off-market" placements were made with the Bank of Japan between 1970 and 1977 for international organizations, notably the World Bank.

Until 1978, Samurai bonds were issued for maturities of 10 to 15 years and private placements for 10 to 20 years, but several five-year maturities were then allowed in the bond market to provide a shorter-term investment for nonresidents, who were at that time barred by the Japanese authorities from investing in Japanese domestic securities with a life of less than five years and one month.

Nonresident income from investment in Japanese domestic securities is subject to withholding for tax while the income of nonresident investment in Samurai and Euro-yen bonds is exempt. From that point, the two instruments are equal for international investors. However, one important distinction is that nonresident investment is limited to 25 percent of Samurai bonds at the time of issue (as already mentioned) while no such limitation exists on the sale of newly issued Euro-yen bonds to nonresidents of Japan. Another distinction is that more than 70 Samurai issues totaling about $7 billion were outstanding by early 1979, compared with only four Euro-yen bond issues totaling $275 million, suggesting a lesser degree of liquidity for investors in the latter at that time. Comparable liquidity would be created only if the Japanese authorities permitted a greatly increased volume of Euro-yen issues, but up to the first quarter of 1979 permission for Euro-yen issues had been given only to the World Bank, the Asian Development Bank, the European Investment Bank, and Eurofima, the railway corporation jointly owned by several European states.

An important development for investors in Samurai bonds was the extension of the international Euroclear system to Tokyo from the beginning of 1979. That greatly improved the efficiency of the secondary market, which had previously required physical transfers of securities between brokerage houses.

From the point of borrowers, two distinctive features of the Samurai market are the hurdles and costs of entry. At the time of writing, prospective borrowers were required to have made at least two bond issues, including at least one public issue, in other markets during the preceding five years or five publicly offered issues within the preceding 20 years, and even that was a relaxation of the previous requirement for three offerings within the preceding five years. On top of that, regulation of issuing volume often forces borrowers to line up; if conditions turn against the borrower while he is waiting in line he is faced with the difficult choice of opting for more favorable terms in another market or paying an effective premium for entry into or continued access to the Samurai market.

Issuing costs present a lesser problem to seasoned Samurai borrowers than new ones, a situation similar to that in the New York foreign bond market. Management fees, underwriting, and selling concessions total only between 1.75 percent and 1.9 percent of the face value of a Samurai issue, compared with a range of 2 percent to $2\frac{1}{2}$ percent in the Eurobond market. But adaptation to Japanese presentation practices and the provision of prospectuses in Japanese adds to costs, especially for first-time borrowers. Another drawback for borrowers is that terms are seldom if ever allowed to rival those on Japanese government issues, even when market conditions might give the Samurai borrower more favorable terms.

As in other international markets, a prime consideration for borrowers and investors in the Samurai market is the relationship between interest rates and exchange rate expectations. It was only in 1977 that Japanese interest rates fell below dollar interest rates and only in 1978 that they did so by a substantial margin. Investors in Samurai bonds therefore got the dual benefit of currency appreciation plus high returns, while borrowers suffered on both counts. An additional complication in the Samurai market during the 1970s was that the funds available to the market seemed out of proportion to the securities in it, and this showed itself in a highly disruptive way in the latter part of 1978. International investors reasoned, correctly as it proved, that the yen had topped out for the time being and the rush to realize exchange rate profits led to a collapse of prices on the Samurai market which threatened the Tokyo domestic bond market as well. Hence the temporary closure of the Tokyo market to new foreign borrowers at that time.

INTERNATIONAL JAPANESE BANK LOANS

In addition to providing international capital through yen bonds and private placements, large sums are provided also in the form of yen-denominated medium- and long-term credits by Japanese banks and institutions to foreign borrowers. It should be noted that these are distinct from the considerable amounts of conventional Eurocredits, usually in terms of dollars, which Japanese banks help to arrange and provide.

As in the case of international yen bonds, the number and value of international yen credits rose very rapidly in 1977 and 1978 on the high liquidity of Japanese banks and sluggish domestic loan demand. The number of publicized yen loans to foreign borrowers rose from nine in 1977 to 33 in 1978 and their total from Y 120 billion to Y 500 billion between the two years. In addition to the equivalent of $2.6 billion provided in publicized yen credits during 1978, another $1 billion was provided in the form of unpublicized credits.

The distinctive feature of yen-denominated foreign loans made by Japanese banks is that they are usually at fixed interest rates for periods of up to 20 years, by contrast with the floating interest rate loans usually provided in the Eurocredits market. For instance, in February 1979, the Canadian government obtained the equivalent of $180 million in the form of a ten-year credit at 7.1 percent plus an equal amount for ten years at a fixed 7.6 percent. The World Bank and Australia had likewise obtained 20-year fixed-interest-rate yen credits from Japanese banks in 1978.

Such Japanese bank credits are, in reality, a hybrid between conventional international syndicated bank credits and private placements in the international bond markets. They resemble conventional bank credits in being arranged and partly taken up by banks. But they resemble private placements in that a large part of such credits are provided through Japanese banks by Japanese fire and casualty insurance companies wishing to acquire some yen-denominated claims on nonresidents. One reason for this is said to be Japan's liability to earthquakes, which puts an additional risk both on the liabilities and the domestic claims of Japanese casualty companies. Unlike most private placements in international bond markets, however, these particular private placements are not normally negotiable among investors.

CHAPTER THIRTY-SIX

THE DUTCH MARKET

As an international center, Amsterdam has the advantages of tradition and a highly developed financial structure. The drawback is that capital controls are periodically adjusted to the country's changing economic circumstances so that the growth of the market in international guilder[1] bonds has been uneven. During a large part of the 1970s, the guilder was the fourth currency in the international bond markets, after the dollar, Deutschemark, and Swiss franc. But it was overtaken by the yen in 1977 and it remains to be seen whether international borrowers will be allowed the same access to the guilder market in the 1980s as in the 1970s.

Tradition helps to explain an exceptional readiness by the Dutch to invest and borrow abroad. They became world traders about four hundred years ago, even before their emergence from Spanish domination; indeed, the British concentrated on India only as a second choice because Dutch adventurers had beaten them to the trading grounds of Java and Sumatra by the start of the seventeenth century. Amsterdam was Europe's main financial center until overtaken by London at the end of the Napoleonic wars. Even today, the city remains one of the world's half-dozen largest international financial centers, ranked by the external assets of banks in the Netherlands.[2] The Dutch banking sector is highly international also in its composition; in 1978, 45 foreign banks were represented directly or indirectly in the Netherlands and 28 of the country's 71 commercial banks were partly foreign-owned. Last but not

---

[1] Also known as the gulden or florin. Money amounts are prefixed by D.fl., as in D.fl. 100 for 100 Dutch florin.

[2] See Appendix 2, page 259.

least is the foundation for an international market provided by the highly developed domestic debt market; in relation to GNP, the volume of fixed-interest debt in Amsterdam is the world's second largest after that in Zurich.[3] Part of the explanation is the supply of investment funds through an exceptionally large flow of contractual savings into life insurance and pension funds.

But although Amsterdam has the historical and structural makings of an international financial center, it has not always been free to develop its potentialities to the full. The central factor in the Dutch economy is that it is the most open in the world. Slightly more than one-half of total output is exported and a roughly equal proportion of national expenditure is devoted to imports. That compares with foreign trade equivalent to about 45 percent of gross national product in Belgium, about 30 percent in the United Kingdom, about 25 percent in Germany, and about 10 percent in the U.S. and Japan.

In a country as open to the world as the Netherlands, the impact of the exchange rate on exports, employment, and domestic prices is correspondingly magnified. The all-important relationship is between the guilder and the Deutschemark, because Germany is the biggest trading partner of the Netherlands, taking about one-third of Dutch exports and supplying about one-quarter of Dutch imports. The link is reinforced because Germany is also the biggest trading partner of Belgium, which, in its turn, is the second trading partner of the Netherlands. The relationship between the two smaller countries therefore yokes each of them even more firmly to their bigger neighbor. It is possible to argue the merits of the joint currency float which several European countries attempted in various forms from 1971; but in the case of the Benelux countries and Germany it was merely an expression of reality.

To say that the Dutch cannot allow the guilder to move too much out of line with the Deutschemark except, perhaps, very gradually over time, is simply another way of saying that the Dutch have limited freedom to run their economy independently. Above all, they cannot ordinarily afford an inflation rate running at about $1\frac{1}{2}$ times Germany's, as during most of the 1970s (an annual average of 7.3 percent compared with 5 percent during the nine years through 1978). The Dutch were able to afford a divergent policy during that time only because of the bonus of natural gas discoveries. A country that had previously had

---

[3]*Financial Market Trends,* OECD, May 1978, p. 104. A special feature of the Dutch domestic market is that about two-thirds of the fixed-interest debt issued in it has usually been in the form of debt certificates which, unlike bonds, are barely negotiable. The certificates carry the name of the borrower, the lender, and the terms of the debt and may be transferred from one creditor to another only with the borrower's consent.

hardly any fuels of its own produced a growing volume of natural gas from 1963 and gained a still further benefit when world energy prices rose to new heights from 1973. But the Dutch knew from the start that their natural gas reserves were limited, and under a policy of conserving resources, output of natural gas was reduced in 1977. The Dutch balance of payments was therefore in substantial current surplus only for the five years through 1976. It moved into approximate equilibrium in the following year and back into deficit in 1978.

During most of the 1970s, natural gas exports kept the guilder above levels at which it would otherwise have been, which helped keep Dutch inflation below the levels it would otherwise have reached. According to their point of view, the Dutch complained that their exchange rate was too high or, alternatively, that their inflation rate was too high. However expressed, the divergence between the exchange and inflation rates was the essence of what was called "the Dutch disease."[4]

That background helps explain the Dutch authorities' attitude toward capital controls. They were uncertain about how long they could rely on current account surpluses and were troubled by the nature of those surpluses. They therefore acted partly like a chronic surplus country, discouraging capital inflows; and partly like a deficit country, welcoming capital imports.

To stimulate capital outflows, or at least limit inflows, the Amsterdam market was reopened to foreign borrowers in 1969, the first time it had been thus opened on a regular basis since 1914. Foreign borrowers were admitted to the extent that it was thought the domestic market could accommodate them, but were generally required to convert their proceeds out of guilders. As a result, the influence on the balance of payments was neutral to the extent that nonresidents invested in the guilder obligations of other foreigners. And there was a net outflow of capital to the extent that Dutch residents invested in nonresident guilder debt.

At the same time, Dutch residents were allowed to borrow on international markets only on condition that the proceeds were invested abroad and not repatriated. Here, too, was the policy of a surplus country limiting capital inflows. But that changed, significantly, from the end of 1978, when restrictions were eased on the repatriation of foreign long-term borrowing by Dutch residents.

Even when they were acting like a surplus country to ward off some capital inflows, the Dutch left the gates open to other flows. Inward and outward portfolio investment was not regulated (nor was it restricted

---

[4]Britain began catching the same "disease" in 1978 on the growing flow of the North Sea oil.

by discriminatory withholding for tax, since the Netherlands has no form of tax withholding). Because the guilder offered international investors the dual attractions of a strong currency and high rates of return during most of the 1970s, freedom for portfolio investment amounted to an invitation for foreign capital to enter the Netherlands. In summary, the authorities had built half a dyke, which is not the sort of thing the Dutch normally build. That they did so in the 1970s was a measure of their uncertainty and their wish to keep capital flows as free as possible. Whether the Dutch decide to extend their dyke or dismantle what there is of it will depend on the future of the country's balance of payments and the guilder. Those fundamentals are more important than the description of market mechanics which follows, because the latter could change.

MECHANICS OF THE AMSTERDAM MARKET

During the 1970s, Amsterdam offered international borrowers an exceptional diversity of financing opportunities and, by contrast with banks in some other centers, those in Amsterdam did not take advantage of cartel-like conditions to bolster costs to borrowers. By 1978, six ways had been evolved of providing guilder capital to nonresidents. They consisted of Euro-guilder notes (listed as guilder Eurobonds in most international data) and traditional foreign bonds issued for nonresident borrowers on the Dutch domestic market. In addition, there were private placements for foreign borrowers in the domestic market and three classes of guilder bank credits available to nonresidents; fixed-interest and floating rate loans in domestic guilders and floating rate credits in Euro-guilders. The main characteristics were the following.

Euro-guilder notes are semiprivate placements made on a best-efforts basis without underwriters or a borrower's prospectus. The practical minimum is D.fl. 30 million or about $15 million.[5] The normal maximum is D.fl. 75 million (or about $37.5 million) but issues of D.fl. 100 million, or about $50 million, have sometimes been allowed for foreign official borrowers, notably the Australian and Norwegian governments and the World Bank. The Dutch central bank has usually allowed only one issue a month, so that borrowers often have to queue.

The maturity of the notes is five to seven years, prepayment is not allowed, and foreign borrowers are required to convert their proceeds into dollars or their own currency on receipt.

---

[5]Dollar conversions here at the early 1979 rate of about D.fl. 2 to $1.

In the absence of a prospectus, access to this market is limited to international borrowers of prime standing and, in the absence of stock exchange listing, trading of the notes depends on the success of issuing banks in making a secondary market. The notes are usually issued in denominations of D.fl. 10,000, or about $5,000 each.

Issuing costs consist of a $\frac{1}{2}$-point managing fee, a 1 percent selling or placing concession, plus about $35,000 of presentation expenses. In addition, the borrower pays banks recurring fees of $\frac{1}{4}$ percent of the value of interest coupons presented for payment on behalf of investors and a commission of $\frac{1}{8}$ percent of the principal when its redemption is arranged. The $1\frac{1}{2}$ percent issuing costs are less than the range of 2 to $2\frac{1}{2}$ percent on the Eurobond market, and the coupon and redemption commissions are about the same as in many centers.

Traditional guilder foreign bonds with maturities of 10 to 15 years are issued for foreign borrowers on the Amsterdam market in amounts of D.fl. 50 million to 100 million, or about $25 million to $50 million. Here, too, issues are usually limited to at most one a month and there is often a waiting list of borrowers. The issues are managed by Dutch banks, but foreign banks may be included at the borrower's request. A prospectus is required in Dutch and issues are listed on the Amsterdam stock exchange. Borrowers are required to convert their proceeds into dollars or their own currency. Prepayment of longer maturities is usually allowed only after 10 years and at 103 percent of face value. The bonds are usually issued in denominations of D.fl. 1,000 (or about $500), but sometimes in denominations of D.fl. 10,000 ($5,000) each.

Issuing costs of $2\frac{1}{8}$ percent ($1\frac{1}{2}$ percent management and underwriting fees plus $\frac{5}{8}$ percent selling concessions) are below the range in the Eurobond market and still more below the 3 to 4 percent range of such costs in the Frankfurt and Zurich foreign bond markets. Commissions of $\frac{1}{4}$ percent charged by banks for arranging payment of coupon interest and $\frac{1}{8}$ percent for arranging redemption are comparable to those in other markets.

Guilder private placements are made for foreign borrowers at final maturities of 10 to 20 years and average maturities of 6 to 13 years, in amounts usually limited to D.fl. 75 million (or about $37.5 million). Prepayment is authorized only in exceptional cases. Borrowers are usually required to convert their proceeds out of guilders. Although the market is open only to prime international borrowers, security in the form of mortgage on property in the Netherlands may nevertheless be required of foreign corporate borrowers in some cases. Issues are placed mainly with Dutch institutional investors, but some placements with foreign investors were authorized early in 1979. Although the Dutch central bank regulates the volume of such placements, it does not limit them rigidly to one a month. A $\frac{1}{2}$-point management fee is payable to Dutch banks; foreign banks advising the borrower may also charge fees, but the total is usually well below 1 percent. In the absence of bonds or notes, there are no recurring coupon or redemption charges.

Guilder Eurocredits are provided for three to eight years in amounts of D.fl. 25 million to 100 million (or about $12.5 million to $50 million) to international borrowers by syndicates of Dutch and international banks. They resemble conventional Eurocredits in nearly every way, except for being granted, in the first instance, in terms of guilders and at interest margins set above the London inter-bank offered rate for guilder deposits. Another distinction is that the Dutch authorities allow the proceeds to be used inside the Netherlands only if invested for 5 years or longer. However, as in the case of most Eurocredits, borrowers can elect to take funds in other currencies at roll-over dates, subject to availability. Commitment fees of $\frac{1}{4}$ percent to 1 percent are charged on undrawn portions of these credits.

Domestic guilder floating rate credits are provided mainly to meet the working needs of Dutch subsidiaries and branches of foreign corporations and are provided in relative small amounts of D.fl. 7.5 million to 10 million (or about $3.75 million to $5 million). The maximum maturities are 10 years and floating interest margins are set above AIBOR (Amsterdam inter-bank offered rate for guilder deposits). Such funds are intended mainly for use in the Netherlands and require authorization for use abroad. Management fees are $\frac{1}{2}$ percent and commitment fees on undrawn portions of credits are $\frac{1}{2}$ percent per annum. Prepayment is allowed against a premium of $\frac{3}{8}$ percent during the first two years and $\frac{1}{4}$ percent thereafter.

Domestic guilder fixed-rate credits are available from Dutch banking syndicates to international borrowers for up to D.fl. 100 million (or about $50 million), usually for 10 years but in some cases for up to 15 years. A fixed-interest rate is payable semiannually, sometimes with an interest revision every five years. For these credits, the requirement that borrowers convert their proceeds out of guilders is applied by the authorities on a case by case basis.

During the 1970s, as already mentioned, the guilder offered international investors the dual attractions of a strong currency (thanks to natural gas exports) plus high interest rates (mainly because of the government's demands on the Amsterdam bond market to finance large budget deficits from 1974 onward). How far those attractions may persist into the 1980s has already been questioned. If the Netherlands can achieve soundly based external surpluses on a close relationship between Dutch and German inflation rates, the currency would remain attractive, but returns on guilder investments would surely fall. Alternatively, high returns may become obtainable only at a growing exchange rate risk.

The position for borrowers is, as always, the reverse. During the 1970s, international borrowers in the guilder markets were mostly international organizations such as the World Bank, the European Investment Bank, and the European Coal and Steel Community, which make a practice of spreading their borrowing among the markets of their member countries; strong currency borrowers like Scandinavians; borrowers having the counterpart of guilder assets or revenues; and also Dutch banks, who joined foreign borrowers in the Euro-guilder note market to diversify their capital base whenever an interest differential between domestic and Euro-guilder rates made it advantageous to tap the latter market. If the guilder strengthens in the 1980s, foreign borrowing will be limited by market forces and, if it does not, then such borrowing may be restricted by the authorities. The growth of Amsterdam's international capital market could be impeded either way.

SOME EURO-MILESTONES

Date	Event	Market impact
1949	Chinese revolution	China starts disguising dollar earnings by placing them with Soviet banks in Western Europe (first Eurodollar deposits)
1950	Korean war; U.S. blocks Peking's dollar balances	Soviet banks start placing dollars with Western European banks
1956	U.S. abandons cheap money for first time since 1932	Conditions for active corporate money management recreated in U.S.
1956	Invasions of Suez and Hungary; sterling crisis; ban on sterling financing of third-country trade	London merchant banks begin bidding for dollars to finance third-country trade (start of active Eurodollar market)
1957		First Eurodollar bond: $5 million for Petrofina SA (Belgium)
1958–1959	30 European and associated countries restore currency convertibility for non-residents	New international asset choices and arbitrage opportunities created
1960	Crisis on London gold market	Early warning of international dollar distrust
1963	Interest Equalization Tax shuts many foreign borrowers out of U.S. bond market for protection of U.S. balance of payments	Major stimulus to issue of Eurodollar bonds on regular basis
1964	IET extended to some international U.S. bank loans	Early stimulus to evolution of Eurocredits market
1964	German "coupon tax" to discourage capital inflows through foreign investment in domestic DM bonds	Stimulus to the regular issue of DM Eurobonds

1965	"Voluntary" U.S. capital export controls force U.S. companies to finance foreign direct investment by borrowing abroad	Further stimulus to growth of Eurocredits market
1966	U.S. credit squeeze limits ability of banks in U.S. to bid for large time deposits at home (under Regulation Q)	U.S. banks bid for dollar deposits abroad; a new rush by U.S. banks to open foreign branches; major boost to growth of Eurodollar market
1967	Sterling devaluation gives new warning of strains in pegged exchange rate system	Several countries start diversifying reserves out of dollars as well as sterling into strong currencies like DM; stimulus to growth of broader Eurocurrencies market
1969	Netherlands starts moving toward strong payments surpluses on exploitation of natural gas	Amsterdam bond market opened to foreign borrowers on regular basis; Euro-guilder notes introduced
1969–1970	New U.S. credit squeeze has same effect on banks as in 1966	Further stimulus to foreign branching and Eurocurrencies business of U.S. banks.
1970	Federal Reserve relaxes Regulation Q after Penn Central collapse	Euromarket sufficiently established to continue growth without artificial stimuli such as Regulation Q
1971	Bretton Woods Agreement collapse; most countries stimulate domestic demand to counter presumed business shock	Start of world boom and its reflection by boom in international bond and credit markets
1972–1973	Western world's monetary boom moves into high gear; world commodity prices soar	Large flows into Euromarkets from world raw materials producers; international bond and credit markets grow as never before
1973	October War in Middle East; quantum rise in oil prices	Conditions created for enlarged "recycling" from surplus to deficit countries through international capital market
1974–1975	Western world's recession	International capital market at first "recycles" funds mainly to Western industrial countries; thereafter to developing countries

1974	Collapse of Bankhaus I.D. Herstatt, Cologne	Temporary panic and near-paralysis of Eurocredits market
1974	U.S. capital export controls lifted	Partial return of U.S. corporate borrowers and foreign borrowers to U.S. markets
1978	U.S. dollar crisis; further diversification of official and semiofficial reserves into strong currencies	Large increase in international yen and DM credits and international yen, DM, and Swiss franc bond issues
1979	Further rise in oil prices	New need for "recycling"

FINANCIAL CENTERS COMPARED

There is no agreed way of ranking world financial centers, let alone defining them. Transactions arranged in one center are often booked through another for tax or regulatory reasons. The Table A-1 is merely one indication of world rankings, derived partly from International Monetary Fund data. Some liberties have been taken. Whereas IMF data refer to countries, Table A-1 equates countries with their main financial centers, despite the unfairness to some countries which have several centers (notably the U.S., West Germany, and Canada). Moreover, while separately identifying the business of the Bahamas and Luxembourg, Table A-1 lumps the former with New York and the latter with Frankfurt because a large part of international lending through the Bahamas is by U.S. banks while a very large part of international lending out of Luxembourg is by German banks.

TABLE A-1
WORLD FINANCIAL CENTERS RANKED, 1978

	External assets ($ billion)	Number of foreign banks
London	173	308
New York	78	274
Bahamas	83	285
	161	559
Frankfurt	61	172
Luxembourg	53	67
	114	239
Zurich	73	111
Paris	58	194
Amsterdam	35	73
Brussels	31	68
Toronto	20	90
Milan	18	40
Tokyo	17	137
Panama	10	111

SOURCE: IMF International Financial Statistics March, 1979. External assets in domestic and foreign currencies of domestic and foreign deposit money banks in member countries at mid-1978, figures rounded and centers listed limited to those having external claims of $10 billion or more. Number of foreign banks includes branches, other offices, subsidiaries, and shareholdings in consortium and domestic banks. Taken from *The Banker,* London, April 1979.

SOURCES OF MARKET INFORMATION

1. OFFICIAL SOURCES
Bank for International Settlements (BIS)

Centralbahnplatz 2
CH-4002 Basel
Switzerland

Eurocurrency and Other International Banking Developments (quarterly)
Coverage: External assets and liabilities of banks in the main industrial countries and their principal offshore branches in relation to 147 countries and territories.

International Banking (twice a year)
Coverage: Expanded version of above plus maturity breakdowns of external assets of banks in the reporting countries.

BIS Annual Reports (June)
Coverage: Includes summarized versions of information and comment contained in the quarterly and half-yearly reports.

Bank of England

Threadneedle Street, London EC 2

Bank of England Quarterly Bulletin
Coverage: Detailed breakdowns of external assets and liabilities of banks in the United Kingdom by class of bank (i.e., British, American, Japanese, and other groups of banks) plus more detailed maturity breakdowns of external assets and liabilities of the banks covered than provided by the BIS for those which the BIS covers.

General Agreement on Tariffs and Trade (The GATT)

Rue de La Lausanne 154
1211 Geneva 21
Switzerland

International Trade (annually, spring)
 Coverage: Particularly useful for information on the trade and trade balances
 of centrally planned economies, providing data not easily obtainable elsewhere.

International Bank for Reconstruction and Development (World Bank)

1818 H Street N.W.
Washington, D.C. 20433

World Debt Tables (annually, October, with updating supplements published
during the year)
 Coverage: Detailed information on volume and servicing of long-term external public and publicly guaranteed private debt of 96 countries; the data are
 derived from the Bank's Debt Reporting System (DRS), started in 1951.

Borrowing in International Capital Markets (quarterly)
 Coverage: Details of new foreign and international bond issues and new
 Eurocredits having maturities of a year or longer, including names of borrowers, managing banks, and terms as well as aggregations of borrowing and
 terms by borrowing countries. Derived from Bank's Capital Markets System
 (CMS) data, whose scope has been continually broadened since the CMS was
 started in 1946.

World Bank Annual Reports (October)
 Coverage: Includes summaries of information and comment on international
 debt and lending trends and extensive information on the economies of
 developing countries.

World Development Report (annually, August)
 Coverage: Published by the Bank in 1978 as "the first of what we expect will
 be a series of annual reports providing a comprehensive assessment of global
 development issues." Includes vital statistics as well as economic data on
 industrial, centrally planned, and developing countries.

International Monetary Fund (IMF)

Washington, D.C. 20431

International Financial Statistics (IFS) (monthly)
 Coverage: The most prompt and internationally comprehensive economic
 and financial data available on the 130 member countries of the IMF; includes
 information on exchange rates, international liquidity, banking and monetary
 statistics, interest rates, prices, national accounts, and international trade and

payments. Also available, as are other statistical publications of the IMF, in the form of computer tapes.

Balance of Payments Yearbook (annual, with monthly updates)
Coverage: Details of international balances of payments and capital flows of 110 countries.

Government Finance Statistics Yearbook (September)
Coverage: Detailed data on revenues, grants, expenditures, lending, financing, and debt of governments in 113 countries.

Direction of Trade (monthly, with expanded issue in September)
Coverage: Exports and imports as reported by 135 countries, showing partner countries.

Organization for Economic Cooperation and Development (OECD)

2 Rue André-Pascal
75775 Paris Cedex 16
France

Financial Market Trends (published five times a year)
Coverage: Detailed statistics, commentary, and analyses of trends in international bond and credit markets, including the OECD staff's forecasts of market trends; special features, published in some issues, describe and analyse individual sectors of the international capital market.

OECD Financial Statistics (annually, autumn, updating supplements every two months)
Coverage: Extensive data on financial and domestic banking and capital market trends in member countries as well as detailed coverage of international bond issues and placements.

Development Cooperation (annually, December)
Coverage: Details of transfers of long-term resources from member countries of the Development Assistance Committe (DAC) of the OECD to 144 recipient countries. Transfers covered include ODA (official development assistance including at least 25 percent grant, or gift, element); OOF (other official flows); private flows at market terms and grants (gifts) from voluntary agencies. Statistics on outstanding long-term debt (one year or longer) and debt service of recipient countries.

Geographical Distribution of Financial Flows to Developing Countries (annually, spring)
Coverage: Flows of disbursed financial resources from DAC members, international agencies, and OPEC countries to more than 160 recipient countries and territories; the flows are given gross and net; data also on external debt of recipients related to their GNP, external trade, and reserves. The 1979 issue covers the years 1971 to 1977.

OECD Economic Outlook (December and July)
  Coverage: Mainly devoted to economic trends in and OECD Secretariat forecasts for the 24 OECD member countries, but also includes attempts at estimating and forecasting global balance of payments trends between industrial, oil-exporting, developing, and centrally planned countries. *Note:* Some OECD data are derived from the Creditor Reporting System (CRS) operated jointly with the World Bank, and there is usually a reconciliation, after time, between the international capital market statistics of the two international agencies.

Special Publication

Manual on Statistics Compiled by International Organizations, published by the Bank for International Settlements, March 1979, gives an extensive description of the information on international capital flows published by official agencies with an analysis of the scope and limitations of the information available.

PRIVATE BANKING SOURCES

Many banks publish market letters on the international capital market. Only two have been singled out here as especially useful:

World Financial Markets (monthly, published by Morgan Guaranty Trust Company of New York)
  Coverage: The most up-to-date totals available for new international bond issues and international bank credits by currencies of denomination, categories and main countries of borrowers; up-to-date estimates of Eurocurrency market size; comparative interest rates and yields in the world's main domestic money and capital markets as well as those in international markets; analytical articles on international economic, exchange rate, and capital market trends.

International Bond Market Roundup (weekly, published by Salomon Brothers, New York)
  Coverage: Details of latest international bond issues and those in course of arrangement; market prices and yields of recently offered and seasoned international bonds; international bond yields and money market rates on covered and uncovered basis (in terms of foreign exchange cover).

Special Publication

Six Possibilities to Raise Loan-Capital in Dutch Guilders
  Published by the Amsterdam-Rotterdam Bank, August 1978, providing an especially useful guide to the Dutch international capital market.

MARKET SOURCE

Association of International Bond Dealers

Inter-Bond Services Ltd.
2 Parway
London NW1

The International Bond Manual (annually, May, with fortnightly updates)
Contents: Full details of borrowers, terms, managing banks, and trustees of
nearly all international bond issues, comprehensively indexed.

NEWSPAPERS AND PERIODICALS

This list is confined to only some of the English language publications specializing in or giving space to coverage of international capital market trends.

The *American Banker*, New York (D)*
The Banker, London (M)
Business Week, New York (W)
The Economist, London (W)
Euromoney, London (M)
The Financial Times, London and Frankfurt (D)*
Financier, New York (M)
The Institutional Investor, International Edition, New York (M)
International Currency Review, London (S)
International Herald Tribune, Paris (D)*
The Money Manager, New York (W)*
The New York Times, New York (D)
The Wall Street Journal, New York (D)

SYMBOLS: D= daily; W= weekly; M= monthly; S= six times a year.

NEWSLETTERS AND SPECIAL PUBLICATIONS

Agefi, London (W)
Financial Report of The Economist, London (F)
Financial Times Euromarket Letter, London (W)
International Insider, Brussels (W)
Trends in International Capital Markets, Banker Research Unit, London (Q,
with monthly updates)

---

*Signifies weekly column on international capital markets besides other daily coverage.

Euromoney Red Book, London (M) (analysis of syndicated loans, borrowers, lenders and terms)

Hambro Euromoney Directory, London, (A) (listings of Eurobanks and key personnel in 75 countries, frequent updatings).

SYMBOLS:W=weekly; F=fortnightly; M=monthly; Q=quarterly; A=annual.

AN INTERNATIONAL MARKET GLOSSARY

acceptance credits Trade credits whose endorsement (or "acceptance") by a bank makes them eligible for trading at a discount. The syndication of some such credits by groups of London banks was one of the precedents for syndication of international bank loans in the Eurocredits market.

advisory funds Funds entrusted to banks for investment on a client's behalf and in the client's name, but only after consultation with the client. Having such funds at their disposal helps a bank place new issues of international bonds with investors. *See also* **discretionary funds fiduciary funds, and in-house funds.**

after-market Trading of bonds immediately after their issue, during the period when the syndicate of selling banks has not yet been formally disbanded; syndicate banks in the U.S. market may not sell bonds below the agreed issue price during this period, but selling banks are not similarly restricted in other international bond markets.

agent bank Bank appointed by members of an international lending syndicate to protect the interests of the lenders during the life of the loan. Its duties resemble those of the trustee of a bond issue. But while a trustee is never an investor, an agent bank is often a major lender itself and is, moreover, usually left free to conduct other business with the borrower as well. The agent's role is therefore open to conflicts of interest.

agio Premium over the issue price which borrowers usually have to pay investors to redeem outstanding bonds before maturity (from the Italian *aggio*).

AIBD Association of International Bond Dealers, founded in 1969 for the establishment of uniform practices in international bond markets. By early 1979, it had 527 member firms in 29 countries. The association's headquarters are in Zurich.

allocation   Amount of a new bond issue allotted for sale to syndicate members by the managing bank or banks; known also as "allotment."

asked   Price sought by the seller in the international bond (and other) markets. *See also* **bid**.

assignment (of a loan)   Banks taking part in a syndicated loan may, with the borrower's consent, assign their share of it to another bank. The bank to which the loan share is assigned then assumes the relationship to the borrower which has been relinquished by the bank which has assigned it.

average life   Measure of the average maturity of a bond issue as a whole after allowing for redemption by the borrower of part of the issue through sinking or purchase funds. *See also* **sinking fund** and **purchase fund**.

Auslandskassenverein   Clearing system for foreign securities in Germany; all sales of traditional DM foreign bonds and DM Eurobonds are cleared through this system.

banque d'affaires   French investment bank, but having far wider latitude than a U.S. investment bank to conduct other forms of banking business as well. The closest analogy is with a British merchant bank. *See also* **merchant bank**.

base rate   Interest rate which banks use as the basis onto which they add their lending spread or margin to borrowers. In the Eurocredits market, the base rate is usually LIBOR. *See also* **LIBOR** and **lending margins**.

basis points   A basis point is $1/100$ of a percentage point and is usually used to describe changes in or differentials between interest rates, rather than the level of interest rates themselves. A rise in an interest rate from 7 percent to 7¼ percent is an increase of 25 basis points; the difference between 5 percent and 5½ percent is 50 basis points.

bid   Price offered by a prospective buyer or borrower as against the asked price sought by prospective sellers in the bond markets or the offered rate quoted by lenders in the inter-bank market.

bonds   Fixed-interest securities issued by official and corporate borrowers and negotiable among investors in secondary markets. Bonds are often secured by a lien on the borrower's property, but most Eurobonds and other international bonds are unsecured and are therefore more accurately described as debentures (although, to add to the confusion, some debentures issued in domestic markets are secured).

bracket   Banks arranging a new international bond issue are grouped into brackets, with the lead manager on top, followed in order by the comanagers, a special bracket for underwriters who have just missed inclusion in the management group, major underwriters, lesser underwriters, and selling group members. Banks in each bracket are listed alphabetically or according to their commitments. Banks in a Eurocredits loan syndicate are similarly bracketed, the lead manager being followed by the comanagers and then by the major and lesser participating banks. *See also* **tombstone**.

bullet   Straight-debt issue without sinking or purchase fund or other arrangements for early partial redemption which would reduce the issue's average life to less than its face maturity.

Cedel   One of the Eurobond market's two clearing systems, owned by several European banks.

certificates of deposit (CD)   Negotiable receipts for time deposits made with banks which can be traded among the holders (i.e., investors). Banks issuing CDs can usually obtain working funds more cheaply than in the inter-bank market while investors, mostly nonbank corporations and institutions, acquire highly rated and highly liquid assets. They were introduced into the U.S. market in in 1961 and London dollar CDs, their Eurocurrency equivalent, were introduced in 1966. London dollar CDs are among the many ways in which banks help to finance themselves in the international bond and credit markets.

comanagers   Banks ranking next after lead managers in the arrangement of international bond issues and international bank credits (i.e., Eurocredits). They help assess the market and discuss terms with borrowers. Comanagers of international bond syndicates are often chosen for their ability to place large amounts of a new issue with investors, while the lead manager is often chosen for having brought a borrower to market. In Eurocredit syndicates, comanagers are usually chosen for their willingness to take a large part of the loan for themselves, or their ability to parcel out a large part to other banks.

concessions   *See* **fees**.

consortium banks   Specialized international banks created by groups of large commercial banks. Nearly 50 sprang up during the 1960s but their number then declined on the realization, in some cases, that the pooling of international business had drawbacks as well as advantages for the partners.

continental depository receipt   Bearer document which is equivalent to and which may be held instead of or exchanged into multiples of an equity issued through the Euromarket.

conversion premium   Premium paid by a borrower to investors to redeem outstanding bonds before maturity. *See also* **agio.**

convertibles   Bonds, in national and international markets, which give investors the option of converting their fixed-interest securities into the common stock of the borrowing company during a stipulated period and at a stipulated price; the conversion price is usually fixed at a premium above the market price of the common stock on the date of the bond issue. By offering investors the hope of obtaining equity below market prices, the borrower is able to obtain fixed-interest capital at a lower interest rate than would otherwise have had to be offered.

convertibility Freedom from exchange control, allowing conversion of one currency into others. In 1958 and 1959, 30 European and associated countries made their currencies freely convertible for nonresidents for the first time in 20 years, thus opening the way for enlarged international capital flows. Free convertibility for residents was introduced only in 1962 and limited to the settlement of current transactions, like trade payments.

coupon most bonds, including international bonds, are provided with coupons which can be detached annually or semiannually and presented by the holder for payment of interest. Hence the folklore about rentiers who do nothing for a living except "clip coupons." The word is used also as shorthand for a bond's rate of interest; a 6 percent bond is often described as a bond with a 6 percent coupon.

coupon tax This tax was announced by the West German authorities late in 1964 and implemented from March 1965, to discourage excessive foreign investment in Deutschemark securities. It amounted to a withholding for tax of part of nonresidents' income from investment in German domestic fixed-interest securities at a basic 25 percent (although the rate sometimes rose closer to 30 percent). Nonresident investment in the DM obligations of other nonresidents was exempt and a large part of international investment in DM bonds was thus confined to those issued by international borrowers as DM foreign bonds or DM-Eurobonds.

covenants Undertakings which borrowers are required to give about their future conduct in the loan agreements governing Eurocredits. Covenants given by corporate borrowers usually stipulate maintenance of given ratios between assets and liabilities while also limiting total debt service and dividends in relation to earnings. Official borrowers often undertake that no liens will be given to new creditors without similarly being offered to existing creditors. Failures to perform covenants are technical defaults, but are often overlooked provided debt service is being maintained. *See also* **representations**.

cover In dumping unsold parts of their allotments of new Eurobonds onto the after-market, some Eurobanks try to disguise their action by selling through small banks which charge a fee for thus providing cover.

cross-default Clauses in loan agreements (including Eurocredit agreements) stipulate that the borrower's default on any loan will be regarded as a default on all. It has the disadvantage of allowing any creditor to bring down the pack, but it does avoid a scramble to get out first and is thus designed to provide equal treatment for all creditors in the event of a default.

currency option clauses Clauses attached to a minority of Eurobonds issued in one currency offering investors the option of taking payment of interest and principal in a second currency. Most such currency option bonds have coupled sterling with the Deutschemark or the dollar. During the 1960s, a number of Eurobonds were issued allowing holders to take payment of interest and principal in sterling or Deutschemark, but only at a rate of exchange fixed for the full maturity of the issue at the time of its initial offering. This put the exchange rate risk heavily onto the borrowers. A second variety of option bond, introduced in 1972, had a floating rate option which could be exercised only at the spot exchange rate between the two option currencies at the time of each payment date. This shared risk and opportunity more fairly between borrowers and investors. *See also* **units of account**.

debt certificates Evidence of debt issued, especially, in the Dutch domestic fixed-interest market. The certificates bear the names of debtor and creditor and the terms of the loan and are not usually negotiable (unlike bonds). As a rule, a debt certificate may be transferred from one creditor to another only with the debtor's consent.

direct investment Building or purchase of a business or plant rather than portfolio investment which consists of the purchase of loan stock or a minority of equity; hence international direct investment and international portfolio investment.

discretionary funds Funds entrusted to banks for investment on a client's behalf and in the client's name. However, the client gives the bank discretion in investing the funds as the bank thinks best, by contrast with advisory funds which banks can invest for clients only after consultation with the clients. Discretionary funds, like advisory funds, add to a bank's placing power in international markets. *See also* **advisory funds** and **placing power.**

discounts *See* **fees.**

double call Sinking fund arrangements under which borrowers assume a legal obligation to redeem a given number of outstanding bonds each year, often allow the borrower to "double" or call at par twice as many bonds as were due for retirement in a given year. *See also* **sinking fund.**

Eurobonds Broadly defined by the market as bonds sold for international borrowers in several markets simultaneously by international groups of banks. This book has preferred the narrow definition of Eurobonds as those issued without restriction outside the jurisdiction of any single national authority, consisting for practical purposes of Eurobonds in U.S. and Canadian dollars and units of account. The argument in favor of the narrow definition is that the unregulated Eurobonds alone have opened up a new and different channel for international capital.

Euroclear One of the Eurobond market's two main clearing systems, operated by Morgan Guaranty for the more than 100 banks which own the system.

Eurocredits Short name for medium-term international credits provided by bank syndicates in currencies which need not be those of the borrower or the banks. Most such credits are provided for agreed periods at agreed margins above an agreed base rate, but the total cost to the borrower is usually reviewed every six months to reflect changes in the underlying cost of money to the banks.

Eurocurrency Foreign currency deposited with a bank outside the country where the currency is issued as legal tender. The decisive factor is the location of the bank, not the ownership of the bank or the funds. Dollars placed with the French branch of an American bank by a corporation in the U.S. are Eurodollars. Some international transactions involve domestic currency for one partner, but foreign (or Eurocurrency) for the other; if a Paris bank advances French francs to a bank in London, the French bank has acquired a domestic currency asset, but the London bank has acquired a foreign currency liability in Euro-French francs. Ultimate settlement is possible only in the country of issue. When a bank in Milan lends dollars to a bank in London, the dollar balances of the two European banks are adjusted accordingly at their correspondent banks in the U.S. The Eurocurrencies market is one in which foreign currencies are lent and borrowed, mostly among banks and mostly at short term. That is its main distinction from the foreign exchange market, where currencies are bought and sold against each other. *See also* **foreign exchange market.**

Eurodollar The most common form of Eurocurrency, usually accounting for about 80 percent of the world market's gross assets. There are markets also in Euro-Deutschemark, Euro-sterling, Euro-French francs, Euro-guilders, Euro-Swiss francs, Euro-yen, and a few other currencies.

facility fee Paid by borrowers on undrawn portions of bank credits, including Eurocredits, especially in the case of revolving Eurocredits. *See also* **Eurocredits.**

fees Front-end fees are paid by borrowers to the managing banks arranging Eurocredits, the lead managers dividing the fee among themselves. Some of the fee is also passed on to other banks in the form of participation fees for taking up parts of a Eurocredit up to agreed minimum levels. In the international bond market, fees are more accurately described as management, underwriting, and selling concessions or discounts, since the borrower pays the costs of distributing a new issue by making the bonds available to managing, underwriting, and selling banks at varying discounts below their face value.

fiduciary funds Funds placed by banks for clients at the client's risk but in the bank's name (as distinct from advisory funds and discretionary funds which are placed in the customers' name).

floating rate notes (FRN) Notes which are unique in being the only Eurobonds which are not fixed-interest securities (the only other exception consisting of Eurobonds convertible into equities). FRNs carry an agreed margin above 6-month London inter-bank offered rate (LIBOR) for dollar deposits and the cost to the borrower (and the return to the investor) is usually adjusted every six months to reflect changes in the LIBOR base. Many FRNs guarantee investors a minimum interest rate. An innovation in April 1979 was an issue of FRNs by Manufacturers Hanover giving holders the option of conversion into fixed-interest debentures. Issue of floating rate notes is especially attractive for nondollar banks and also for banks in those countries where the authorities allow banks to count the proceeds toward capital.

floating rate option bonds *See* **currency option clauses.**

foreign exchange market Market in which currencies are bought and sold against each other (as distinct from the Eurocurrencies market in which currencies are lent and borrowed, mostly among banks). However, Eurocurrencies business was grafted onto the foreign exchange business of banks from the first, partly because many Eurocurrency loans are covered in the forward exchange market.

foreign exchange and currency deposit brokers In most large centers foreign exchange and Eurocurrency transactions between banks are arranged through brokers, who describe their clients in general terms but do not disclose their identity until serious interest in a transaction has been shown by the other party.

foreign bonds Often referred to also as "classical" or "traditional" foreign bonds to distinguish them from Eurobonds. Foreign bonds are issued for a nonresident borrower in the domestic capital market of another country under the laws and regulations of the country in which they are issued. Such issues are arranged by syndicates consisting exclusively or at least predominantly of banks registered in the country where the issue is being made. There is seldom any bar to the international distribution of foreign bonds; on the contrary, international investment in them is usually encouraged.

fungible Both major Eurobond clearing centers handle most bonds on a fungible basis. This means the bonds are not individually earmarked as belonging to any particular holder, but that the clearing systems merely credit banks with the number of bonds to which they are entitled, the banks in turn similarly crediting their customers.

in-house funds Funds which clients have entrusted to banks for investment are known as in-house funds and enhance the bank's placing power in international bond markets (i.e., the bank's ability to place large amounts of a new issue with its own clients). In addition to advisory and discretionary funds, Swiss banks in particular are responsible also for the administration of fiduciary funds. *See also* **advisory funds, discretionary funds,** and **fidicuary funds.**

issue price Price at which a new issue of bonds is sold to the public on the offering day. The issue price is sometimes adjusted at the last moment to compensate for a misjudged interest coupon. If the coupon has been pitched too high, the bond may be issued above par (or face value) to bring down the yield; conversely, the bond may be issued at a slight discount if the coupon is judged to have been set too low to attract enough market interest.

Interest Equalization Tax   Introduced by President Kennedy in July 1963 and levied on the income of U.S. investors from the new and outstanding securities of designated foreign borrowers in the U.S. market. It was intended to reduce foreign borrowing in the U.S. bond market by effectively shutting out many foreign borrowers, mainly European and Australasian borrowers. It gave a major impulse to the regular issue of offshore dollar bonds, i.e., Eurodollar bonds. The tax was lifted, with other U.S. capital export controls, at the start of 1974.

Kassenobligationen   Issued by Swiss banks in their domestic market to help them finance Swiss exports and mortgage loans. They are roughly equivalent to stretched out certificates of deposit, having maturities of three to eight years.

Koffergeschäft   Literally: suitcase business. Applied to the smuggling of German domestic bonds to nonresidents, similar smuggling of Swiss franc securities abroad, and the smuggling of lira bank notes from Italy into Switzerland.

lead manager   Bank with the main responsibility for arranging a bond issue or an international bank credit. It has the main responsibility for agreeing terms and conditions with the borrower, for assessing the market, and for recruiting other banks into the selling or lending syndicate *See also* **comanager**.

lending margins   Fixed spread which borrowers agree to pay above an agreed base rate, usually LIBOR, to banks providing a Eurocredit. The total rate of interest paid by the borrower is adjusted, usually every six months, to reflect changes in LIBOR.

LIBOR   London inter-bank offered rate for short-term dollar deposits; i.e., three-month, six-month, nine-month, and one-year LIBOR. Three- and six-month LIBOR are most commonly used as the base rate for Eurocredits and floating rate notes. LIBOR is the rate at which dollar deposits are offered to banks in London, by contrast with the bid rate quoted by banks seeking such deposits.

listing   Most international bonds are listed on stock exchanges to provide regular public quotations and to make them eligible for institutional investors who are often restricted to investment in listed securities only. But most Eurobond trading takes place over the counter on telephone lines between market makers registered with the AIBD. *See also* **AIBD.**

London dollar certificates of deposit   Certificates of deposit introduced in London in 1966 as an international variant of the CDs introduced in the U.S. five years earlier. Most London dollar CDs are "tap" issues made according to market demand. They are issued in minimum amounts of $25,-000, but usually in blocks of $2 million or more and usually have maturities of three to six months. Most are issued by big banks to obtain funds at margins slightly below LIBOR from other banks or institutional investors willing to hold highly rated and highly liquid paper. A minority of London dollar CDs are issued in maturities of two to three years, some of them at floating rates of interest. *See also* **certificates of deposit.**

Luxibor   Luxembourg inter-bank offered rate for Deutschemark deposits (equivalent to LIBOR for dollar deposits in London).

market makers   Banks undertaking to make a secondary market in Eurobonds by taking bonds offered onto their own books or by finding takers for them among or through other banks active in the secondary market. They act both as principals and brokers. Most market makers specialize in groups of stock or categories (like convertibles or floating rate notes).

merchant bank   British institution also known as an accepting house for its business of "accepting" or endorsing trade bills. Roughly equivalent to U.S. investment banks, but with far greater freedom than their American counterparts to engage in nearly any form of specialized banking business. The closest equivalent is the French banque d'affaires (q.v.).

negative pledge   Undertaking by a borrower that no future loans will be raised on terms giving new creditors preference over existing creditors.

overallocation   Practice among lead managers of international bond issues of allocating to the selling group a larger sum of bonds than that actually planned for issue; the approach is used when the managers believe that an issue will be oversubscribed by the public.

overseas banks   British banks having their head offices in London but their main operations in countries which used to be part of the British empire or in which British investment was especially large (such as parts of Latin America).

participation certificates (also known as sub-participation certificates)   A bank helping to provide a syndicated loan may grant a participation in its share of the loan to another against a participation (or sub-participation) certificate. The relationship of the certificate holding bank is with the bank that issued it, and not with the borrower. In this, the granting of a participation differs from loan assignment. *See also* **assignment**.

placing power   Ability of a bank to place large amounts of newly issues securities with investors. *See also* **advisory funds, discretionary funds, fiduciary funds,** and **in-house funds.**

praecipium   Part of the total front-end fee paid by a Eurocredit borrower which is kept by the lead managing bank or banks for themselves after payment of participation fees to other members of the lending syndicate (from the Latin *praecipere:* to take a prerogative share).

prime rate   Rate of interest charged by banks in the U.S. on loans to their biggest and most creditworthy customers. It has sometimes been used instead of LIBOR as the base for dollar loans made by groups of U.S. banks to foreign borrowers.

protection   Promise given by lead managers during the syndication period to allocate certain amounts of new bonds to favored underwriters and selling group members.

purchase fund   Fund set aside by a borrower to repurchase some outstanding bonds in the market up to a stipulated amount in any given year of the issue's life. The borrower is under no legal obligation to use the purchase fund (as in the case of a sinking fund). Hence the phrase that an issue's average maturity will be X years "if the purchase fund is used in full." *See also* **sinking fund**.

reallowance   Practice by which banks in a bond issuing syndicate "reallow" some of their discounts to strong or favored investors; in plain English, a selling bank sacrifices part of its discount to pass on a discount to its customer.

redemption   Many international bond issues provide for early redemption by borrowers who might wish to switch to other forms of borrowing in changing circumstances. A purchase fund allows but does not oblige a borrower to repurchase a given amount of outstanding bonds in any year; a sinking fund legally obliges one to do so; in some cases borrowers also have an option to "call" all or part of their outstanding bonds from a given year at a premium over their face value, the premium declining in each subsequent year that calls are made. *See also* **purchase fund**.

reference banks   Banks chosen as a representative cross-section of banks in a Eurocredit lending syndicate to determine the base LIBOR which will be deemed to apply to all members of the syndicate at each six-monthly roll-over date. This meets the difficulty that LIBOR quotations differ according to the size and status of the bank to which dollars are being offered, so that LIBOR will seldom be the same for all banks at any moment.

reference rate   LIBOR chosen as applying to a Eurocredit syndicate as a whole by its reference banks.

representations   Statements made by a Eurocredit borrower about the state of the borrower's affairs at the time the credit is being sought (by contrast with covenants, in which the borrower gives undertakings about future behavior). Also known as "warranties." Falsifications of representations and warranties are regarded as technical defaults, but are often overlooked as long as debt service is maintained. *See also* **covenants**.

revolving credit   Kind of Eurocredit resembling an overdraft facility or credit line made available for a given period either as a standby in case of need or to meet temporary but recurring financial requirements. Borrowers may draw such credits up and down as circumstances dictate, paying full interest only on the amounts actually drawn while they are drawn and a nominal facility or standby fee on unused portions of the credit. *See also* **term credit**.

Samurai bond   Nickname of yen bonds sold for foreign borrowers on the Tokyo market (i.e., foreign bonds in Japan).

secondary market   Market in which outstanding bonds are traded through banks acting as market makers. The after-market exists during the short period between the formal issue of new bonds and the disbanding of the issuing syndicate. The secondary market comes into being thereafter. In the Eurobond secondary market bonds are traded in minimum lots of 10, equivalent to $10,000 in the case of Eurodollar bonds.

selling group   All banks marketing a new Eurobond issue.

selling period   A week or ten days during which managing banks canvas demand for a new issue among underwriters and other selling group banks on the basis of provisionally indicated coupon and issuing price. These terms are formally agreed at the end of the selling period on the basis of demand expressed.

sinking fund   Fund set aside by the borrower to repurchase a given number of outstanding bonds in the market during each year that the issue is outstanding; the borrower is under a legal obligation to use the sinking fund in full, by contrast with his optional use of a purchase fund. *See also* **purchase fund.**

small investor   Defined as Eurobond investors holding less than 15 or 20 Eurobonds, or about $15,000 to $20,000. Sales to them are sometimes referred to as the retail market.

spread   *See* **lending margins.**

straight debt   Fixed-interest securities without provision for conversion into the borrower's common stock.

syndication   Act of marketing a bond issue or an international bank loan through a syndicate of banks acting jointly for that special purpose (as distinct from banks permanently grouped together).

SLOB   "Substantial lender on own book"—the mocking acronym applied to themselves by large banks which take up a substantial portion of a syndicated international bank credit they have helped to manage.

term credit   Most common variety of Eurocredit. It usually provides for a schedule of drawings at the beginning, a schedule of repayments toward the end, and an intervening period of grace during which the full amount is available to the borrower. It contrasts with the revolving credit. *See also* **revolving credit.**

tombstone   Advertisement placed by banks shortly after a new bond issue or syndicated credit to record their part in its arrangement.

trustees   Independent agents, often accountants or lawyers, appointed to look after the investor's interests in a bond issue. The trustee is never an actual investor. *See also* **agent bank.**

underwriting group   Full amount of any new Eurobond issue is always underwritten by the managers and underwriters, but since part is usually marketed by selling group banks who are not underwriters, the underwriters in the group need rarely take up their full commitments (although they still get their full underwriting concessions). In other markets, notably New York, underwriters are legally forbidden to sell newly issued securities below issue price until the selling syndicate has been formally disbanded.

units of account Multicurrency units used to denominate a small proportion of Eurobond issues. It is claimed that they provide equality of currency risk to investors and borrowers. In practice they have proved more useful in getting around the control of new issuing volume in some markets, notably that for external Deutschemark bonds, and many units are regarded as little more than "disguised" DM international bonds. Units used include the EUA (European Unit of Account), originally based on the parities of the 17 members of the European Payments Union and later on the currencies of countries participating in various forms of European joint currency floats; the ECU (or European Currency Unit), based on the parities of the active participants of whatever European joint-float happens to be alive; the EURCO (or European Composite Unit), valued at daily market rates of a group of European countries rather than on central rates or parities as in the EUA and ECU); and SDR units valued in terms of the International Monetary Fund's (floating) Special Drawing Rights.

warrants Attachments to bond issues which can be converted into the borrower's equity under given conditions, though without the surrender of the bond itself, as in the case of conventional convertible bonds. The warrants can be detached and either converted into common stock or traded separately.

warranties *See* **representations.**

Yankee bonds Nickname for bonds sold in U.S. domestic markets for nonresident borrowers (i.e., U.S. foreign bonds).

yield Return provided by investment in a financial asset. The running yield is the one available at any given moment; the yield to redemption is that which would accrue if the investment were held to maturity.

yield curve Measure of the difference between yields at any given moment.

yield differential Measure of difference between yields over time.

BIBLIOGRAPHY

Bell, Geoffrey, *The Euro-dollar Market and the International Financial System,* Macmillan, New York, 1973.

Chalmers, E.B., ed., *Readings in the Euro-dollar,* W.P. Griffith and Sons, London, 1969.

Clendenning, E. Wayne, *The Euro-dollar Market,* Clarendon Press, Oxford, 1970.

Coombs, Charles A., *The Arena of International Finance,* John Wiley and Sons, Inc., New York, 1976.

Davis, Steven I., *The Euro-Bank; Its Origins, Management and Outlook,* Macmillan, New York, 1976.

Delaume, Georges R., *Legal Aspects of International Lending and Economic Development Financing,* Oceana Publications, New York, 1967 (for the Parker School of Foreign and Comparative Law, Columbia University).

Donnerstag, Hans-Christian, *The Eurobond Market,* Financial Times, Ltd., London, 1975.

Einzig, Paul, *The Euro-Dollar System,* Macmillan, 1964 (revised editions up to 1973).

Einzig, Paul, and Brian Scott Quinn, *The Euro-Dollar System,* Macmillan, New York, 1977 (successor to the late Paul Einzig's earlier book of the same title, above).

Einzig, Paul, *Foreign Dollar Loans in Europe,* Macmillan, New York, 1965.

Einzig, Paul, *The Eurobond Market,* Macmillan, New York, 1969 (successor to *Foreign Dollar Loans in Europe*).

Fisher, F. G., *The Eurodollar Bond Market*, Euromoney Publications Ltd., London, 1979.

Friedrich, Klaus, *The Euro-dollar System*, Cornell University Press, Ithaca, 1968.

Gehrmann, Dieter, *Die Effizienz des Euro—Kapitalmarketes Funktionsmechanismen und internationale Kapitalallokation*, Weltarchiv, Hamburg, 1978.

Hermann, A.H., ed., *Banking and Sources of Finance in Comecon*, Banker Research Unit, London, 1978.

Hirsch, Fred, *Money International*, Allen Lane and the Penguin Press, London, 1967.

Horsefield, J. Keith, *The International Monetary Fund 1945–1965*, IMF, Washington, D.C., 1969.

Johnson, Brian, *The Politics of Money*, John Murray, Ltd., London, 1970.

Little, Jane Sneddon, *Euro-dollars*, Harper and Row, New York, 1975.

Martenson, G. Carroll, *The Euro-dollar Market*, The Bankers Publishing Co., Boston, 1964.

McKenzie, George W., *The Economics of the Euro-Currency System*, Macmillan, New York, 1976.

Park, Yoon S., *The Euro-bond Market: Foundation and Structure*, Praeger, New York, 1974.

Prochnow, Herbert V., ed., *The Euro-dollar*, Rand McNally and Co., Chicago, 1970.

Roosa, Robert V., *The Dollar and World Liquidity*, Random House, New York, 1967.

Schacht, Hjalmar, *The Magic of Money*, Oldbourne Book Co., Ltd, London, 1967.*

Solomon, Robert, *The International Monetary System 1945–1976*, Harper and Row, New York, 1977.

Stem, Carl H. (ed.) with John H. Makin and Dennis E. Logue, *Eurocurrencies and the International Monetary System*, American Enterprise Institute for Public Policy Research, Washington, D.C., 1976.

Taylor, A.J.P., *The Course of German History, 1815–1945*, Capricorn Books, New York, 1964.*

---

*Included for descriptions of Germany's hyper-inflation of 1923.

INDEX

Advertisement of bond issues, 164, 232
Africa, savings rates in, 43
Agio, Eurobond premium, 148
AIBD market centers, 195–196
Albania, distrust of Western finance, 104
Algeria, Eurocredit borrowing by, 66
Amsterdam, financial center, 247
    (*See also* Netherlands)
Amsterdam inter-bank offered rate
    (AIBOR), 252
Amsterdam market, mechanics of, 250–
    253
"Arab funds," Eurobond investment, 176
Argentina, 19
    Eurocredit borrowing by, 108, 110
Asian Development Bank, Samurai bond
    markets, 243
Association of International Bond Dealers,
    185, 192
Auslandskassenverein, Eurobonds, 139
Australia, Eurocredits, 67

BAII (Banque Arabe et International d'In-
    vestissement), 81
Balance(s) of payments:
    composition of, 4
    estimates of, 43–44
    Eurobond markets, 35, 172
    Eurocredit markets, 66, 127
    Eurocurrency markets, 28–29, 50
    imbalances in, 57, 59
    industrialized countries, 55
    Japan, 25, 32, 240–241
    Netherlands, 249
    Switzerland, 225

Balance(s) of payments (*Cont.*):
    United Kingdom, 156
    United States, 22, 28, 33, 35, 54, 136, 209
    (*See also* Surplus countries)
Bank for International Settlements (BIS)
    (Basel), 26, 31, 48, 58, 261
    costs, 134
    markets, 93, 94, 174
    risk analysis, 123
Bank of America, 19, 88, 122
Bank of England, 49, 261
    controls of, 46
    monetary system and, 8, 20, 21
Bank of Japan, 244
Bank of London and South America, 20
Bankers Trust, Eurocredit earnings of, 130
Bankhaus Herstatt, collapse of, 47, 48, 73,
    75
Banking system (Western):
    bond markets, 194–195, 216
    capital markets, 3, 5–7
    control of, 125
    dollar rate differentials, 30
    Eurobond markets, 141, 159, 173–174,
        177, 183–184, 186, 190, 192–197
    Eurocredits markets, 51, 66–67, 71, 80–
        82, 83–86, 87–91
    Eurocurrencies markets, 17, 18, 29
    Euromarket controls, 45–46
    Germany, 25, 237
    innovation in, 24
    Japan, 241–242
    Netherlands, 247–248, 251–252
    pension funds of, 176
    politics and, 60–61, 87–91, 128, 132
    protection for, 122–126

281

Peru, 14
  Eurocredit borrowing by, 76, 108, 110, 111
Philippines, Eurocredit borrowing by, 108, 110, 111
Poland, Eurocredit borrowing by, 106
Politics:
  banking system and, 60–61, 87–91, 128, 132
  default, 133
  (*See also* Governments)
Praecipium, Eurocredits, 75
Prices:
  Bretton Woods collapse, 13–14
  Eurobonds, 151, 153, 177–178
  oil (*see* Oil prices)
  prosperity, 12
  raw materials, 12–13
  rise in, 55
  stability in, 23
  (*See also* Inflation)
Pringle, Robin, 240*n*.
Private investors, capital markets, 16
    (*See also* Investors and investment)
Private sector, capital markets role, 5, 52
Productivity increases, 11–12
Protectionism, trade, 58, 217
    (*See also* Trade)
Publicity:
  Eurobonds, 164
  Swiss bond markets, 232
Purchase funds, Eurobonds, 162
Putnam, G. E., 90

Radcliffe, Lord, 21*n*.
Raw material prices, 12–13
Real estate prices, Eurobond investment, 179, 180
Recession:
  capital markets, 8, 57
  debt payment, 133
  Eurocredit market, 101
  industrial countries, 5, 15
  Interest Equalization Tax, 33
  Japan, 241
  oil price rise, 14
  Switzerland, 225, 226
  U.S., 22, 33
Recycling of funds, 55, 57, 209
Redemption of convertibles, Eurobonds, 163–164
Regulation Q, U.S. Federal Reserve Board:
  Eurocredit markets, 33
  interest rates, 24
  suspension of, 25

Reserve requirements:
  Eurocredits market, 34
  Euromarket, 47*n*.
  usefulness of, 50
Reserves:
  of dollars (U.S.), 168
  Eurocurrency markets, 46
  world, of eurocurrencies, 26
Revolving credit, Eurocredit market, 76–77
Risk:
  Eurobond markets, 156, 157, 167
  Eurocredits, 66, 130
  German bond markets, 236
  protection against, 122, 123
Riyal (Saudi Arabia), Eurobond markets, 170
ROBOT, Eurocurrency development, 20
Rockefeller, John D., 206*n*.
Roll-over, Eurocredits, 71, 74
Roosa, Robert V., 35
Roosevelt, Franklin D., 49
Roosevelt, Theodore, 206
Rothschild, Nathan Mayer, 123
Rowan, Sir Leslie, 20

S. G. Warburg Bank, 194
Salomon Brothers, 133, 194
Samurai bonds, 242
  issues of, 244
  markets of, 245
  regulation of, 243
San Francisco (Calif.), financial center, 206
Saudi Arabian Monetary Agency (SAMA), Eurobond investment, 176
Savings:
  Eurobond investment, 179
  recycling of, 55, 57
  self-sufficiency in, 43
  transfer of, 3
Scandinavian countries, Eurocredit borrowing by, 101
Schacht, Hjalmar, 11*n*.
SDR (*see* Special Drawing Rights)
Sears Roebuck, Samurai bond market, 243
Securities and Exchange Commission (SEC):
  bond markets, 137, 138, 218
  Eurobonds, 138, 177, 184
  foreign bond markets, 54, 231
  Yankee bonds, 212, 213
Securities firms:
  Euromarkets, 17, 39
  Japan, 243
  U.S., 207
Senate Subcommittee on Foreign Policy (U.S.), Eurobanks, 48